What's God Got To Do With It?

Burt Flannery

First published in Great Britain in December 2012 by Geoffrey Publications, Kingswinford, West Midlands

Copyright © Burt Flannery 2012

The moral right of Burt Flannery as author of this work has been asserted by the Copyright, Designs and Patents Act of 1988.

ISBN 978-0-9557220-9-7

Printed and bound in Great Britain by T. J. International Ltd.

To Tolerance and Kindness

Contents

Preface

Nowhere in the human condition are logic and reason suspended so evidentially as when they are concerned with matters of religion. It seems that a person buoyed by religious faith can believe almost anything irrespective of implausibility. Closed minds cannot healthily debate contentious religious issues so, perhaps, we would all benefit from a willingness to accommodate an alternative point of view and a positive shift in our thinking. The alternative is stagnation and a continuing polarisation which keeps people of the world apart.

In all communities, children learn initially from their parents before going on to receive wisdom from a wider environment. Religious conviction is automatically handed down to children before they extend their knowledge in the wider world by attending places of worship and Sunday school, for example. All religions have wonderful tales to tell and, generally, children are enthralled by what they hear and learn from the ancient scriptures. Many make the journey into adulthood without modifying their beliefs in any way, without ever asking, "Why?" Others, motivated by inquiry and, by applying thought and reason, begin to see incongruities and inconsistencies in what they had hitherto accepted as fact and explore further. Benjamin Franklin, the noted scientist, politician, and one of the most iconic figures of American history, explained:

"My parents had given me betimes religious impressions, and I received from my infancy a pious education in the principles of Calvinism. But scarcely was I arrived at fifteen years of age, when, after having doubted in turn of different tenets, according as I found them combated in the different books that I read, I began to doubt of Revelation itself."

Some people advise that one's politics and religion should not be discussed, that views pertaining to these should be held in private. Nowadays, of course, politics is widely debated, particularly on television programmes, so why not religion? This book is about thinking the unthinkable, laying bare some of the mysteries that cloak religion and establishing the probability of the existence of God. There are many questions to be asked, not all of them answerable, but it's worth a try. The only prerequisite is an open mind.

A young Muslim dental nurse recently asked her mother to explain some of the anomalies she had perceived within her faith. Her mother became uncomfortable, even nervous, as if afraid that any discussion might induce some form of divine retribution to befall them. Her daughter saw no problem in seeking answers as she believed her intelligence came from God and, if he did not intend that she used it, he would not have provided it in the first place. Just because something is written, doesn't make it true, she thought. She was on a journey of discovery but as her mother couldn't help, she had to look elsewhere. Throughout, the nurse maintained her opinion that, wherever the journey led, knowledge gained from the experience and views of other free thinking people would always be preferable to ignorance. Over centuries, ecclesiastical authorities have fed their congregations a diet of ritual and dogma, stifling freedom of thought. Breakaway groups expressed any discontentment at their peril yet, despite all the imposed constraints, it was freedom of thought that encouraged the rise of Protestantism, for example. Perhaps it's time to scrutinise the role of religion in a modern society and encourage debate, hopefully devoid of the fear that a mere point of view might invite threats of reprisal or ostracism.

Religious tolerance would be a good starting point. If it were able to supplant the natural hostility that is felt by some people when confronted with an alien ideology, that would, indeed, be progress. In January 2006, Professor Richard Dawkins, the prominent evolutionary biologist, author and renowned atheist, presented a television documentary entitled, *The Root of All Evil?* It included a discussion of what the professor saw as a conflict between faith and science. He pointed out that science involves a process of constantly testing and revising theories in the light of new evidence, while faith makes a virtue out of believing unprovable and, more often than not, improbable propositions. Given this stance, there was unlikely to be any consensus when he visited Colorado Springs to discuss the rise of fundamentalist Christianity in the United States. At the New Life Church, an $18 million centre for worship, he met Pastor Ted Haggard who presided over a congregation of 14 thousand. Haggard was, at that time, chairman of the National Association of Evangelicals and, according to Professor Dawkins, claimed to undertake weekly conference calls with President George W. Bush. Haggard also claimed that the literal word of the Bible is true and does not suffer from contradiction in the way that science does. Dawkins countered by pointing out the many advantages of science and, gradually, the exchanges affirmed that common ground was unlikely to be found.

Haggard maintained that American evangelicals fully endorse scientific methodology, expecting it to show how God created the heavens and the Earth. In other words, if science can prove the Bible's account of the creation, he will fully embrace science but if a different conclusion is derived, his contention will be that science must be mistaken. As a check on the pastor's open-mindedness, Dawkins asked if he accepted the scientific exposition that the Earth is 4.5 billion years old but, predictably, Haggard contended that this was merely a view accepted by but a portion of the scientific community. He went on to remark that Dawkins' own grandchildren may laugh at him upon hearing his assertion. The meeting degenerated with more wild Haggard claims and an accusation that Dawkins was guilty of intellectual arrogance. Professor Dawkins, to his credit, maintained a professional composure, resisting any urge to become angry, to laugh, or even to cry with frustration. The term, 'talking to a brick wall' comes to mind, doesn't it? As Dawkins and his film crew were preparing to leave, there was a brief dispute in the car park when, it seems, Haggard ordered them off his land threatening legal action and confiscation of their technical equipment. Clearly, the New Life Church was not a good place to start in the hope of religious tolerance, benevolence and Christian expression.

Next came a visit to Jerusalem where the professor met representatives from both sides of the religious divide before concluding that the Jewish and Muslim views appeared irreconcilable. Hoping to meet someone who might be sympathetic to both viewpoints, Dawkins interviewed Yousef al-Khattab, formerly known as Joseph Cohen, an American-born Jew who came to Israel as a migrant before converting to

Islam. After making Dawkins welcome, al-Khattab explained his views
with regard to the decadence of western values. He had two major
concerns. Firstly, he wanted all non-Muslims to leave the lands of the
Prophet Muhammad. Secondly, he expressed his concern about the
manner in which western women were dressed. He objected to seeing
women dressed 'like whores' or 'bouncing around on television topless'.
When asked for his thoughts on the September 11th atrocities, he traced
the blame back to the partition of Palestine and the creation of the State
of Israel. He also took the opportunity to advise Great Britain to:
"Take your forces off our lands, correct yourselves, fix your society, fix
your women."

From a friendly start, al-Khattab's demeanour became increasingly
aggressive and Dawkins' hopes of finding a conciliator were well and
truly extinguished. The professor had interviewed a Christian and a
Muslim and both had become irritated by his questioning. Why is it that
religious debate so frequently and unnecessarily evokes intolerance and
frayed tempers? Why can't a little patience and forbearance be
exercised?

In February 2010, Professor Dawkins, perhaps believing that he
would have more empathy with a woman, interviewed Wendy Wright, a
creationist and Chief Executive Officer of *Concerned Women For
America*. This time, thankfully, there were no displays of aggression,
only a series of brain-numbing exchanges. Try as he might, though
armed with mountains of scientific evidence supporting the evolutionary
process, Dawkins failed to make any impression on Wright who
remained implacable throughout, refusing to accept any of his arguments.
He exercised commendable restraint even when faced with the most

nonsensical of retorts. She believed that all people deserved to be treated respectfully as if, in some way, evolution contravened this sentiment. Also, that God created us all. When Dawkins asked her for evidence of the creation, she stated it was the fact that everyone is an individual, everyone is different. Doesn't this sound like the perfect argument in favour of evolution? Ironically, she accused Dawkins of closed-mindedness but remained infuriatingly pleasant throughout the interview. It was as if, in her condescension, she was thinking:

"I pity you because you can't see what I see."

By the end of the interview, Professor Dawkins seemed to be losing the will to live. He had tried his best.

Achieving religious tolerance is, clearly, a monumental challenge. For example, consider the case of Asia Noreen Bibi, a Pakistani Christian woman, sentenced to death by hanging after having been convicted of blasphemy by a court in Pakistan. In June 2009, Asia Noreen, a farm labourer from the village of Ittan Wali, was asked to fetch some water. A quarrel erupted when, after Noreen's return, some of her Muslim co-workers refused to drink, believing Christians to be 'unclean'. One can't help wondering why, as a Christian, she was allocated the task in the first place. Subsequently, a number of Muslims complained to a cleric that Noreen had made derogatory comments about Prophet Muhammad. If this were true, she had encroached into an area of great sensitivity. Perhaps she could have exercised more care in her remarks but the disproportionate response that followed was shameful. Noreen and members of her family, when at home, were beaten by a mob before being rescued by police. Following the violence, the police initiated an investigation into her remarks which culminated in her arrest and prosecution under Section 295 C of the Pakistan penal code. She spent more than a year in jail and, in November 2010, Muhammed Naveed Iqbal, a Punjabi judge, sentenced her to death by hanging. On the 4th January 2011, Salmaan Taseer, Governor of Punjab, was assassinated by a member of his own security team simply because he had expressed sympathy with Noreen and opposed the blasphemy laws. Thousands paid their respects to Taseer at his funeral in Lahore whilst later, to demonstrate their support for the country's religious laws, a similar number of people was amassed. Is there anything more divisive and, simultaneously, more incomprehensible than religious prejudice? When nations go to war, people generally die in the cause of freedom which, to the normal human mind, is fathomable. However, when members of the same community are prepared to kill each other because of a mere difference of opinion or interpretation of a religious doctrine, we are faced with the impenetrable; in particular, when differences perceived as fundamental are, in reality, quite miniscule.

The killing didn't end there. Shahbaz Bhatti, Pakistan's Minority Affairs Minister and the only Christian member of the country's cabinet, was next to be assassinated. On the 2nd March 2011, he was shot dead by gunmen who ambushed his car near his home in Islamabad. On the 26th August, the 28-year old son of Salman Taseer, Shahbaz, was kidnapped and Noreen's family went into hiding while she remained in custody awaiting the decision of a superior court. It is truly ineffable.

Can anyone take any pride in this catastrophic chain of events? It was Noreen who was, initially, insulted and provoked into allegedly making unguarded remarks about Muhammad. As a Christian, Muhammad meant little to her. She voiced her opinion and Muslim hypersensitivity sent a mindless juggernaut into motion. Why the physical violence? Wouldn't a reprimand have sufficed for a Christian who was less accustomed to their traditions and their reverence of Muhammad? After all, was it not Muhammad who directed Muslims to be good to women during his last sermon? Of course, it is highly likely that his beneficence didn't extend to women of a different faith but, if not, it should have done. Do people have to die because they hold a particular point of view? When will we realise that religion, in general, is man-made; that it has not been ordained by a divine power? If it had been, there would be a single universal religion, not the vast array of denominations and sects in evidence today. Does anyone seriously believe that God decided:

"What I'll do is direct the people on planet Earth to establish a multiplicity of religions. That way, there'll always be conflict and millions of people will be killed as a consequence?"

When will people the world over be open-minded enough to stop believing that their religion is the right one? There is no right and wrong, only preference. Surely, Islam is not so flimsy that it cannot countenance any form of scepticism or criticism. It would be helpful if, when offensive remarks are made by persons of a different faith, Muslim academics could dampen the flames of outrage by advising:

"Treat these words with the contempt they deserve by ignoring them. They are only words. We have confidence in our faith."

This would discourage violence. People and places would not be defiled and Islam, which purports to be a peaceful religion, would be more admired by the rest of the world. The next time some Christian preacher decides to draw attention to himself by burning a copy of the Quran, perhaps he could be denied the publicity generated by Muslim enragement. The greater the reaction from the Muslim community, the greater the air time afforded the preacher. If the academics could counsel their fellow Muslims by saying:

"This is clearly a crackpot; ignore him and he'll go away. It's beneath the followers of Islam to be provoked," they would be sending a clear message of religious tolerance.

Religious hatred is rather like racial hatred in that both are based on emotion and both banish logic and reason from the mind. Neither makes any sense. Stephen Lawrence was a fine young man who was stabbed to death on the evening of the 22nd April 1993, while waiting for a bus. He was the victim of an unprovoked attack by a gang of thugs who simply objected to the colour of his skin. It is an unfortunate fact that, just as it is beyond the realms of reason that an innocent life should be lost on such a premise, the cerebral faculties of some members of humanity are regrettably deficient. For all we know, the gang may have had cause to dislike some black people. They had no reason to dislike Stephen but when the mind is closed and emotion gains the upper hand, the consequences are invariably tragic. In this case, the emotion seems to have been a pointless hatred. It needed at least one gang member to stop, think and say:

"Hang on a minute, this guy's done nothing to us. Leave him alone."

That way, the situation might have been defused and a decent teenager would still be alive. Unfortunately, without the presence of that kind of reason or a superior force, the hate-fuelled intentions of a crowd are virtually impossible to extinguish. The ability to control random and arbitrary emotion requires a certain level of intellect, the ability to think logically. If people can ask of themselves, "Why am I being so intolerant?" there is every chance that greater tolerance will follow. The aspiration must be that better education will gradually help to fill the gap and encourage thought, questioning, dialogue and the emergence of greater forbearance.

The Right Reverend David Jenkins was an academic and Bishop of Durham between 1984 and 1994. He caused outrage when he expressed views that questioned Christ's resurrection and virgin birth yet today many clerics would concur with him. Is it absurd to consider a virgin birth and a resurrection impossible? Just because these events were recorded in scriptures by persons in thrall to a great man for consumption by a gullible, impressionable audience does not make them real. The events were not witnessed as, indeed, they could not be witnessed and, by not blindly accepting them, do we invalidate a great religion? The story of Jesus Christ is sufficiently extraordinary – it does not need embellishments which elevate it to the supernatural.

Thomas Jefferson, the third president of the United States, was one of the most remarkable men in history. He was a man of towering intellect and a polymath. Polymaths have such intellectual capacity and energy that they cannot obtain sufficient stimulation from specialising in only one or two subjects. As such, Jefferson spoke five languages, was a politician, an architect, an inventor, a horticulturalist, a prolific writer and theologian. To provide an indication of the esteem in which this man is held, we can recount the words of President John F. Kennedy. In 1962, the president welcomed 49 Nobel Prize Winners to the White House. He addressed them thus:

"I think this is the most extraordinary collection of talent gathered at the White House with the possible exception of when Thomas Jefferson dined here alone."

It is always worth taking the insights of men such as Jefferson into consideration just as he himself learnt from other intellectual giants and philosophers such as John Locke, Francis Bacon and Isaac Newton. By religious conviction, he was a deist. Deists typically reject supernatural events such as prophecy and miracles and, whilst accepting a Creator (or Supreme Architect), believe that he (or she) does not interfere in the affairs of human life. Jefferson wrote the Jefferson Bible in which he extracted the doctrine of Jesus (of which he was a great admirer) by removing all supernatural events and misinterpretations attributable to the Four Evangelists. Had Jefferson been aware of today's knowledge of science and the cosmos, it is highly likely that his views would have veered towards atheism.

In many respects, the inspiration for this book came from John Lennon's brilliant song, *Imagine*, arguably the zenith of his achievements. It is widely regarded as one of the greatest songs of all time and it is highly probable that only Lennon could have crafted this composition – he had that unique combination of song writing talent, intellect, irreverence and rebellion. He wrote the words (shown below) when he was about 30 years old, demonstrating a perception beyond his relatively young age:

Imagine there's no Heaven
It's easy if you try
No hell below us

Above us only sky
Imagine all the people
Living for today

Imagine there's no countries
It isn't hard to do
Nothing to kill or die for
And no religion too
Imagine all the people
Living life in peace

You may say that I'm a dreamer
But I'm not the only one
I hope someday you'll join us
And the world will be as one

Imagine no possessions
I wonder if you can
No need for greed or hunger
A brotherhood of man
Imagine all the people
Sharing all the world

You may say that I'm a dreamer
But I'm not the only one
I hope someday you'll join us
And the world will live as one.

Imagine, he says, a world without a Heaven and a Hell. Imagine a world without religion (or religious hatred) replaced by a brotherhood of man. In other words, he sees a world that is predicated on cooperation and kindness. In the recipe of life, it is kindness that is the all too often missing ingredient.

There is no foreseeable end to the current Israeli – Palestinian conflict. Imagine a different dynamic which focuses on the futility of the interminable loss of life on both sides. Then imagine an Israeli prime minister saying to the Palestinians:

"You are not only our neighbours, you are our brothers. We wish to divert the money we spend protecting our borders against your attacks to improving the infrastructure of your territory and raising your standard of living and quality of life. We believe this is the best way of securing a lasting peace between us and mutually protecting all our citizens. Peace, thereby nullifying threat, is the greatest security we can have."

The line, 'You may say I'm a dreamer' fits here, doesn't it? Equanimity will occur one day, though perhaps not before the adversaries have been driven to exhaustion and their religious encumbrances become ever more diluted. The prize for Lennon's vision, a brotherhood of man, is the realisation of peace and harmony.

Chapter 1

The Beginning

Science and Conjecture

Around 13.75 billion years ago, an event took place which cosmologists call the Big Bang, the beginning of our universe. The theory holds that all the matter and energy that make up the cosmos were once concentrated into a space no larger than the head of a pin and that, suddenly, an inconceivably vast explosion took place to begin the formation of the universe in evidence today. Containing billions of galaxies, each containing hundreds of billions of stars, it is of a scale and complexity far beyond the comprehension of the normal human mind. It has been estimated that the diameter of the universe is at least 93 billion light years (where a light year equates to the distance travelled by light in one year at a speed of 186,000 miles per second). Alternatively, the universe is 8.8×10^{26} metres or 547 billion billion miles across. It is, in short, so vast that we might consider it virtually infinite. A further estimation is that there are fewer grains of sand in the world than there are stars in the universe. This again is incomprehensible as one has only to stand on a beach and contemplate the grains of sand thereon to conclude that scarcely anything could be more plentiful. This means, however, that in relation to the universe, planet Earth is less significant than a single grain of sand amongst all the grains of sand in the world.

Our solar system and, therefore, planet Earth was formed over 9 billion years after the Big Bang. Using radiometric age dating techniques, scientists have estimated that the age of the solar system is 4.54 billion years. Professor Stephen Hawking, the theoretical physicist and cosmologist, once said:

"The Big Bang didn't need God."

In the minds of millions of people throughout the world, however, God the Creator is the architect of the universe and the guardian of all that lies within. The inherent power required to monitor trillions upon trillions of celestial bodies is beyond description though it may be that much of the universe requires little or no intervention. Perhaps, it looks after itself. It may be that God is concerned, primarily, with planets that support intelligent life forms (such as Earth) and it is a near statistical certainty that our planet is not unique in this respect. The probability of the life forms being identical to ours is exceedingly slim, some being more advanced than ours, others less so. Hundreds of millions of other bodies in the universe may readily support life though we may never be aware of them because they are, simply, too far away. If we consider planet Earth to be part of a special group which supports life, then its significance greatly increases and instead of it being a 'single grain of sand', we might consider it to be more analogous to a single rock amongst all the rocks contained in the world. Either way, in terms of the universe, we seem very insignificant indeed.

It may be that God has trillions of other subjects to watch over besides ourselves. Could it be, consequentially, that disasters occur here on Earth whenever God is too busy dealing with the problems of other far flung civilisations? Or, are there many gods and a supreme God as depicted in Norse, Egyptian, Greek and Roman mythologies? Perhaps there is a god for each group of galaxies or, perhaps, the division of labour is arranged by groups of civilisations. Whichever way it is, it is virtually certain that we on Earth comprise a very small portion of God's work.

A sportsman recently underwent a minor operation and as the effects of the anaesthetic began to wear off, amidst the shining lights, he thought he was in Heaven. He noticed a member of the theatre staff who was typically dressed and outlined in brightness causing him to believe he was in the presence of God. Then, a second staff member who was taller than the first came into view and the sportsman thought that this was a greater God before, eventually, realising where he was and that he was still alive. Could his subliminal thoughts have identified a supernatural hierarchy that exists in the universe; who knows? In any case, these events show that things are not always what they seem.

What of all the other civilisations that are present outside our world? Some, no doubt, will be pagan cultures and, if our experience is any yardstick, will remain so unless there is an emergence of prophets. It seems that, on Earth, God has only ever revealed himself to prophets providing them with a direct line of communication. Without them, perhaps, he would have remained outside our consciousness. The more advanced civilisations would probably have a unified religion, complete religious tolerance or, perhaps, no religion at all – only a moral code developed through intuition and experience. They would have realised that it was not worth killing each other just because of a difference of opinion. They would, further, have realised that lifetimes are limited, that they should be constructive and filled with as much happiness as possible. They would have learned that there was enough potential for sorrow in their world owing to illness, accident and natural disasters without exacerbating that potential.

The Book of Genesis

Genesis is the first book of the Christian Old Testament and of the Tanakh, the Hebrew Bible. Tradition tends to credit Moses with its authorship. The divergence between the basic scientific treatise mentioned earlier and the scriptures could scarcely be more pronounced. For example, we know that the Earth took billions of years to cool down before it could support any form of life yet, according to Genesis, God required only six days to create the universe and establish the first human. On the seventh day, apparently, he rested.

It is written that Moses was in communion with God but why would God advise Moses that he had taken six days to create the universe when it had, in fact, taken very much longer. One possibility is that God was 'pulling his leg'. However, this can probably be discounted because the God of the Old Testament didn't appear to have much of a sense of humour. Another possibility is that Moses sincerely believed that he heard God's voice but was mistaken such that his communion with God was an illusion. The third and most likely scenario is that Moses used his imagination to craft a fiction making many assumptions along the way. One assumption is that God would need a rest on the seventh day but this is barely credible. Given his awesome power to create billions of galaxies it would be most surprising if he needed a rest. It is more likely that Moses worked hard and thought it would be most convenient if he could have a day off every week. With God setting the precedent, who would oppose this proposition becoming law? On the other hand, if God needs a rest like everyone else, it would explain the interminable disasters that befall the world. Perhaps they occur when he's asleep.

The Bible provides a complete genealogy all the way from Adam, via Abraham and Moses, to Jesus. By scrutinising the genealogies and accumulating the years, we arrive at a figure of 4,000 years. When added to the time since Jesus was born (about 2,000 years), it is clear that according to the Bible, the Earth is a mere 6,000 years old. Adam was the first man on Earth and he was, apparently, created from dust. Now, in terms of sheer absurdity, this must rank alongside the birth of Athena, the goddess of war, who emerged fully armed from the forehead of the primary god, Zeus, after he had swallowed her mother, Metis. Both are fascinating stories but while Athena of the ancient Greek religion has been consigned to mythology, many people still accept the materialisation of Adam as a literal truth. It is, of course, also rendered a myth not least because human skeletons have been discovered that are thousands of years older than the biblical Earth. If that were not enough, bones from hominids (man's ancestors) have been dated to millions of years.

Many theologians faced with facts such as these argue that Genesis is to be taken symbolically, not literally. They recognise that it was written by someone who, though intelligent, was fanciful and unaware of the scientific laws governing his environment. On this basis, it would appear that Moses has provided a largely fictional account of events, as long suspected. The problem is that millions of people throughout the world, particularly in the United States, actually take Genesis literally.

Creationism, as it is known, is taught in some schools as an entity distinct from the subject of religious instruction; sad, but true.

A recent television debate featured three panellists, one of whom was an American preacher. A theological discussion ensued in which the preacher stated:

"All you need to know about the beginning of the world is in Genesis."

He was so emphatic that neither of the panellists (both journalists) confronted him with an alternative point of view. It was not clear whether they were cowed by his evident passion, whether they were overawed by this disciple of God, or whether they simply considered this man to be incapable of persuasion. Bigotry seldom finds any common ground.

Members of the Flat Earth Society believe that the Earth is flat and not, as is universally accepted, an oblate spheroid. No amount of physical, scientific or photographic evidence will persuade them otherwise. All one can say in situations such as this is:

"Feel free to believe what you like and enjoy your meetings. Please don't disrupt our meetings and please don't be unkind to those that disagree with you, particularly old people and children; and please don't frighten any horses."

Imagine that it is the first day of the Wimbledon Tennis Championships and the protagonists are on court ready to start their singles match. Before play commences, however, Player A objects to the height of the net saying it looks higher than the regulation three feet at the centre. The umpire checks the measurement and agrees with the line judges and Player B that it is precisely three feet but still Player A does not concur.

The umpire calls for the referee to adjudicate. The referee confirms that the height is correct and asks Player A to start the match but he refuses, still feeling the net is too high. The referee has no alternative but to disqualify Player A and award a bye to Player B saying:

"Player A, it is with regret that I have to disqualify you. I hope you continue to play tennis with opponents who see the height of the net as you do."

It is rather like this with Genesis. Even when faced with incontrovertible evidence, some people cannot be persuaded – they seem afraid that if they opened the door to logic it would, in some way, devalue their faith.

Chapter 2

The Onset of Religion

Before Mankind

It is estimated that modern man, Homo sapiens, the species of which we are a part, has roamed the Earth for around 200,000 years. In terms of the age of the Earth this is a very short time, relatively no more than the blink of an eye within a time period of one day. When compared to the age of the universe it is even shorter, more analogous to the time taken up by the single beat of the wing of a fly when in flight. To put this yet another way, imagine a clock face depicting the usual 12 hours. If the clock face is equivalent to the passage of time since the beginning of the universe, modern man would have first appeared less than one second ago. Though we may consider ourselves important, standing at the pinnacle of the animal kingdom, it is perfectly clear that we (excluding our predecessors such as Homo erectus and Homo heidelbergensis) did not begin to inhabit the Earth until very, very recently in the timescales of our solar system or the cosmos.

There is a conflict here. It is the conflict of 'intelligent design', a branch of creationism, versus evolution. Design would suggest that a creator God, the architect of the universe, must have had a blueprint for mankind well before he instigated the cosmic creation, that is, he must have known what his end product would look like. The end product would clearly have included all the stars in the universe and, specifically, all life on Earth including humans. If God has the awesome power to create the universe, then it follows that he has the power to deploy humans on Earth in a short time period (like the six days in Genesis, for example). Whatever the precise time period, it seems reasonable to assume that God would be capable of implementing his design well within a year, certainly within 100 years. But, it took much longer than that – not millions, but billions of years involving billions of superseding designs. With so many modifications, this is a far cry from 'right first time' and, therefore, cannot possibly be entitled 'intelligent design'. The only plausible explanation for the vast timeline with its immense array of adaptations is the gradual process of evolution. With evolution comes the appearance of one design following another even though no design exists at all.

Imagine the scene in the boardroom of a successful manufacturing business when the engineering director announces that his department had just designed a product that will revolutionise the company.

"When can we have this product?" asked the chief executive.

"Well, it'll take about 50 years," the engineering director replied.

As his jaw dropped, the chief executive said:

"That's not a design, it's a forecast. A design that we can't bring to market in our lifetimes is worthless. It's evolutionary, not revolutionary; now get to work on something we can bring to market in the next five years."

Clearly, any would-be design which fails to incorporate a reasonable timescale for its implementation is too nebulous to be considered a real design, let alone an intelligent one.

The Evolutionary Timeline

One can only marvel at the way our world has evolved and the immensity of the time period required by the transformation from the beginning to the present day. Palaeontology is the study of prehistoric life in general and, particularly, includes the evolution of organisms and their environmental interactions. The primary types of evidence used to decipher ancient life are body fossils and trace fossils (the result of biological activity). Geochemical evidence relating to rocks, water and soils has helped to provide clues to the evolution of life before organisms were large enough to leave fossils. By using radiometric age dating techniques, palaeontologists have been able to discover much of the Earth's history extending back over 3,800 million years. It was around this time that the Earth first became capable of supporting its earliest life forms. For almost half of that time, single celled micro-organisms lived within ecosystems with a thickness of only a few millimetres. The diversity and complexity of life began to accelerate around 2,400 million years ago with the oxygenation of the Earth's atmosphere. Multi-cellular plants and fungi have been found in rocks dated in a range from 1,700 million down to 1,200 million years ago whilst the earliest multi-cellular animal fossils have been dated to some 620 million years later. A table of events is shown next to provide a basic appreciation of the complexity involved.

Period Beginning (millions of years ago)	Period	Event
4,540	Pre-Cambrian	Formation of Earth Prokaryotes then Stromatolites appear
570	Cambrian	Hard-Shelled Molluscs First Trilobites Earliest Vertebrates
500	Ordovician	Earliest Cartilaginous Fish
435	Silurian	First Spiders and Scorpions
410	Devonian	Amphibians emerge from the water
360	Carboniferous	Earliest Reptiles
290	Permian	Reptiles become dominant
248	Triassic	First Dinosaurs
205	Jurassic	Dinosaurs become dominant
138	Cretaceous	First Flowering Plants Dinosaurs become extinct (65 million years ago)
63	Tertiary	Primates appear
24	Tertiary	Hominins descend from trees
2	Quaternary	Ice Ages occur Man emerges (towards end of period)

DNA (deoxyribonucleic acid) provides evidence which independently corroborates that provided by fossils. It is DNA that constructs the genetic code which identifies us and influences the way our bodies are built. It is made up of nucleic acid strands and we are all the product of a unique code inherited, about equally, from our parents. The most interesting aspect of DNA, however, is that it not only provides a link to our immediate parental ancestry but also a history that can be traced back much farther. Scientists are able to visualise our deep history by studying our DNA as it is copied from one generation to the next. At times, copying errors (or mutations) become imbedded. If these mutations are not harmful, they are retained in the DNA pattern and transferred to future generations. By examining the changes over time and observing how they have accumulated, scientists are able to establish relationships between people and their distant ancestors.

It has been discovered that our DNA is very similar to that of our closest primate relatives. Calculations show that we share over 98 percent of our DNA with chimpanzees and, though the physical and mental differences between humans and chimps are self-evident, our genetic codes are remarkably similar. We are equally related to the two species of chimpanzees, common chimpanzees and bonobos, and DNA studies have clearly demonstrated that of all the apes, chimpanzees are our nearest relatives, closely followed by gorillas, orang utans and gibbons. The order of divergence is reflected in this way. On the basis of the evidence, it is believed that humans share a common ancestor with apes (hominoids) and that the different species split off accordingly. First to branch off were the gibbons followed by the orang utans, then the gorillas and, finally, the chimpanzees leaving humans with their own line of evolution. Scientists, in analysing the difference between human and chimpanzee DNA, have estimated that in order to accumulate the measured difference, the two species must have split between five and seven million years ago.

The evidence for the evolutionary process is, clearly, overwhelming but suppose for a moment that we owed our existence today to intelligent design. Human beings regard themselves as important, the zenith of the animal kingdom but, if we are so important, why do we appear so much later than all the other forms of life depicted in the table of events? Why did dinosaurs come before us and roam the Earth for over 150 million years? What caused the extinction of the dinosaurs? Was it a cataclysmic event such as an asteroid or meteor collision? Whatever the cause, it is highly likely that had the dinosaurs not died out, we would not be here at all. In this context, doesn't the claim for intelligent design appear muddled and incongruous, if not downright absurd?

One suspects, looking at the timeline, the most plausible explanation for our existence is that it is attributable to chance as well as evolution by natural selection, the survival determinant of the most adaptable and capable of Earth's creatures. Just as the dinosaurs, trilobites and millions of other species have become extinct, mankind will also die out one day. It may take a million years, perhaps longer, but it is inevitable. Everything in the universe progresses in cycles. Stars such as our Sun are born and, eventually, die to be replaced by other stars. Because the Sun is slowly heating up, within a billion years or so the surface of the Earth will become too hot for liquid water to exist. All terrestrial life will end at this time if it has not, for other reasons, already ended. When mankind faces extinction, no amount of prayers or religious fervour will make any difference, just as they made no difference to the millions of victims of man's inhumanity, earthquakes, flood and volcanic eruptions that have occurred through the ages.

A Basic Need

Religion can be defined as the belief in and worship of some supernatural or divine power, especially in a personal God or gods. Because writing was developed only about 5,000 years ago, it is impossible to tell when religion actually started though it is most likely that it has existed in some polytheistic form (a worship of multiple gods) for tens of thousands of years. The discovery of the contents of ancient burial grounds has provided some evidence to suggest that religious rituals had taken place.

It is easy to imagine a primitive people being overawed and beguiled by the Sun and Moon, both constants in their lives. The Sun gave them warmth and was so powerful they could not behold it without causing damage to their sight. The shape of the Moon was ever changing and, occasionally, it was even powerful enough to blot out the Sun for short periods. They would have felt insignificant against these alien entities and, because of the influence they held over their lives, it would not have taken long before they began to appease and worship them as gods. Other gods would follow with unbridled zeal; one for thunder, one for rain, one for the forests, one for the sea and so on. The scope would have been unlimited.

Belief in a god or gods would have originated primarily out of fear. From their primitive forms of religion the ancients would have derived consolation, comfort and a sense of security. Their religion would have fostered togetherness, binding them to something much greater than their group or tribe and, in addition, it would have satisfied their innate requirement for leadership. The need for leadership has a long evolutionary history and applies to most species of the animal kingdom,

including man. We have long looked to different kinds of leaders
(meritocratic, military, spiritual, political and so on) to help maintain our
security and general well-being. Of course, the leaders have their own
need of leadership, ultimately in the guise of some divine power.
According to Bertrand Russell (1872 – 1970), the great British
philosopher and mathematician:

"Religion is based, I think, primarily and mainly upon fear. It is partly
the terror of the unknown and partly, as I have said, the wish to feel that
you have a kind of elder brother who will stand by you in all your
troubles and disputes."

Soon, individuals would have emerged who believed they could interpret
the will of the gods and, more importantly, were so articulate that they
could convince suggestible others of their art. To have someone
alongside who could become a spiritual leader and provide a conduit to
the gods must have seemed particularly desirable to an ancient people. It
would become the job of these early priests to develop a multiplicity of
rituals and incantations (to be enacted at appropriate times of the year) to
convince their congregations to worship and pray. It is a sobering
thought that these were the forerunners of the clergy of today. If life was
good for the congregation, thanks would be given to the gods but, if not,
they would be exhorted to worship more steadfastly next time. Some
things never change.

Ritual sacrifice crept in along the way but how did it become so
widespread? It appears to have been inherent in human culture,
proliferated by migration and absorbed by one religion from another. It
was practised by adherents of many religions as a means of appeasing a
god or gods or changing the course of nature. The start may have been

innocuous enough as a gift of flowers or food but if, seemingly, it was rejected as unworthy, the perceived value of the gift would have had to be raised to another level. The slaughter of animals would have come next and from there it would have been but a short step to the ultimate sacrifice, that of a human being. Evidence of sacrificial mutilation has been found by archaeologists in diverse parts of the world. Through the ages, this ritual became commonplace and, surely, ranks as the most abhorrent practice that can be laid at religion's door especially when, at its worst, it was actively encouraged by the priesthood. Polytheistic religions have existed for many thousands of years and are still widespread today. However, seminal events ostensibly took place around 4,000 years ago during the life of the Hebrew, Abraham, and the advent of monotheism. It is as if, at this time, God thought to himself:

"Well, thousands of millions of years have elapsed since I created planet Earth. Polytheism's had a good run so I think it's high time the Earthlings knew about me. I need someone to spread the word. I don't think I'll choose a polymath, a scientist or philosopher; it's an itinerant tribesman for me. Of course, the other way would be for me to appear before everyone at the same time to ensure a unified religion but I think I'll go with the single tribesman route. That way, millions of people will end up killing each other to defend their version of the truth. All I will have to do is sit back and watch."

Abraham

According to Jewish tradition, Abraham was born (as Abram) in the city of Ur in Babylonia around 1800 BC. He was the son of Terach, an idol merchant, but came to believe that the universe was the work of a single Creator and began to convey his belief to others. Abraham tried repeatedly to convince his father of the folly of idol worship without success. One day, when his father was away, he smashed all of the idols except the largest. When his father returned and asked for an explanation, Abraham said:

"The idols got into a fight and the big one smashed all the others."

"Don't be ridiculous," his father exclaimed, "these idols have no life or power. They can't do anything."

Apparently, Abraham replied:

"Then why do you worship them?"

From these humble beginnings, Abraham rose to become regarded as the father of the Hebrew nation. Jews are descended from the ancient Hebrew people of Israel (the Children of Israel) who settled in the land of Canaan, an area between the eastern coast of the Mediterranean Sea and the Jordan River. They share a lineage through their common ancestors to Abraham, his son Isaac, and grandson Jacob. The Children of Israel consisted of 12 tribes, each descended from one of Jacob's 12 sons, Reuven, Shimon, Levi, Yehuda, Yissachar, Zevulun, Dan, Gad, Naftali, Asher, Yosef and Benyamin.

Abraham was not a great leader in the sense that vast multitudes followed him during his lifetime but it is written in the Book of Genesis that he communed with God, a significant progression given that Abraham's antecedent, Noah, only listened. Was this communion real or imaginary? From its account of the creation, we know that Genesis should be viewed with healthy scepticism but the whimsy doesn't end there. What are we to make, for example, of the tale that the wife of Abraham's nephew, Lot, was turned into a pillar of salt for simply casting a backward glance when taking leave of the city of Sodom? Wasn't that a little harsh or was it, simply, a biographer's attempt to shock? Whatever the answer, perhaps it is fair to assume that Abraham was sincere and really believed he had entered into a covenant with God. It was in this covenant that God promised to make Abraham's descendents into a great nation. The covenant was sanctified by the rite of circumcision in accordance with God's command but why God, after tens of thousands of years of human existence, suddenly decided it was essential that the foreskin of an eight-day old child's penis should be sliced off with the aid of any proximate sharp implement remains a mystery.

During another communion, God commanded Abraham to offer his son, Isaac, as a sacrifice. Why is it that human sacrifice was so imprinted in the mindset of the servants of God? Whilst polytheistic ritualised killing might be excused on the grounds of palpable ignorance, surely greater enlightenment would be expected with the benefit of God's guiding hand. After a journey of three days, Abraham and Isaac began to climb Mount Moriah. Along the way, with natural curiosity, Isaac repeatedly asked his father where they would find the sacrificial animal and Abraham replied that God would provide one. At the end of the journey, however, it was Isaac who was bound and placed on an altar. Just as Abraham was about to slit his son's throat, an angel appeared, stayed his hand and provided a ram which was summarily dispatched. Because of his obedience, Abraham received further promises from God.

What a harrowing tale this is. Abraham must have been in enormous mental anguish for three days knowing that he was required to kill his son. Moreover, what kind of God is it that encourages the ritual of sacrifice? It is believed that it was God's way of testing Abraham's loyalty but this cannot have been necessary as an omniscient God would know everything there is to know about his servant's character. The test would have been entirely superfluous.

According to the Book of Exodus, Hebrews are God's 'chosen' people and from them will come the Messiah, the redeemer of the world. However, following Abraham's covenant with God, the Jews became one of the most conquered and persecuted nations on Earth. Even before the Holocaust, they were enslaved by the Egyptians for 400 years, then persecuted and forced to flee to different parts of the known world by the Romans. The Roman General, Julius Severus, ravaged Judea (part of Israel) during his savage repression of the Bar Kokhba revolt of 132 – 136 AD. His legions destroyed 985 villages and most of the Jewish population of central Judea was extirpated, sold into slavery or dispersed. Initially conquered by the Roman military leader, Pompey, in 63 BC, the Jewish kingdom did not again achieve independence as a sovereign state for over 2,000 years. During this period, Jews suffered further persecution at the hands of both Muslims and Christians. If Abraham could see what happened to his nation during four millennia, it is likely that he would be very dismayed and say:

"God, this is not what I had in mind when you promised me a great nation."

Woody Allen, the film director, wouldn't have been surprised as he once said:

"If there is a God, he's an under-achiever."

Albert Einstein (1879 – 1955), the great theoretical physicist and developer of the general theory of relativity stated:

"For me the Jewish religion like all others is an incarnation of the most childish superstitions. And the Jewish people to whom I gladly belong and with whose mentality I have a deep affinity have no different quality for me than all other people. As far as my experience goes, they are no better than other human groups, although they are protected from the worst cancers by a lack of power. Otherwise I cannot see anything 'chosen' about them."

Moses

Moses is regarded as the most important prophet in Judaism and is, furthermore, revered in the religions of Christianity and Islam. He is reputed to have led his people, the Children of Israel, out of enslavement by the Egyptians as described in the Book of Exodus. The existence of Moses as well as the veracity of the flight from Egypt is disputed amongst academics but, whatever the truth, it is clear that centuries of oral and written transmission have raised the story to the level of pure fantasy.

If we are to believe the account in Exodus, Moses must have had the persona of a religious fanatic and a bloodthirsty tyrant. In his early life in Egypt, he killed an Egyptian slave master, concealed the body and fled across the Red Sea to Midian. There he became a shepherd, an occupation he held for several years until one day he encountered a burning bush. Miraculously, the bush was not consumed by the fire. Moses believed that God spoke to him from the bush commanding him to return to Egypt and free his countrymen from bondage.

Moses and his brother, Aaron, held a number of audiences with Pharaoh, the Egyptian ruler, during which, in a display of power, they transformed a rod into a serpent, turned the river Nile into blood and enticed thousands of frogs from the river in a threat to overrun Egypt. None of this sorcery had much effect and the Israelites were permitted to leave only after God had visited 10 vile plagues on the Egyptians. The 'last straw' was the tenth plague which 'passed over' Hebrew houses but slew all first-born Egyptian male children, an event which is today commemorated as Passover, a Jewish holiday and festival.

Moses led his people eastwards on the long journey towards Canaan. The Red Sea was an impassable barrier so Moses stretched out his hand and the waters parted in two walls enabling the Israelites to pass through. In the meantime, God had encouraged an Egyptian army to follow in hot pursuit and, as they made their crossing, he released the walls of water. Pharaoh and his entire army perished but one wonders why God couldn't simply have convinced the unfortunate Egyptians stay at home. Hadn't they suffered enough already?

During the onward journey, Moses continued to impress his followers with his wizardry by once turning water from bitter to sweet and, on two occasions, striking a rock with his staff causing water to gush forth. On reaching the region of Midian, a dispute occurred with the Midianites who, subsequently, sent their most beautiful women to infiltrate the Israelite camp. Once within, the women seduced the young men and persuaded them to take part in idolatry. When Moses discovered what had happened, he ordered a mass execution of all culpable Israelites and then sent an army to wreak vengeance on the Midianites. According to the Book of Numbers, Moses instructed his soldiers to kill all Midianite women, boys and non-virgin girls leaving the virgin girls to be shared amongst his men. Clearly, this was not a man to cross.

Moses was summoned by God to Mount Sinai where he remained for 40 days. During this time, he received the Ten Commandments directly from God inscribed onto tablets of stone. Moses believed he heard God's voice enunciating the commandments, numbered as follows:

1.   I am the Lord your God, who brought you out of the land of Egypt, out of the house of bondage. You shall have no other gods before Me.

2.   You shall not make for yourself any carved image, or any likeness of anything that is in heaven above, or that is in the earth beneath, or that is in the water under the earth; you shall not bow down to them nor serve them. For I, the Lord your God, am a jealous God, visiting the iniquity of the fathers on the children to the third and fourth generations of those who hate me, but showing mercy to thousands, to those who love Me and keep My commandments.

3.   You shall not take the name of the Lord your God in vain, for the Lord will not hold him guiltless who takes His name in vain.

4.   Remember the Sabbath day, to keep it holy. Six days you shall labour and do all your work, but the seventh day is the Sabbath of the Lord your God. In it you shall do no work: you, nor your son, nor your daughter, nor your manservant, nor your maidservant, nor your cattle, nor your stranger who is within your gates. For in six days the Lord made the heavens and the earth, the sea, and all that is in them, and rested the seventh day. Therefore the Lord blessed the Sabbath day and hallowed it.

5. Honour your father and your mother, that your days may be long upon the land which the Lord your God is giving you.

6. You shall not murder.

7. You shall not commit adultery.

8. You shall not steal.

9. You shall not bear false witness against your neighbour.

10. You shall not covet your neighbour's house; you shall not covet your neighbour's wife, nor his manservant, nor his maidservant, nor his ox, nor his donkey, nor anything that is your neighbour's.

There is little that is revelatory here. Even an ancient people would fully comprehend the validity of the last five or six commandments without having to be reminded. The first three are much like the ranting of a demented warlord clearly intended to instill fear whilst the fourth claims God's approval for the author's well-earned day of rest. So who really crafted these laws, bearing in mind that there is something very human about them in style? Was it Moses, God, or someone else?

The first commandment begins by reminding the people that it was God who brought them out of bondage in Egypt whilst drawing a veil over the fact that it was God who caused their enslavement in the first place.   God had revealed to Abraham centuries before that his descendants would lose their freedom in Egypt for a very long time. Some things are quite incongruous aren't they?

When Moses returned to his people with the Ten Commandments he was enraged to find them indulging in revelry and the worship of an idol in the form of a golden calf. In a terrible anger he broke the commandment tablets and ordered his tribe, the Levites, to kill every guilty person, no exceptions being made for family and friends. In all, the Levites slaughtered 3,000 people before Moses returned to Mount Sinai for a further 40 days to inscribe new tablets. The point at which he delivered the commandments to his people marked the beginning of formal Judaism and the foundation of the first Abrahamic religion. Can there ever have been a greater irony than this? The sixth commandment states clearly 'You shall not murder', yet just before the birth of Judaism, 3,000 people were put to death on the explicit order of its greatest prophet. Given Moses' human rights record, it would have been surprising if anyone stepped out of line again.

But why was it necessary for so many people to die? Why does God always have to communicate via a messenger? Clearly, in this case, the people were not sufficiently persuaded by Moses that idolatry was forbidden and just thought they'd have a good time. If God had spoken to them directly via thunder and lightning or, simply, from a dark cloud, the impact would have been everlasting and so many lives would have been saved. Instead, for reasons unfathomable, God chooses to speak with an efficacy debilitated by the words of the prophets.

Other Prophets

After Moses, there came a procession of prophets too numerous to mention. All were said to have the power of prophesy, were able to commune with God, whilst the most gifted were able to perform miracles. Elijah struck the water of the River Jordan causing it to part so that he could walk on dry land. He was the first prophet in recorded scripture to bring the dead back to life and, when it was his turn to die, horses and a chariot of fire appeared before he was raised up to Heaven in a whirlwind. As he was elevated heavenwards, his mantle fell to the ground to be picked up by Elisha.

Elisha was no less prolific than his mentor when it came to working miracles. When King Jehoram's army was faint from thirst, he filled trenches with water. A poor widow's jar of oil was automatically and continually replenished saving her family from hardship. He resurrected the son of the woman of Shunem and multiplied 20 loaves of barley into a supply sufficient to feed a multitude. During the military incursions of Syria into Israel, he cured Naaman the Syrian of his leprosy.

Ezra is revered in Jewish scripture even though he appears not to have performed any miracles. He led a large body of exiles back to Jerusalem where he discovered that Jewish men had been marrying non-Jewish women. In despair, he tore his garments and confessed the sins of Israel to God before braving the wrath of his own countrymen as he resolved to purify the community by enforcing the dissolution of sinful marriages. It is impossible to say whether the principal figures of the scriptures were simply dreaming or suffering hallucination but it is interesting to note that, nowadays, nobody claims to work miracles or regularly commune with God. If they did, a more educated and, therefore, more sceptical public would be quick to ask for proof. There are plenty of preachers who, on the basis of analysis and deduction, claim to interpret the word of God for the benefit of their congregations but they fall short of claiming that they have received the word of God directly in the way of Abraham or Moses. If they made such claims, it would not be too long before they were confronted by men in white coats who would accompany them to an asylum and dress them in suitable attire.

Chapter 3

Religion Takes Hold

Jesus of Nazareth

With the coming of Jesus, people were presented with a very different way of looking at their lives. From this new perspective, even God's persona seemed to change from one preoccupied with punishment, instilling fear of retribution and vengeance to one whose disposition seemed to emphasise a more compassionate and loving approach to his subjects. When referring to the God of the Jews under Moses, Thomas Jefferson wrote:

"That sect had presented as the object of their worship a being of terrific character, cruel, vindictive, capricious and unjust."

This may be considered in stark contrast to his sentiments about the teachings of Jesus when he said:

"Of all the systems of morality, ancient or modern, which have come under my observation, none appear to me so pure as that of Jesus."

He added that they were:

"The most sublime and benevolent code of morals which has ever been offered to man."

No evidence of historical authenticity exists from the period spanning the lifetime of Jesus. There are no artefacts or self-written manuscripts, no dwellings or carpentry nor is there a contemporaneous Roman record of a Pontius Pilate sentencing a man called Jesus to death. All documents about Jesus were written well after his lifetime though, despite doubts about his historicity, it is generally accepted that he did exist some 2,000 years ago and that he was of exceptionally good character. The most authoritative accounts of an historical Jesus come from the four canonical gospels of the Bible written by the evangelists Matthew, Mark, Luke and John. The problem with these, however, is that much of the content appears fictional, mythological or falsified. In this regard, Thomas Jefferson wrote:

"We find the writings of his biographers a ground work of vulgar ignorance, of things impossible, of superstitions, fanaticisms and fabrications."

With the passage of time, an original work, perhaps already inaccurate, can become embellished by design or otherwise with more and more incredible accretions until it becomes unrecognisable from its state at inception. Thomas Paine, the 18th century English American author and philosopher, wrote in his book *The Age of Reason*:

"When the Church mythologists established their system, they collected all the writings they could find and managed them as they pleased. It is a matter altogether of uncertainty to us whether such of the writings as now appear under the name of the Old and New Testaments are in the same state in which those collectors say they found them, or whether they added, altered, abridged or dressed them up."

It is quite clear that Thomas Jefferson felt the same way. In a letter to former president John Adams, he wrote:

"The whole history of these books (the gospels) is so defective and doubtful that it seems vain to attempt minute enquiry into it: and such tricks have been played with their text, and with the texts of other books relating to them, that we have a right, from that cause, to entertain much doubt what parts of them are genuine. In the New Testament there is internal evidence that parts of it have proceeded from an extraordinary man; and that other parts are of the fabric of very inferior minds. It is as easy to separate those parts, as to pick out diamonds from dunghills."

The birth of Jesus, the Nativity, is a prominent element in the gospels of Luke and Matthew. According to both, Jesus was born in Bethlehem to Joseph, a carpenter, and his betrothed, Mary. Both accounts support the doctrine of the virgin birth in which Jesus was miraculously conceived in Mary's womb by the Holy Spirit. From where did the apostles derive this fanciful information bearing in mind that their writings did not take place until several decades later? At no time in their presence did Jesus say, "I am the Son of God," but they may have been convinced by implication or on hearing the testimonies of other apostles, particularly Peter. Could it be that Matthew and Luke assumed that Jesus was the Son of God and, therefore, that Mary must have been a virgin when she gave birth? Whatever the reason, immaculate conception has been quite commonplace in ancient religions. For example, the ancient Greek myth of Heracles has unmistakeable parallels with the story of Jesus. After a union with Zeus, king of the gods, the mortal and chaste Alcmene, mother of Heracles, gave birth to him. The wife of Zeus, the goddess Hera, plotted the death of Heracles just as King Herod wanted to kill Jesus. Also like Jesus, Heracles lived itinerantly as a mortal, assisting his fellow man and performing miraculous deeds. Both had excruciating deaths and whilst Jesus rose to Heaven, Heracles rose to Mount Olympus, becoming a god. The ancient Greeks wrote stories about him, worshipped him and built temples which they dedicated to him so the birth of Jesus is, most likely, a story borrowed from other religions and a long line of virgin births, differing only in the detail. Many of those religions died along with the civilisations that had initially enabled them to flourish and entered into the realms of mythology. They are no longer the focus of blind faith. Why should the virgin birth of the Christian religion be any more likely than those proclaimed in ancient Greek or Aztec beliefs, for example, and which were long ago consigned to fantasy and fable?

With no rooms available anywhere in Bethlehem, Mary and Joseph had to reside in a stable and lay their newly born son in a manger. They were visited by the Three Wise Men (or Magi) bearing gifts for the child they believed to be the King of the Jews. To arrive at the stable, they had followed a star but no normal star in the night sky would be much help in this regard. Perhaps it was a comet but, then again, comets do not tend to linger, travelling at many times camel speed. Nowadays, the story of the Nativity is portrayed in plays and celebrated every Christmas but, in reality, it can be no more than that, a wonderful story.

According to the gospels, King Herod, feeling threatened by the birth of a child proclaimed to be the King of the Jews, ordered the massacre of every boy child under the age of two years. In his dreams, an angel warned Joseph of the impending slaughter so he and his family fled to Egypt, returning to live in Nazareth only on Herod's death. It must be emphasised that none of these events has ever been confirmed by historians, thereby arousing suspicion as to their authenticity. Disbelief in the story of the Nativity and, in particular, the virgin birth is by no means new. Around 200 years ago, Thomas Jefferson wrote:

"The day will come when the mystical generation of Jesus, by the Supreme Being as his father, in the womb of a virgin, will be classed with the fable of the generation of Minerva in the brain of Jupiter."

That said, millions of people still believe the word of the gospels literally and are encouraged to do so by churches throughout the world.

The Miracles of Jesus

According to the gospels, Jesus was a miracle worker par excellence. He was much more prolific than any of the prophets that had gone before him and, it is apparent, the recorded miracles form but a fraction of those that he performed. In the first of well over 30 recorded miracles, Jesus attended a wedding feast and when there was only water left to drink, he turned it into wine. Was this circumstance worthy of a miracle? When his disciples could catch no fish in the Sea of Galilee, Jesus advised Peter to let down his nets further out. Peter did so and returned with nets bulging with fish. Of course, this is one miracle that could be explained by coincidence. Many of Jesus' miracles were associated with the healing of the blind, deaf and infirm as well as those with leprosy. All that was necessary was a command or the laying of hands. He restored a man's completely severed ear in an instant and brought Lazarus back to life after he had been dead for four days. By this time, Lazarus would have passed the stage of rigor mortis and decomposition would have commenced before Jesus attended to him.

Jesus rebuked the wind and waves to calm a storm and, in a separate incident, walked on water to reach the boat of his disciples. He fed a multitude of 5,000 men and their families who had come to hear him preach with only five small barley loaves and two fish. When the leftovers were gathered up, there was more food than at the beginning and to prove that this was no fluke, he repeated the feat on another occasion with 4,000 men and their families present.

When Jesus climbed up a mountain with Peter and two other apostles, it is written that he was transfigured, his face shining as the Sun and his garments as white as the light. Moses and Elijah also appeared on the mountain and as Jesus talked with them, a bright cloud appeared from which a voice said:

"This is my beloved Son with whom I am well pleased; listen to him."

Once again, of course, this begs the question that if God was prepared to address himself to three apostles, why doesn't he ever address himself directly to all of mankind? Everyone would then understand the standards of behaviour expected of them making life much less complicated and confrontational. Instead, we have had prophets throughout history delivering mixed messages, creating factions in every corner of the world.

Everyone will have their own views on the subject of miracles but it is a truism that people in the time of Jesus were much more susceptible to the possibility of miracles than we are today. On the 19th December 2009, John Paul II was proclaimed venerable by his successor Pope Benedict XVI to begin the process of his canonisation to sainthood. The canonisation can only take place if two miracles attributable to John Paul can be identified and though these would not be expected to have the majesty of the miracles of Jesus, they could still take a long time to find. Also, it should be pointed out that they are likely to be perceived miracles rather than de facto miracles. For example, consider a disastrous earthquake in which 10,000 people lose their lives and a little girl is saved after three days of being entombed. Most call it a miracle but it is, of course, pure chance. Out of 10,001 people, it is quite likely that at least one could live in an air pocket for several days before being rescued. If the child says that during her incarceration she prayed to John Paul and that he was her saviour, it is likely that the Catholic Church would consider this 'miracle', even posthumously, to be attributable to John Paul. The church would, no doubt, be satisfied by this kind of evidence. The negative thought that 30 other people also prayed to John Paul but were not so lucky would be cast aside as far too logical and distracting for miracle contemplation.

Throughout history, the church has endeavoured to control the faithful by telling them what they should think, what they should believe. Faith cannot tolerate profound thought and thought is stifled by faith so until one of these becomes sovereign, they will always be in conflict. One is reminded of the excellent television period drama, *Downton Abbey*, written by Sir Julian Fellowes, when Lady Mary, attempting to defend her sister, asserted:

"Lady Sybil is entitled to her opinion."

Her grandmother, Countess of Downton, replied:

"No she isn't, not until she is married, and then her husband will tell her what her opinions are."

Nowadays, people are a little more inclined to establish their own opinions though there remains a reluctance to challenge the ecclesiastical hierophants. Their views should be subjected to scrutiny, not allowed a 'free ride' simply because they claim to interpret the word of God.

Thomas Aquinas (1225 – 1274), a Dominican priest and exemplar of the Catholic Church, considered its greatest theologian and philosopher, was pronounced a saint 50 years after his death by Pope John XXII on the 18th July 1323. When at the canonisation process, the devil's advocate raised the objection that there were no miracles, one of the cardinals replied that there were as many miracles in the life of Aquinas as there were articles in his *Summa Theologica*, meaning thousands. It seems no provenance was required, the miracles being so abundant. One wonders what would have happened had the child from Hans Christian Andersen's fairy tale, *The Emperor's New Clothes*, been present at the canonisation. He might have said:

"But I still can't see any miracles, the *Summa* is only words."

There was probably more chance of seeing a snowman in the Sahara than witnessing a cardinal raise a continued objection. No cardinal would have welcomed the inevitable cries of infidelity, the threats to his comfortable way of life and possible excommunication. Discretion and silence frequently constitute the best policy.

What is the likelihood that the Jesus miracles are factual? Is it really likely that they happened or is it, simply, that more and more revisions of an original text have brought us to this metaphysical position? Some studies have provided evidence of a correlation between intelligence and religiosity. Highly intelligent (usually better educated) people are less likely to harbour religious beliefs whilst less well educated people are more likely to believe everything they read in the scriptures. It follows that the latter will be inclined to believe in the miracles of Jesus whilst the former, being more sceptical, will tend to consider them impossible. For example, less well educated people will see no reason to doubt that Jesus could bring the dead back to life. Better educated people will be more likely to believe that nobody can or ever could raise the dead. The contrast is hardly surprising in that teachers of higher education encourage their students to question continually, to research and think before arriving at a conclusion. The correlation between educational achievement and astrology or phasmophobia, a fear of ghosts, is probably quite similar. Millions of people actually believe that their futures can be predicted by planet alignment and, furthermore, that headless apparitions roam around in haunted places. Any cosmologist or astrophysicist would, of course, regard such popular opinion as mere bunkum. Advising caution in relation to our beliefs, Bertrand Russell pointed out:

"This state of mind is rather difficult: it requires a high degree of intellectual culture without emotional atrophy."

To emphasise the point, in 1998, the United States National Academy of Sciences issued a statement that asserted:

"Science can say nothing about the supernatural. Whether God exists or not is a question about which science is neutral."

However, according to a survey carried out in the same year, 93 percent of the members of the academy stated that they did not believe in a personal God. Roughly the same percentage of all U.S. citizens have asserted that they do believe in God so what is it that led the elite of U.S.

scientists to differ so dramatically from the general population? Apart from science, the difference can only be ascribed to the level of educational attainment which largely depends upon a propensity for enquiry and rational thought. Whilst the majority of scientists do not believe in any god, however, most are reluctant to challenge the religious beliefs of others even though they are fully aware of the human mind's proclivity for self-delusion.

René Descartes (1596 – 1650), the great French philosopher and mathematician of the 17th century, is well known for the statement, "Cogito ergo sum" or, "I think, therefore I am." Though Descartes attached a deeper meaning to this statement, it does emphasise the importance of being able to think rather than simply perceive. Bertrand Russell once declared:

"Most people would rather die than think; many do."

The thought process must, of course, be rational and well-informed otherwise we can end up with the wrong result. After all, "What did Thought do?" According to the old adage:

"It followed a muck cart and thought it was a wedding."

Descartes also stated that:

"All beliefs must submit to being proved beyond doubt."

He might have added:

"Except when it comes to religious faith."

The line between belief and rational thinking can become blurred so that exceptions to the correlation mentioned earlier will always exist. Pope Benedict XVI and Dr. Rowan Williams, Archbishop of Canterbury, are both highly educated but probably believe in the miracles of Jesus. If they do, it may simply be that their powers of deductive reasoning are outweighed by their faith. If they do not, then as pointed out by Bertrand Russell, it would not be in their interests to profess this disbelief. The Right Reverend David Jenkins, by expressing his doubts, has long been considered somewhat of a maverick by the established church. His views, of course, are shared increasingly by many others. During a street survey carried out in the English Midlands, the interviewer asked people if they believed that Jesus actually performed the miracles described in the scriptures. One humorist replied:

"Well, I think it's all a bit far-fetched; about as far-fetched as a bucket of rice from China."

Popes, archbishops and clerics in general, of course, have always seen it quite differently. It is as if they have been imprisoned inside a metaphorical box with the word 'faith' emblazoned on each of six sides. People inside the box are of three types – those that can't think rationally, those that can but refuse to do so, and those that can but, despite their doubts, are prevented by faith from taking a first step outside. The loyal priesthood and the faithful have remained inside the box whilst outside, changes are gathering pace.

Jesus Christ's Teachings

The teachings of Jesus were delivered, primarily, in sermons, allegories and parables that had an underlying message. His was a benign, benevolent ministry which emphasised peace and kindness. Have more kindly sentiments ever been expressed than, 'love your neighbour', 'be good to those that hate you', 'turn the other cheek', 'pray for those who persecute you'? We are reminded that because of his inherent goodness, he single-handedly transformed the perception of the vile, spiteful, vengeful God of Moses into a God of love and compassion. Despite this, he was regarded as a threat by the established church and the Sanhedrin, a council of judges, who conspired against him. The high priest accused Jesus of blasphemy and, after a protracted trial separately involving King Herod and the Roman Governor, Pontius Pilate, Jesus was sentenced to death. Remarkably, during his ministry, the only blood that was spilled was his own.

During a recent TV debate, an Anglican bishop stated that Jesus had died so that we might all be saved. He didn't say from what we were saved – a plethora of Old Testament plagues, perhaps. He was referring to the Book of Ephesians 1:7 in which, according to Paul the Apostle, Jesus died so that our sins might be forgiven. What does this actually mean? Does it make any sense? Is this not the most preposterous concept and does it not raise a number of questions? For example, whose sins are being forgiven precisely? Was it just the Jews at the time of Jesus or did it include the Romans as well? Is the whole of mankind to be forgiven, even those that clearly do not deserve to be forgiven and those that have no belief in God? Is there an expiry date on the forgiveness or does it apply in perpetuity? Not all sins are candidates for forgiveness, however, because on the day of judgement, God still decides who goes to Heaven and who is condemned to Hell. Confusing isn't it?

In any case, what kind of trade-off is it that demands someone's life in exchange for forgiveness? No doubt, Paul had a vision of God saying: "Well, here's the deal. If you murder my son and ensure that he has an agonising, lingering death in the process, I'll forgive all your sins - just like that."

It really stretches belief to breaking point, doesn't it? What kind of loving father would do this to his son, especially when he could have saved his son and forgiven everyone unconditionally? Does God always require a quid pro quo and isn't this whole concept of vicarious redemption an absurdity of egregious proportions?

According to the Book of John 14:6, Jesus said:

"I am the way, the truth and the life, nobody comes to the Father except through me."

It seems a rather curious comment to make and one wonders whether Jesus was right to claim such exclusivity. Where, for example, does it leave all the Muslims, Buddhists and Orthodox Jews? In Mark 10:25, Jesus says:

"It is easier for a camel to go through the eye of a needle than for a rich man to enter the Kingdom of God."

The implication seems to be that a rich man should give away his wealth if he wishes to enter the Kingdom of God, a sentiment that will not be lost on Sir Cliff Richard, one of Britain's most famous singers and a devout Christian. Cliff is, clearly, a very rich man so how does he reconcile his faith with his comfortable lifestyle especially when, if reports are true, he continually agonises over whether he has enough money? Perhaps he intends to give away all his money when he is a very old man or, perhaps, he doesn't consider himself rich, anyway. Or, it may be that he considers this an aspect of Jesus' teachings that need not be taken too seriously providing that one leads a good life in most other respects. There seems to be some merit in this point of view. Andrew

Carnegie (1835 – 1919), the great industrialist and the second richest man in history after John Davison Rockefeller, was one of the foremost philanthropists of all time. He believed passionately that wealth should be used to enrich society and, in verification of his conviction, he gave nearly all of his vast fortune away before he died at 83 years of age. The remainder was appropriated to various foundations and charities. When Andrew Carnegie died, he was still a very rich man but if anyone deserved to enter the Kingdom of God, it is he. Perhaps Jesus got it wrong when he denigrated a man for being rich instead of recognising compensating factors such as his compassion, benevolence and the way he led his life.

There is no doubting that Jesus sincerely believed he communed directly with God. Suppose, however, that Jesus was mistaken in believing this discourse actually took place. If so, what could have caused this misunderstanding? Could he have seen God in his dreams, in a trance, or in some other subconscious way? Could it have been hallucination or visions caused by intense, prolonged meditation and solitude? Most people have thought that they were in another world at some time in their lives (like the sportsman regaining consciousness after his operation and believing he was in God's presence). Crazy Horse was a famous American Red Indian (or Native American) war chief. His contemporary tribesman and cousin, in his classic text, *Black Elk Speaks: being the life story of a holy man of the Oglala Sioux,* provided an account of Crazy Horse's vision from which he derived his name:

"When I was a man, my father told me something about that vision. Of course he did not know all of it; but he said that Crazy Horse dreamed and went into the world where there is nothing but the spirits of all things. That is the real world that is behind this one, and everything we see here is something like a shadow from that world. He was on his horse in that world, and the horse and himself on it and the trees and the grass and the stones and everything were made of spirit, and nothing was hard, and everything seemed to float. His horse was standing still there, and yet it danced around like a horse made only of shadow, and that is how he got his name, which does not mean that his horse was crazy or wild, but that in his vision it danced around in that queer way."

Could Jesus have experienced something akin to this? Or, could he simply have been convinced by his own fertile, vivid imagination? The power of imagination should not be underestimated. It was none other than Albert Einstein who stated:

"Imagination is more important than knowledge. Knowledge is limited. Imagination encircles the world."

There is, of course, no way of knowing what the cause of any delusion might have been so the matter simply rests on belief; people either believe, if not undecided, that Jesus actually communed with God, or they do not. Many scientists have had their doubts. Charles Darwin, one of the great scientists of the 19th century, is one of them. He went so far as to say that:

"Science has nothing to do with Christ, except insofar as the habit of scientific research makes a man cautious in admitting evidence. For myself, I do not believe that there ever has been any revelation. As for a future life, every man must judge for himself between conflicting vague probabilities."

The Birth of Christianity

After the crucifixion of Jesus, Christianity saw its beginnings as a Jewish sect around the middle of the first century in the eastern Mediterranean. Its earliest development took place under the leadership of the Twelve Apostles, particularly that of Saint Peter, as well as Paul of Tarsus. From the start, Christians were persecuted by some Jewish religious authorities who disagreed with the apostolic teachings of the new movement. Punishments included death and in consequence, Stephen and James, son of Zebedee, became the first of the Christian martyrs.

Persecution on a much greater scale ensued at the hands of the Romans, firstly in 64 AD when Emperor Nero blamed the Christians for causing the Great Fire of Rome. It was under Nero's oppression that the early church leaders, Peter and Paul of Tarsus, were both martyred in the city. Further widespread persecutions took place under nine subsequent Roman Emperors, especially under Decius and Diocletian. During this period, Christians had to endure all manner of torture which included being thrown into amphitheatres to be torn to shreds by wild animals.

The plight of the Christians changed during the early part of the fourth century under the reign of Constantine I (Constantine the Great) (272 – 337). Before being able to assume total control of the Roman Empire, Constantine, the foremost general of the time, engaged in a number of civil wars. During one of these, against Emperor Maxentius, it is said he had his soldier's shields and standards marked with the labarum, a sign of Christ. Though vastly outnumbered, Constantine won a series of battles and, to demonstrate his gratitude, issued an edict of toleration known as the Edict of Milan, in 313 AD. The edict stated that

Christians should be allowed to freely practise their faith and from that point onwards they were absolved from state persecution. Constantine proclaimed his Christianity when he was around 40 years old but was not baptised until his final illness in 337 AD, a full 25 years later. On the 27th February 380 AD, the anniversary of Constantine's birth, Emperor Theodisius I enacted a law which instituted Christianity as the official religion of the Roman Empire. The second of the great monotheist religions was now well and truly underway.

Muhammad and Islam

Muhammad (570 – 632) is the founder of Islam, the third of the Abrahamic religions, and is widely considered to be one of the most charismatic and influential figures in history. He is regarded by Muslims to be a messenger and prophet of God and the restorer of an unadulterated original monotheistic faith as practised by Adam, Noah, Abraham, Moses, Jesus and other prophets. He was also active in a number of other guises including social reformer, diplomat, merchant, philosopher, orator, legislator, philanthropist and military leader.

Around the time of Muhammad, the Arabian Peninsula was largely arid making agriculture burdensome except near oases or springs. The landscape was speckled with towns and cities, the two most prominent being Mecca and Yathrib (later called Medina). Mecca was a large flourishing agricultural settlement whilst Yathrib became renowned as a financial centre patronised by many of the surrounding tribes. Communities were indispensable for survival in the harsh environment and tribal groupings developed out of necessity, based on the bond of kinship by blood. Indigenous Arabs were either nomadic or sedentary, the former constantly seeking water and pasture for their flocks whilst the latter settled and focused on trade and agriculture.

In pre-Islamic Arabia, individual tribes viewed gods and goddesses as their protectors, their spirits being associated with sacred trees, stones, wells and springs. Being the site of an annual pilgrimage, a cuboid-shaped building known as the *Kaaba* shrine in Mecca housed 360 idols of tribal patron gods. Today, the *Kaaba* is surrounded by the Grand Mosque and is regarded as the most sacred site in Islam. Aside from these gods, the Arabs believed in a supreme deity called Allah who was remote from their everyday lives and, consequently, was not the object of cult or ritual. The daughters of Allah, three goddesses, were called Allat, Manat and Al-'Uzza. A minority of monotheistic communities existed alongside their idol-worshipping neighbours including Christians and Jews whose forbears had, almost certainly, settled there as a consequence of Roman persecution. According to Muslim tradition, Muhammad was one of a small number of native Arab monotheists known as Hanifs.

Muhammad was born around 570 AD and belonged to the Banu Hashim, one of the most prominent families of Mecca. His father, Abdullah, had died almost six months before his son's birth so it was not long before Muhammad was sent to live with a Bedouin family in the desert. He stayed with his foster mother and her husband until he was two years old (though the historicity of this assertion is sometimes disputed). At the age of six, Muhammad became fully orphaned when, after a period of ill health, his mother, Amina, also passed away. For the next two years he was raised under the guardianship of his paternal grandfather, Abd al-Muttalib, of the Banu Hashim clan of the Quraysh tribe. When Muhammad was eight years of age, his grandfather also died and care passed to Abu Talib, the new leader of the Banu Hashim.

Muhammad was nurtured but it was a difficult upbringing, particularly as the fortunes of the Banu Hashim were in decline at the time. As a teenager, he often accompanied his uncle on trading missions to Syria where he gained commercial experience. In later years, he became a merchant travelling widely and because of his honesty and integrity he acquired the sobriquet *al-Amin*, meaning faithful and trustworthy. Accordingly, he was in demand as an impartial arbitrator and, when he was 25 years old, his reputation attracted the attention of Khadijah, a 40-year old widow. He and Khadijah married in 595 AD.

After some time, Muhammad began meditating alone for several weeks each year in a cave on Mount Hira near Mecca. On one of these visits around 610 AD, the angel Gabriel appeared to him and commanded him to recite the following verses by saying:

"Read: In the name of thy Lord and Cherisher, Who created,

Created man, out of a clot of congealed blood.

Read: And thy Lord is Most Bountiful,

He Who taught the use of the pen,

Taught man that which he knew not."

This was the first of Muhammad's revelations and he was to undergo several throughout his life but is it not curious that, of all the blessings God had bestowed on mankind, reference should have been made to 'the pen'? Muhammad, apparently, was illiterate so was this anything more than a self-conscious craving for literacy being brought to the fore subliminally? His revelations were accompanied by violent seizures causing his whole body to shake and, after the first of these, he returned home to his wife deeply distressed. Khadijah and her Christian cousin, Waraqah ibn Nawfal, consoled him and helped to interpret recent events concluding that he had been chosen by God to be his messenger. It is fascinating to note that had a different interpretation been derived, the whole of world history would have been immeasurably altered. A similar experience today would, most likely, be ascribed to a rather vivid dream but seventh century minds were inclined to be more credulous.

There is no doubt, given Muhammad's reputation for honesty, he sincerely believed that the angel Gabriel had visited him during the first revelation. A possible explanation, of course, is that the seizure caused him to imagine all that had transpired and made it seem very real. Who knows what might have been induced by a long period of solitary confinement and meditation high up in a cave? So what do we know? We know that Muhammad travelled to other lands where he would have learned about other religions, was acquainted with monotheism and that his experiences could have conditioned him to be receptive to a divine message. We also know from Muhammad's revelation that the first man on Earth being created from a clot of blood conflicts with the Book of Genesis in the Old Testament which claims that Adam was created from dust. So, which account is the right one? Well, almost certainly, neither because we now know from rafts of evidence that humans came into existence tens of thousands of years ago and are descended from primates. God, via Gabriel, would not have imparted the wrong information to Muhammad so the logical conclusion is that whatever Muhammad saw, it was a figment of his imagination. This remarkable and sincere man would have had no way of differentiating the real from the unreal so he could easily have been mistaken. To him, the visions, dreams or apparitions he experienced would have seemed totally authentic. How could he be expected to differentiate the visions emanating from his subconscious and divine revelation? The other possibility is that Muhammad knew from Christianity and Judaism that Adam was created from dust and, simply, forgot. In the second revelation which came three years after the first, he was commanded to begin preaching.

Along with the onset of Muhammad's preaching, around 613 AD, came the beginnings of the Quran, the holy book of Islam. According to the Quran, one of Muhammad's primary roles was to warn unbelievers of the final judgement and their eschatological punishment. He was also the bearer of good tidings for all those that abandon evil, listen to the divine word and serve God. According to the Quran, he was required to proclaim and praise the name of his Lord and not to worship idols or associate other deities with God. The key themes of the early Quranic verses related the responsibility of man towards his Creator, the resurrection of the dead and God's final judgment including vivid descriptions of the tortures in Hell and the pleasures of Paradise. Religious duties required of believers around this time were few. They encompassed an unconditional belief in God, asking for the forgiveness of their sins and the offering of frequent prayers. Furthermore, it was expected that they should assist those in need, reject cheating and the love of wealth and observe chastity. It was also stated that they were not to kill newborn girls.

It was Muhammad's wife, Khadijah, who first believed he was a prophet though, initially, most Meccans ignored his attempts to preach to them. His early followers comprised friends and family, sons of merchants, those out of favour within their tribe and the downtrodden. Opposition to Muhammad was aroused when he delivered verses that condemned idol worship and all forms of polytheism. As the number of his followers increased, he was seen as a threat by local tribes and the rulers of the city whose wealth depended upon the *Kaaba*. Muhammad's own tribe and guardians of the *Kaaba*, the Quraysh, were particularly offended by his denunciation of their traditional religion. He was offered several inducements to abandon his preaching but was unmoved. As a consequence, his followers were persecuted and it was during this period that Sumayyah bint Khayyat, a slave, was murdered by her master, a Meccan tribal chief. She became the first Islamic martyr when she refused to denounce her faith. Others were tortured but most suffered from a trade ban announced by tribal leaders that prohibited the citizens of Mecca from providing food and medicine to any supporters of the new movement. Muhammad, as a somewhat privileged member of the Banu Hashim clan, was not subjected to physical harm but suffered a continual spate of insults.

In 615 AD, some of Muhammad's followers emigrated to the Ethiopian Askumite Empire where they founded a small colony under the protection of the Christian Ethiopian emperor, Ashama ibn Abjar. In 617 AD, the leaders of two leading Quraysh clans declared a public boycott of the Banu Hashim in an attempt to coerce a withdrawal of its protection of Muhammad. The boycott lasted three years but, gradually, collapsed as a failed imperative. In 620 AD, there followed, arguably, the most momentous event of Muhammad's life. The angel Gabriel once again visited him and took him on a trip during which he was carried by a winged horse. The *Isra* and *Mi'raj* are two parts of a night journey, the first part transporting Muhammad from Mecca to a mosque in Jerusalem (a distance of some 800 miles) in the blink of an eye. Inside the mosque, he met a number of prophets including Abraham, Moses and Jesus and led them in prayer. During the second part, the *Mi'raj* (aptly named according to unbelievers), a celestial ladder descended and Muhammad climbed through the seven heavens whereupon he communed directly with God. God instructed Muhammad that he expected the faithful on Earth to offer prayers five times a day.

Whilst in Heaven, Muhammad is said to have seen an angel with 70,000 heads, each head having 70,000 mouths, each mouth having 70,000 tongues, each tongue speaking 70,000 languages and every one involved in singing Allah's praises. This would mean that the angel spoke 24 quintillion (24×10^{18}) or 24 billion billion languages for the praise of Allah. How much praise does Allah need? Was there ever a tale more likely to engender mistrust and scepticism regarding Muhammad's revelations? Nevertheless, many Muslims actually believe that the night journey was a physical one even though most Islamic academics, realising that such a position is devoid of credibility, claim it was spiritual. They do not tend to go further, however, and offer the most likely explanation that Muhammad was dreaming or was undergoing some other imaginary experience, perhaps influenced by a cataleptic stupor. In the minds of many, Muhammad's biographers have, in common with those of Christianity and Judaism, perpetuated myth and superstition depicted in all manner of numinous events. There aren't many winged horses in all the world's mythologies but if the ancient Greek religion could have Pegasus, then why shouldn't Islam adopt a version of its own? For all we know, Pegasus might have been offered an inducement to make a comeback, being brought out of retirement specifically for the event. Islamists regard the Quran to be the literal word of God but, for those unaware, the amount of it that is borrowed and plagiarised from other religions, most notably Christian and Jewish, would be a source of astonishment.

Muhammad's beloved wife, Khadijah, and his uncle, Abu Talib, both died in 619 AD. With Talib's death, the leadership of the Banu Hashim clan was passed to Abu Lahab, one of Muhammad's inveterate enemies. Soon afterwards, Abu Lahab rescinded the clan's protection from Muhammad, thereby, placing his life in danger. Consequently, Muhammad had no choice but to look for a new home for himself and his followers outside Mecca and, after several unsuccessful negotiations, he found potential in Yathrib. The inhabitants of the city were familiar with monotheism primarily because of its thriving Jewish community. So it was that Muhammad encouraged his followers to leave Mecca for Yathrib and, although the Quraysh attempted to repress the emigration, most Islamists managed to escape. The emigration is known as the *Hijra* and marks the beginning of the Islamic calendar (622 AD).

Yathrib had witnessed bloody feuds for at least the past century between the Arab and Jewish communities. Such was the esteem in which Muhammad was held by his new neighbours that a delegation representing 12 important clans invited him to serve as chief arbitrator, investing him with the authority to adjudicate in cases of dispute. Not long after Muhammad's arrival, Yathrib became Medina which literally means, 'city'. Among the first actions Muhammad took to calm longstanding grievances between the tribes was to draft a document known as the Constitution of Medina. It established an alliance or federation between the tribes of Medina and the migrants from Mecca specifying the rights and duties of all citizens including the Jews. In effect, the first Islamic state had been established and this was followed by a general acceptance of Islam by the largely pagan population.

Following the *Hijra*, the Muslim migrants were dispossessed of their abandoned assets by the Meccans. Living in penury because of a dearth of available professions, the Muslims turned to raiding Meccan trade caravans. This enabled them to acquire wealth, power and prestige whilst inching towards their ultimate goal of compelling Mecca's submission to the new faith. Mecca regarded the raids as acts of war and to legitimise the attacks on the Meccans, Muhammad delivered Quranic verses permitting the Muslims to engage in armed conflict.

The Quran is regarded by Muslims as 'the Word of God' so the verses must have been conveyed to Muhammad in some way. However, there is more than a suspicion of convenience here, isn't there? To initiate robbery and bloodshed, Muhammad needed God on his side, so this would appear to be a most appropriate time for a self-induced revelation. Did God convey his thoughts to Muhammad or did he, simply, convince himself that God condoned the thoughts that were already in his mind? Either way, Muhammad saw his way clear to wage war against the unbelievers.

In 624 AD, Muhammad led some 300 warriors in a raid on a Meccan merchant caravan only to be confronted by a larger force that had been sent as protectors. The antagonists met at Badr. The Battle of Badr, fought in the Hejaz region of Arabia (present day Saudi Arabia), was highly significant in the early days of Islam and a turning point in Muhammad's struggle with the Quraysh tribe. The battle has been recorded in Islamic history as a decisive victory attributable to divine assistance or, by secular sources, to the strategic genius of Muhammad. It is one of the few battles specifically mentioned in the Quran. Though outnumbered by more than three to one, the Muslims were victorious killing at least 45 Meccans and taking 70 prisoners. With only 14 Muslims losing their lives, the crushing triumph provided confirmation of their faith for Muhammad's followers and strengthened their position in Medina. When a series of disputes and revenge killings took place between the Muslims and Jews, Muhammad blamed the Jews for contravening the Constitution of Medina. He, subsequently, expelled the Banu Qauynuqa, one of the three primary Jewish tribes from the city.

The Battle of Badr committed Muhammad to total war with the Meccans, particularly the Quraysh. After the battle, he continued to attack caravans and led expeditions against any tribes sympathetic to his enemies. In response, Abu Sufyan, the leader of the Quraysh, formed an army of some 3,000 men and advanced on Medina. He met Muhammad's force by the mountain of Uhud. The Battle of Uhud was fought in 625 AD and, although the Muslims had the better of the early encounters, indiscipline led to their eventual defeat. Though 75 Muslims had been killed, including Muhammad's uncle, Hamza, the Quraysh failed to press home their advantage and returned to Mecca, content with their victory.

The defeat had to be explained so Muhammad delivered some more Quranic verses, presumably after yet another revelation. The message was predictable, indicating that the reason for the loss was in part due to a punishment for disobedience and also as a test of fortitude. With another attack on Medina in mind, Abu Sufyan attracted the support of nomadic tribes to the north and east of the city. In the meantime, Muhammad's policy was to discourage as many of these alliances as possible by mounting expeditions against any tribes hostile to him. Anyone known to have transgressed was dealt with severely. The chieftain of Banu Nadir, a Jewish tribe, was assassinated and about a year later the tribe was expelled from Medina.

By 627 AD, with the aid of the Banu Nadir, Abu Sufyan had mustered an army of some 10,000 men. Muhammad had a force of only

3,000 and adopted a defence unknown in Arabia at that time. The initiative for the defence, a deep trench dug wherever Medina was vulnerable to cavalry attack, is credited in Islam to Salman the Persian. The siege of Medina lasted several weeks but, as it was ineffectual, Abu Sufyan elected to return to Mecca. During the battle, known as the Battle of the Trench, the Jewish tribe Banu Qurayza had entered into negotiations with the Quraysh with the intention of revolting against the Muslims. The dialogue was never completed. Immediately after the retreat, however, the Muslims accused the Banu Qurayza of treachery and besieged their forts for 25 days before the tribe capitulated. During the siege, the Qurayza leaders offered to surrender on two occasions. Initially, they requested permission to depart from their stronghold with one camel load of possessions per person. When Muhammad refused this request, they asked to leave without any property, taking with them only their families. Again, Muhammad declined their request, insisting that they surrender unconditionally and submit to his judgement.

There followed one of the most controversial incidents in Muhammad's entire life. Compelled to surrender, the Qurayza were led to Medina where Muhammad appointed an arbitrator to determine the tribe's fate. Sa'd ibn Mu'adh was acceptable to the captives as they felt he was trustworthy and fair. His harrowing verdict, quickly served, was that the men should be put to death, the women and children sold into slavery and the spoils divided amongst the Muslims. Muhammad ratified the judgement stating that Sa'd's ruling was a decree of God pronounced from above the seven heavens and thus, some 800 men from the Qurayza were led to the marketplace. Trenches were dug and all were beheaded, a massacre that is, virtually, unimaginable by the standards of today. The decapitated corpses were buried in the trenches as the Muslims crowded to watch. Male youths who had not reached puberty were spared and they, along with the women and other children, were sold into slavery or distributed as gifts amongst Muhammad's companions. Muhammad chose one of the Qurayza women, Rayhana, for himself and all property and possessions were divided and appropriated as booty to the Muslims. The Qurayza had been exterminated, never to rise again.

The extant enmity and hostility between Jews and Muslims can be traced back to these events as their origin. Certainly, many would consider the punishment, namely annihilation, wholly disproportionate to the crime. Would Muhammad have been a greater man had he acted with magnanimity instead of such brutality? What if he had spared the lives of the Jews despite the verdict of Sa'd? He could, for example, have taken a number of hostages in order to discourage any further duplicity on behalf of the Qurayza. However, unwilling to risk the Qurayza's joining forces with the Quraysh, he chose to have the tribe slaughtered and proclaimed that it was decreed by God. But what did God have to do with it all? Could he have had his back turned dealing with an even greater crisis unfolding on some other planet millions of light years away? This seems unlikely given the number of prayers that would have been offered to him during the 25-day siege, and thereafter. They would have amounted to hundreds of thousands, but to no avail; God permitted the massacre, anyway. It should also be borne in mind that the Jewish nation had been worshipping God and only God for centuries, yet even this counted for nothing. This was a conflict between believers.

There was no evidence of the merciful God of Jesus anywhere to be seen. Centuries later, during World War II in one of the death camps, a

Jewish rabbi called out to God, pleading with him to save his people. There was no response, whereupon the rabbi proclaimed:

"There is no God."

If he were right, it would explain the lack of intervention and the reason why prayers never seem to be answered. Of course, if you ask another cleric to make sense of it all, he'd probably say:

"Well, they're now in a better place," to which the response might be:

"Well, couldn't they have gone to that better place after having lived full lives?"

Trying again, he might say, "God moves in mysterious ways." This is the catch-all, intended to explain everything that defies explanation and it derives from an eighteenth century hymn by William Cowper, the first lines of which are:

God moves in a mysterious way
His wonders to perform

One is left contemplating what it is that's so wonderful about the extinction of the Qurayza and further Jewish persecution throughout the Holocaust.

During the siege of Medina, the Quraysh had exerted their utmost force with the aim of destroying the Muslim community. Their failure resulted in a considerable loss of prestige and their trade with Syria was nullified. Muhammad continued to lead raids to the north of Medina and it was on returning from one of these that an accusation of adultery was made against his wife, Aisha. Aisha was exonerated from the accusations when Muhammad announced that he had received a revelation confirming Aisha's innocence and directed that the charges of adultery had to be supported by four eyewitnesses. The matter was closed.

In 628 AD, Muhammad ordered his followers to prepare for the *Hajj*, the pilgrimage to Mecca. About 1,400 Muslims set out on an unsuccessful journey as its completion was prevented by the Quraysh. Subsequent negotiations resulted in a treaty between the two sides signed at al-Hudaybiyya, primarily including an end to hostilities, the deferral of the pilgrimage and an agreement to send back any Meccans who had defected to Medina after the *Hijra*. The truce of Hudaybiyya had been in force for two years when it was annulled following further tribal conflict. Consequently, Muhammad, by this time the most powerful leader in Arabia, marched on Mecca with an army said to exceed 10,000 and, with minimal casualties, took control of the city. He declared an amnesty for all past offences excepting 10 men and women who had previously mocked him in both song and verse. Most Meccans converted to Islam and Muhammad, subsequently, had all the statues of Arabian gods in and around the *Kaaba* destroyed.

In 630 AD, at the Battle of Hunayn, Muhammad defeated the Banu Hawazin and Banu Thaqif. Not long afterwards, other tribes submitted to Muhammad and converted to Islam. Bedouin tribes also yielded but wished to maintain their independence, their established code of virtue and their ancestral traditions. In this case, Muhammad demanded that they enter into military and political agreements according to which they recognized the suzerainty of Medina and paid the *zakat*, a Muslim religious levy. So it was that, in the later years of his life, Muhammad first subjugated and then united the disparate tribes of Arabia into a single Muslim religious polity.

In 632 AD, Muhammad and his followers completed the *Hajj* after which he delivered a famous speech known as the Farewell Sermon. In this, he reminded his followers of their duties as Muslims, that all blood feuds should be abolished and that they should be good to women. Men should be entitled to discipline their wives, he said, but they should do so with kindness. He also forbade his followers to leave their wealth to a testamentary heir. A few months after the pilgrimage, Muhammad fell ill in Medina and suffered for several days before dying on the 8th June, 632 AD at 63 years of age. Against all odds he had, by sheer moral force and a large slice of luck, propagated the religion of Islam and set the foundation for its permanency, yet problems ensued immediately his towering presence was no more.

Sunni and Shia are the two major denominations of Islam. The historical background to Shia-Sunni antagonism lies in the schism that occurred on Muhammad's death because of a dispute over succession. Sunnis believe that Abu Bakr, the father of Muhammad's wife Aisha, was Muhammad's rightful successor as he was the most gifted candidate. Abu Bakr became the first Caliph of Islam. Shias, however, believe that Muhammad divinely ordained his cousin and son-in-law, Ali ibn Abi Talib, to be the next caliph and since then, they have not recognised the authority of elected Muslim leaders choosing, instead, to follow a line of imams they believe have been appointed by Muhammad or God himself. As a consequence, sectarian violence persists to this day. They have the same prophet and the same God, yet the extremists among them are prepared to maim and murder in the name of their cause; surely, it is religion gone mad.

Chapter 4

Other Religions and Beliefs

Polytheism

The sheer diversity of culture, religion and belief among the people of the world is truly astonishing, culminating in all manner of different customs and ritual. Take an example from the culture of the American Red Indian. It was customary among the Lakota Sioux to allow a woman to divorce her husband whenever she wished. She did so by moving in with relatives or with another suitor, or by placing the husband's belongings outside their lodge. Although some compensation might be required to smooth over any hurt or embarrassment, the rejected husband was expected to accept his wife's decision. At the other end of the spectrum, imagine what would happen in an Islamic country if a woman behaved in a similar way. There would be no hearing to establish any mitigating circumstances, death by stoning being the likely outcome.

The world is served by around 50 different religions and within each of these there can be a large number of denominations and sects. The result is a vast array of disparate beliefs and ways of worship that is simply breathtaking, yet God never seems to intervene to encourage unification or consensus. Around one third of the world's population don't even believe that a supreme god exists and, amongst the two thirds that do, there is a lack of consistency; God, Brahman (from Hindu) and Shangdi (of the Chinese Folk religion), for example, are all quite different. One can't help but wonder whether two or three billion people are destined for eternal damnation. If they are, does it seem fair that they should be disenfranchised because God hasn't given them any irrefutable signs? There have been no significant prophets for the last 14 centuries. Does this mean that God regards prophets irrelevant for the modern age? Or, does he feel that too many prophets and spiritual teachers have, paradoxically, been part of the problem in that they have been bearers of mixed messages? Surely, a single teacher would have been enough but, instead, we've had Moses, Elijah, Gautama Buddha, Lao Tzu, Jesus, Muhammad and Guru Nanak, to name but a few. Better still, why doesn't God cut out the middle man altogether and tell us very clearly how he expects us to conduct our lives? The misery that would have been averted by such a manifesto is incalculable.

Only about 50 percent of humanity is monotheistic with around one-third embracing polytheism and one-sixth, no religion at all. The major monotheistic religions, numerically, are Christianity and Islam with these accounting for around 99 percent of all those that believe in 'the one true God'. Judaism and Sikhism are minority religions forming the bulk of the remaining one percent. Numbers so disproportionate do not imply evidence of value or intrinsic worth; they are rather a reflection of the warlike nature and imperialist ambitions of the Christian and Islamic nations. Christianity spread throughout Europe and parts of Asia once it had become the official religion of the Roman Empire. Thereafter, the propensity for exploration shared by several European states was the catalyst for the success of their religion in distant continents such as Africa, the Americas and Oceania. A number of technical and geographical factors coalesced to make Europeans the most likely people to explore the Atlantic, for example, and develop its commerce. They had the drive and ambition to find new and profitable commercial opportunities outside of Europe as well as the necessity to create an alternative trade network to the one controlled by the Muslim Empire of the Middle East. Muslims were viewed as a commercial, political and religious menace to European Christendom. In particular, the Europeans wished to trade for gold to be found in Western Africa and also to find a sea-faring route to India where they could trade for luxury goods such as silks and spices without having to bargain with Middle Eastern Islamic traders. Missionaries frequently followed initial conquest to convert a subjugated people to the Christian faith. Jews and Sikhs never had the expansionist ambitions of Christian and Muslim states nor did they exhibit any yearning for exploration. Accordingly, their religions remained more parochial and their numbers relatively static.

Muslim expansion began with Muhammad and continued for centuries after his death in 632 AD. It was, initially at least, motivated by a desire to convert a conquered populace to Islam and within the space of a century, the Muslim Empire had become the largest ever seen, twice as large in land area as the Roman Empire of the 2nd century AD and the seventh largest in history. Muhammad's conquest of the Arabian Peninsula was followed by the Rashidun and Ummayad Caliphates, the latter of which held sway over an area stretching from the borders of China and India, across Central Asia, the Middle East, North Africa,

Sicily and the Iberian Peninsula to the Pyrenees. The conquest of the Visigothic Iberian Peninsula began in 711 AD and, after an eight-year campaign, most of Iberia was subjected to Islamic rule. In 732 AD, the Frankish commander, Charles Martel, defeated a 60,000-strong Muslim army at the Battle of Tours, effectively halting the northward Islamic advance. The retaking of lost lands by Christian forces began over three centuries later but was not completed until 1492 during the reign of Queen Isabella I of Castille and Ferdinand II of Aragon when the Muslims surrendered in Grenada. Subsequently, any Muslims not wishing to be expelled were ordered to abandon their Muslim faith and become Catholic.

The modern era, the period just after the Middle Ages, saw the rise of three powerful Muslim empires. The demise of the caliphates was followed by the Ottoman Empire in The Middle East and Europe, the Safavid Empire of Persia and Central Asia and the Mughal Empire of India. The territory controlled by these three empires was even larger than the Muslim Empire of the Ummayad Caliphate. The Mughal Empire began to decline after 1707 and was officially dismantled by the British after the Indian Rebellion of 1857. The Safavid Empire ended in 1760 with the death of its last ruler, Ismail III, and the Ottoman Empire collapsed in 1918 during the aftermath of World War I.

Islam had been introduced to India in the 7th century with the arrival of Arab traders and the conquest of parts of the province of Sindh. However, it only began to become a major religion during the later Muslim conquests of the Indian subcontinent between the 13th and 16th centuries. During this period, Buddhism and Hinduism declined rapidly when many adherents were forcibly converted to Islam. In 1398, Tamerlane, the Mongol warlord, penetrated deeper into India than any of his predecessors. As a Muslim, he detested the Hindu 'idolaters' and his army fell upon them with a savagery not seen since Genghis Khan's invasions of Eurasia almost two centuries earlier. Tamerlane's conquests paved the way for his illustrious descendant, Babur, to become the first ruler of the Mughal Empire.

By the beginning of the 20th century, despite the impact of the Mughal Empire, polytheistic Hinduism was still the dominant religion in India. This was largely due to the fact that some Mughal rulers were tolerant of religious differences as were the British (the British Raj) between 1858 and 1947. The British Empire, before its dissolution, was the largest in history and, though loss of life is inevitable whenever an indigenous people are subjugated, religious oppression was not a British imperative. Tensions increased between Hindus and Muslims until, in 1906, the All India Muslim League (AIML) was founded out of suspicion of the Hindu dominated Indian National Congress. The AIML complained that its members did not have the same rights as their Hindu counterparts. Among the first to make demands for a separate state was the writer and philosopher, Allama Iqbal, who, in his presidential address to the 1930 convention of the Muslim League, said that a separate nation for Muslims was crucial. By 1946, public order had broken down across Northern India and Bengal and thousands were killed or injured. To avoid full scale civil war, the pressure increased to seek a political solution incorporating a partition of territories. So it was that the Partition of India based on religious demographics led to the creation, on the 15th August 1947, of the sovereign states of the Dominion of Pakistan (later the Islamic Republic of Pakistan and the People's Republic of Bangladesh) and the Union of India (later the Republic of India). The partition was promulgated in the Indian Independence Act 1947 and hastened the dissolution of the British Indian Empire. Massive population movements occurred between the newly formed states in the ensuing months. About 14.5 million people crossed the borders to new homelands where they hoped to find the relative safety of religious majority. Muslims left India for Pakistan and Hindus and Sikhs left Pakistan for India. The newly formed governments were completely overwhelmed by migrations of such staggering magnitude and violence and slaughter occurred on both sides. The number of deaths was estimated at more than 500,000 and the ineffable violence created an atmosphere of mutual hostility and suspicion between India and Pakistan that plagues their relationship to this day.

Islam is the dominant religion of Indonesia which has the largest Muslim population in the world. Currently, there are over 200 million Muslims in this country of islands accounting for about 85 percent of all the inhabitants. The remaining 15 percent are, primarily, Christians. The spread of Islam began at the end of the 13th century and, by the beginning of the 17th century, it had supplanted Hinduism and Buddhism as the dominant religion. Both Hinduism and Buddhism have largely faded away. In complete contrast to the advance of Islam elsewhere in the world, success was achieved largely through trade and assimilation rather than bloodletting. The result is a much less austere form of Islam than that practised in the Middle East.

Polytheism has been with us for tens of thousands of years and, despite the most strenuous efforts by monotheists, still accounts for over two billion people worldwide. When regarding the choice of some governments to regulate religion and thought, the great Thomas Jefferson, a firm advocate of religious freedom, stated:

"The legitimate powers of government extend to such acts only as are injurious to others. But it does me no injury for my neighbour to say there are twenty gods, or no god. It neither picks my pocket nor breaks my leg."

The first commandment, said to have been delivered by Moses on a tablet of stone, states:

You shall have no other gods before Me.

Perhaps this has been misunderstood. Could 'before Me' be the same as, 'ahead of Me' or 'higher than Me', implying that God was willing to accept other gods as long as he was considered the Supreme God? Like so many others, this commandment arouses the suspicion that it was man-made, if only because an omniscient deity would not have fallen prey to such ambiguity. Or, perhaps God is tolerant of other gods, after all. If this were not the case, how else could polytheism have lasted for so long? For that matter, how could any religion have lasted so long? The fact is that beliefs such as those in God or gods that cannot be falsified empirically continue to form the basis of religion, the essence of which is drawn primarily from emotion. Once emotion is the overriding factor rather than logic and reason, conclusions drawn can be random, unpredictable and frequently absurd.

Polytheism is usually convened into a pantheon of gods and goddesses replete with ritual and mythology. It was the typical form of religion during the Bronze Age and Iron Age and is well documented in the religions of classical antiquity, especially those of Greece and Rome. It persists today in traditions such as Hinduism, Buddhism, Shintoism and Chinese folk religion. The deities of polytheistic religions are often portrayed as a hierarchy of complex personalities having individual skills, needs and ambitions and are usually seen as anthropomorphic in their character traits but with additional powers and knowledge. They are the highest echelon in a continuum of supernatural beings and spirits.

Greek resistance against the Roman Empire ceased after the Battle of Corinth in 146 BC.   Thereafter, the Romans assimilated Greek polytheistic culture to such an extent that the same deities were renowned with different names: Zeus (Greek) and Jupiter (Roman), for example. Other examples of polytheistic pantheons include the gods of Sumeria and Egypt and post-classically, the Norse and Aztec gods.   Ancient Greek religion was based on a wide spectrum of deities with Zeus, the king of the gods, exerting his power over the other gods, though not with complete sovereignty.   Some deities had dominion over nature's phenomena with Zeus, as the sky god, initiating thunder and lightning and Poseidon ruling over the sea and earthquakes.   Hades had jurisdiction over the dead and the Underworld whilst Helios controlled the Sun.   The principal deities of the Greek pantheon, residing at the summit of Mount Olympus were Zeus, Hera, Poseidon, Demeter, Athena, Hestia, Apollo, Artemis, Ares, Aphrodite, Hephaestus, and Hermes, with Dionysus later taking Hestia's place.   The gods, though immortal, were not omnipotent as they had to obey fate. After the Trojan War, for example, it was the fate of Odysseus to return home to Ithaca on a journey which some gods sought to impede but could not prevent.   The Greek deities behaved like humans, had the same vices and often interacted with humans, even spawning children with them.   At times, gods would confront each other as they vied for supremacy.   According to Homer's *Iliad*, Zeus, Aphrodite, Ares and Apollo championed the

Trojans during the Trojan War while Hera, Athena and Poseidon lent their support to the Greeks.

The ancient Greek religion, supplanted by Christianity, has long since been consigned to the realms of mythology. Few believe that the gods of the Greek pantheon ever really existed even though many aspects of their religious structure survive in the monotheism of today, no doubt handed down through the generations. But, weren't the gods immortal? If so, they must still be living on Mount Olympus feeling unwanted and eating ambrosia. Or, maybe they never really existed other than in the minds of a fickle, religious people who discarded them amidst the contagion of a new, though equally fanciful, ideology. Perhaps this is what happens to all religions in the fullness of time: their relevance ceases when something better comes along. There is little doubt that there are more extinct than extant religions. If a religion is not based on fact, only on misappropriated belief, the erosion of popular opinion can occur at any time. If there is no redress, that religion will be relegated to mythology along with all the rest.

Whilst as a religion it lies in disrepute, Greek mythology has exerted an extensive influence on the culture, arts and literature of western civilisation and remains an integral part of its heritage and language. Poets and artists through the ages have derived inspiration from the vibrancy of the stories, myths and legends and have never failed to discover contemporary significance in the mythological themes.

In contrast, very much alive, Hinduism is the predominant and indigenous religion of the Indian subcontinent and is regarded as the world's oldest major religion with over 900 million followers. It evolved organically and spread over a large territory marked by considerable ethnic and cultural diversity. Without a single founder, it is formed of a multiplicity of traditions and is an accumulation of distinct philosophical and intellectual observations rather than a rigid, common set of beliefs. It grew both by innovation from within the movement and by assimilation of external traditions or cults. The result is a vast array of religious practices, ranging from innumerable small, unsophisticated sects to major religious groups with millions of adherents. Consequently, the identification of Hinduism as an independent religion distinct from Buddhism or Jainism hinges on the affirmation of its followers. Hinduism grants absolute freedom of belief and worship and conceives the whole world as one family that deifies a single truth. The embodiment of Hinduism is affirmed in the ancient text of the *Rig Veda* as follows:

"There is one reality, the wise call it by many names; there is one truth, reached by many paths."

This statement defines the starting point of Hinduism and the Hindu way of life. The Hindu mindset considers the sacred books of all religions, its own included, as nothing more than limited human perspectives on an unlimited reality. Though each perspective captures an aspect of the truth, no single view is capable of conveying it totally. It, therefore, accepts all forms of beliefs and dismisses the identities of distinct religions. Hence, Hinduism is devoid of the concepts of apostasy, heresy and blasphemy for which so many people have died within the Christian and Islamic faiths. With so much mutability, Hinduism is difficult to classify but it is sometimes referred to as henotheistic, involving devotion to a single god whilst tolerating the existence of others. The primary god is Brahman, the cause and foundation of everything.

Brahman has three distinct forms: Brahma (the Creator), Vishnu (the Preserver) and Shiva (the Destroyer) under which are aligned a panoply of lesser gods.

Hindus believe in reincarnation, that the soul is eternal and lives many lifetimes in a succession of bodies. The soul, ostensibly, is at times born in a human body or in the bodies of animals, plants or other life forms. The cycle of repeated reincarnation is known as *Samsara* which is governed by *Karma*, the determinant of a particular destiny. The belief is that the next incarnation is always dependent upon the previous one, with current misfortunes governed by acts in a past life. Consequently, present actions will impact subsequent lives, thus stimulating Hindus to live in a better way than they did during previous incarnations.

The spiritual goal of a Hindu is to become in unison with Brahma, a freedom known as *Moksha*. Until *Moksha* is achieved, Hindus believe that they will be repeatedly reincarnated in order that they may realise the truth (that only Brahman exists, nothing else). For many Hindus, there are four goals in human life: *Moksha, Dharma, Artha* and *Karma*. *Moksha* releases the soul from the cycle of rebirth and *Dharma* is the code for leading one's life. *Artha* is the pursuit of material gain by lawful means and *Karma* determines that through pure acts, knowledge and devotion, a higher level of reincarnation can be achieved. Hindus can choose one or all of four different paths to the realisation of *Moksha*: the paths of spiritual knowledge, meditation, devotion and good works. In comparison with the major monotheist religions, Hinduism practises a welcome tolerance as implied by the words of Sita Ram Goel, a 20th century Hindu historian. When after reading a book on monotheism, he wrote:

"It was a profound study of monotheism, the central dogma of both Islam and Christianity, as well as a powerful presentation of what the monotheists denounce as Hindu polytheism. I had never read anything like it. It was a revelation to me that monotheism was not a religious concept but an imperialist idea."

Buddhism could, in many ways, be viewed as a guide to a philosophical or ethical way of living rather than a religion. It began around 2,500 years ago in North East India, founded on the teachings of Siddhartha Gautama (the Buddha or 'awakened one') and currently numbers about 400 million adherents. Gautama was born around 563 BC into a royal family in the village of Lumbini in Nepal. For many years, he lived within palace walls shielded from most of the sufferings of life. One day, in adulthood, after marrying and fathering a child, he ventured outside and saw, for the first time, an old man, a sick man, a corpse and, finally, an abstinent holy man. Worried by this experience, he learned that sickness, age and death were the inevitable fate of all human beings. In search of a way to escape from the certainty of pain and death, he abandoned royal life to begin a spiritual quest. He studied with famous religious teachers, underwent prolonged fasting, breath-holding and exposure to pain but failed to find a way to end suffering. At the age of 35, he allegedly sat in meditation under a sacred fig tree (known as the Bohdi tree) in the town of Bohd Gaya and vowed not to rise before achieving enlightenment (the knowledge into the true nature of reality). After many days, he finally escaped the shackles of his mind, thereby, liberating himself from the cycle of suffering and rebirth to arise a fully enlightened being. Soon after, he attracted a band of followers and instituted a monastic order. By this time, as the Buddha, he spent the rest of his life teaching his discovered path of awakening and travelling throughout the northeastern part of the Indian subcontinent. He died at the age of 80 in Kushinagar, India. Two of his disciples inspired the main schools of Buddhism that were inaugurated at least 200 years after he died. Sariputta inspired the Theravada school, considered to be analytical and monastic, whilst Maudgalyayana was the instigator of the Mahayana school which propounds compassion and democracy. Amongst other denominations are Tibetan, Chinese and Japanese including Soto and Zen.

Buddhists believe that there is a cycle of birth, life, death and rebirth which continues in perpetuity. They believe that up to the point that someone gains enlightenment, they will be reborn after death. Breaking out of the cycle is known as *Nirvana*, the end of imperfection, freedom from suffering and the achievement of perfect peace. Buddhists attempt to reach *Nirvana* by following Buddha's teachings and by meditating, emptying the mind of all thoughts to enable them to see with clarity. They believe that nothing in the world is perfect and that Buddha understood the reasons.   Buddhists worship at home or in a temple facing an image of Buddha whom they regard as a person, not a god. They do not believe in a personal creator God and, though they recognise god-like beings (*devas*), they tend not to worship them.

Buddha's teachings are frequently divided into three parts; the Three Signs of Being, the Four Noble Truths and the Noble Eightfold Path. It is in the first of these parts that Buddha proposed nothing in life is perfect because of its many deficiencies such as boredom and general discomfort. The view that Buddha's recognition of life's imperfections could not be reconciled with the notion of an omnipotent creator may account for the Buddhist lack of belief in God.   In a remarkable perception of the evolutionary process, Buddha stated that everything in life, even solid things such as mountains, is in constant change. He, furthermore, posited that there is no soul and that a person's life force (*Karma*) is conveyed to a subsequent life. The cumulative consequence of a person's actions during one existence influences his or her destiny in the next.

Buddha's thoughts were amplified in The Four Noble Truths. The first of these, *Dukkha*, notes that suffering exists and life includes pain, disease, ageing and, ultimately, death. We also endure psychological forms of suffering such as loneliness, frustration, boredom, fear, embarrassment, disappointment and anger. The second truth, *Samudaya*, states that the cause of suffering is craving and the need for control. It can take many forms such as the desire for fame, popularity, power, wealth and prestige. *Nirodha*, the third truth, evinces that there is an end to suffering; that it can be overcome and true happiness and contentment attained. If we release our craving and live each day at a time (not dwelling in the past or an imagined future) then we can become happy and free. We then have more time and energy to help others and this, ultimately, leads to the state of *Nirvana*. Finally, *Magga* simply states that in order to end suffering, one must follow the Noble Eightfold Path.

The Eightfold Path focuses the mind on being fully aware of our thoughts and actions and the development of wisdom. Buddha advised that people should avoid extremes, that the 'Middle Way' is best and that the path to enlightenment comes through the practice and development of wisdom, morality and meditation. He advocated a purity of view (understanding), intention, speech, action, livelihood, effort, mindfulness and concentration.

The basic Buddhist code of ethics is encapsulated in the Five Precepts which are formulated not as imperatives but as training rules for lay people to undertake voluntarily. Adherents profess that they will refrain from taking the life of a sentient being, from stealing, from sexual misconduct, from lying and becoming intoxicated.

Of the world's religion's, Buddhism must surely be the most kindly and benign with the first of the precepts setting Buddhism apart from all major religions. Animals have always been regarded in Buddhist thought as sentient beings, different from humans in their intellectual ability but no less capable of feeling suffering. Furthermore, animals possess Buddha nature (according to the Mahayana school) and, therefore, an equal potential to become enlightened. Moreover, the doctrine of rebirth posited that any human could be reborn as an animal, and any animal could be reborn as a human. On this basis, an animal might be a dead relative reborn and, looking back through an infinite series of lives, the perception is that every animal would be related to a specific person in some way. The Buddha expounded that sentient beings living in the animal realm have been our mothers, brothers, sisters, fathers, children and friends in past rebirths. One could not, therefore, make a definite distinction between moral rules applicable to animals and those applicable to humans. The interconnectivity means that, ultimately, humans and animals are part of a single family.

Cosmologically, animals were believed to inhabit a distinct world, separated from humans not by space but by state of mind. Rebirth as an animal was considered to be one of the unhappy rebirths, usually involving more suffering than that of humans. Buddhist commentarial texts depict many sufferings apposite to the animal world. They note that, even where no human beings are present, animals are attacked and eaten by other animals, live in fear, endure extreme changes of environment and have no security of habitation. Those that live among humans are often slaughtered for food or forced to work, being regularly beaten before they are killed towards the end of their lives. In addition, they suffer from ignorance, not understanding what has befallen them, unable to alter their circumstances and having to rely almost exclusively on instinct.

Concern for animals is confirmed at the beginning of Buddhist history. The first Buddhist monarch of India, Ashoka the Great (ca. 304 BC – 232 BC), expressed concern in his Edicts for the animals that had been killed so that he might eat. Accordingly, he implemented a number of restrictive and protectionist measures to improve animal welfare. Both wild and domesticated animals were beneficiaries of his reform programmes. All young animals and mothers still feeding their young were decreed safe from harm and the burning of forests was outlawed to protect the creatures living within. Ashoka, one of the earliest conservationists, is renowned for safeguarding the interests of countless animals, even going so far as to construct veterinary hospitals.

Interpretation of the Buddhist sutras regarding vegetarianism has, at times, caused some contention. Not all Buddhists, including monks, are vegetarians but the basic precept of non-harm to animals is upheld. Some monasteries strictly forbid the eating of meat whilst others are more flexible and permit monks to accept donated food. However, they are forbidden from accepting animal flesh if they know, believe or suspect that the animal was killed especially on their behalf. They must not, in other words, be the reason for an animal's slaughter. Other interpretations permit the eating of meat on the condition that the animal died of natural causes. Some sutras fundamentally condemn meat consumption because of the distress caused to animals when in the presence of a meat-eater. Others simply consider vegetarianism as an ideal state from which some humans descended and, as a result of their increasing wickedness, began to live by hunting, a demeaning occupation.

In contrast to its monotheistic counterpart, polytheistic thinking posits that issues of morality are relative to the individual or culture. Each believer is free to worship a god of choice in a personal manner without any emphasis being placed on the hope of eternal salvation.

Pantheism

Pantheism is based on the view that the universe, or nature, and divinity are identical. Thus, pantheists do not believe in an individual, anthropomorphic or creator God but express the idea that 'God' is best seen as the universe itself. Although there are divergences within pantheism, the central concepts found in practically all versions see the cosmos as an all-encompassing entity, the sacredness of which is to be treated with reverence. The term 'pantheist' was purportedly first used in English by the writer and philosopher, John Toland, in *Socinianism Truly Stated, by a pantheist*, his work of 1705. He referred later in a 1710 letter to:

"The pantheistic opinion of those who believe in no other eternal being but the universe."

Pantheistic ideas, however, were by no means new having been expressed much earlier by writers, schools of philosophy and various religious movements, including Taoism. Pantheism retreated when it was regarded as heresy during the Christian dominated years between the

4th and 15th centuries. The first open revival came during the late 16th century with the work of Giordano Bruno (1548 – 1600), an Italian Dominican friar, philosopher, mathematician and astronomer, whose cosmological theories went beyond the others of his time when he by proposed that the Sun was essentially a star. Moreover, he expounded that the universe contained an infinite number of inhabited worlds populated by other intelligent beings. He was burned at the stake by the secular authorities in 1600 after having had a metal spike driven through his tongue as decreed by the Roman Inquisition that had found him guilty of heresy for his pantheistic views. The fact that he was largely correct was never likely to provide any guarantee of immunity from the church obscurantists who, rather than allow him the benefit of the doubt, decided he'd be better off dead. Posthumously, he gained considerable fame, particularly among 19th and early 20th century commentators who regarded him as a martyr for freedom of thought and modern scientific theory. Good people perform good deeds and bad people perpetrate bad ones but for good people to do bad things, a strong dose of religion seems to be a prerequisite.

In 1633, the Italian physicist and astronomer, Galileo Galilei (1564 – 1642), was hauled before a panel of holy men who accused him of heresy. By observing the movement of planets with his own telescope, an enhanced version of an earlier Dutch invention, he had found conclusive evidence for heliocentrism. In direct contravention of biblical text (now known to be nonsense) and possessing a lesser resolve than Bruno, Galileo recanted. He feigned acceptance when the priests told him he could not have seen what he claimed to have seen, that his eyes had deceived him. He was spared Bruno's fate and spent the rest of his life under house arrest, ordered to read seven penitential psalms once a week for the first three years.

Also highly influential was Baruch Spinoza's magnum opus, *Ethics,* published after his death in 1677. Spinoza (1632 – 1677) was a Dutch Jewish philosopher and scientist and one of the greatest minds in history, respected and admired by all the foremost thinkers of his time and thereafter. The breadth and importance of his work was not fully realised until years after his death but by laying the groundwork of the 18th century Enlightenment and modern biblical criticism, he became one of the great rationalists of 17th century philosophy.

He was raised in a Jewish community and gradually developed highly controversial views regarding the authenticity of the Hebrew Bible, the Tanakh, and the nature of the divine. In July 1656, the Jewish religious authorities issued a writ of *cherem* (a kind of excommunication) against him, effectively banishing him from Jewish society at only 23 years of age. His works were later listed on the Catholic Church's Index of Forbidden Books. Whilst the language of the *cherem* was particularly harsh, the exact reason for the expulsion of Spinoza was not stated. However, the 20th century philosopher, Steven Nadler, stated it is likely that:

"He was giving utterance to just those ideas that would soon appear in his philosophical treatises. In those works, Spinoza denies the immortality of the soul; strongly rejects the notion of a providential God - the God of Abraham, Isaac and Jacob; and claims that the Law was neither literally given by God nor any longer binding on Jews. Can there be any mystery as to why one of history's boldest and most radical thinkers was sanctioned by an orthodox Jewish community?"

Spinoza was, in Bertrand Russell's words:

"Cursed with all the curses in Deuteronomy and with the curse that Elisha pronounced on the children who, in consequence, were torn to pieces by the she-bears."

Spinoza lived a quiet, saintly existence as a lens grinder, turning down rewards and honours throughout his life including a number of prestigious teaching positions. He gave his share of the family inheritance to his sister. He preached a philosophy of tolerance and benevolence and his accomplishments and righteous character prompted the 20th century philosopher, Gilles Deleuze, to name him 'the prince of philosophers'. He died at the age of 44, allegedly of a lung illness such as tuberculosis or silicosis exacerbated by fine glass dust inhaled while grinding optical lenses. He is buried in the churchyard of the Christian Nieuwe Kerk in The Hague. Albert Einstein revered Spinoza and wrote a poem in his honour, part of which goes:

How much do I love that noble man
More than I could tell with words
I fear though he'll remain alone
With a holy halo of his own.

For a time during the 19th century, pantheism was the religious viewpoint of many leading writers and academics including William Wordsworth and Samuel Taylor Coleridge in Britain and the German philosophers, Schelling and Hegel. However, in the 20th century, it was somewhat supplanted by political ideologies such as Communism and Fascism and by the traumatic disruption of two world wars. It was left to eminent pantheists such as the novelist D. H. Lawrence, scientist Albert Einstein, poet Robinson Jeffers, architect Frank Lloyd Wright and historian Arnold Toynbee to keep it alive. In the late 20th century, pantheism began its revival when it seemed to accord with the growing ecological awareness in society and the media. The Universal Pantheist Society was founded in 1975 and the larger, naturalistic World Pantheist Movement in 1999. The latter's Statement of Principles is as follows:

- We revere and celebrate the Universe as the totality of being, past, present and future. It is self-organizing, ever-evolving and inexhaustibly diverse. Its overwhelming power, beauty and fundamental mystery compel the deepest human reverence and wonder.

- All matter, energy, and life are an interconnected unity of which we are an inseparable part. We rejoice in our existence and seek to participate ever more deeply in this unity through knowledge, celebration, meditation, empathy, love, ethical action and art.

- We are an integral part of Nature, which we should cherish, revere and preserve in all its magnificent beauty and diversity. We should strive to live in harmony with Nature locally and globally. We acknowledge the inherent value of all life, human and non-human, and strive to treat all living beings with compassion and respect.

- All humans are equal centres of awareness of the Universe and nature, and all deserve a life of equal dignity and mutual respect. To this end we support and work towards freedom, democracy, justice, and non-discrimination, and a world community based on peace, sustainable ways of life, full respect for human rights and an end to poverty.

- There is a single kind of substance, energy / matter, which is vibrant and infinitely creative in all its forms. Body and mind are indivisibly united.

- We see death as the return to nature of our elements, and the end of our existence as individuals. The forms of 'afterlife' available to humans are natural ones, in the natural world. Our actions, our ideas and memories of us live on, according to what we do in our lives. Our genes live on in our families, and our elements are endlessly recycled in nature.

- We honour reality, and keep our minds open to the evidence of the senses and of science's unending quest for deeper understanding. These are our best means of coming to know the Universe, and on them we base our aesthetic and religious feelings about reality.

- Every individual has direct access through perception, emotion and meditation to ultimate reality, which is the Universe and Nature. There is no need for mediation by priests, gurus or revealed scriptures.

- We uphold the separation of religion and state, and the universal human right of freedom of religion. We recognize the freedom of all pantheists to express and celebrate their beliefs, as individuals or in groups, in any non-harmful ritual, symbol or vocabulary that is meaningful to them.

In 2008, Albert Einstein's 1954 German letter, in which he dismissed a belief in God, was auctioned off for more than $330,000. Einstein wrote:

"The word 'God' is for me nothing more than the expression and product of human weaknesses, the Bible a collection of honourable but still primitive legends which are nevertheless pretty childish."

"I do not believe in a personal God and I have never denied this but have expressed it clearly," he wrote in another letter, also in 1954. He related his belief to pantheism by stating:

"If something is in me which can be called religious then it is the unbounded admiration for the structure of the world so far as our science can reveal it."

Atheism

The word 'atheism' comes from 'a', meaning 'without' and 'theism', meaning belief in a god or gods. Therefore, it follows that atheists are those who believe that gods, spiritual or other supernatural beings are man-made constructs, myths and legends or who believe that such concepts are not meaningful. They don't use a creator God to explain the existence of the universe and believe that mankind can devise suitable moral codes to live by without a reliance on God or spurious scriptures. They apply the same values as monotheists, believing that the benevolent teachings of all religions are worth retaining even though they are based on myth and fable.

Atheists tend to be tolerant of religion even though they believe it has no basis in truth, causes people to live their lives on falsehoods and fetters their proclivity to think in a rational and objective way. They believe that religion is divisive, frequently causing conflict and war, hinders progress and offends human rights, particularly in its treatment of women and homosexuals. Most atheists, however, concede that there are many aspects of religious inspiration to be admired such as art and music, charities and good works, moral teaching and fellowship. They also recognise that they have many friends who would describe themselves as religious and accept that friendship does not insist on like-minded clones.

Atheism dates back to the time of classical antiquity when several Greek and Roman thinkers became the first atheist writers. Among these were Epicurus, Diogenes, Aristophanes, Democritus and Lucretius. Without the benefit of modern scientific discovery, some of their observations were truly remarkable. Epicurus (341 BC – 270 BC), a foremost Greek philosopher, maintained that the purpose of philosophy was to enable the attainment of a happy, tranquil life characterised by peace, freedom from fear, the absence of pain and by self-sufficiency surrounded by friends. He taught that pleasure and pain are the measures of good and evil, that death is the end of the body and the soul and should, therefore, not be feared. Furthermore, that the gods do not reward or punish humans, that the universe is infinite and eternal and that events in the world are ultimately based on the motions and interactions of atoms moving in empty space. He propounded the theory of 'materialism', suggesting the only things that exist are bodies and the space between them. He taught that the soul is also made of material objects so that when the body dies, so too does the soul, and if gods existed, they did not interact with humans. He believed there was no afterlife and stated:

"The soul cannot survive separation from the body, since it is necessary to understand that it too is a part. By itself the soul cannot ever either exist (even though Plato and the Stoics talk a great deal of nonsense on the subject) or experience movement, just as the body does not experience sensation when the soul is released from it."

With regard to religion, he said:
"Fabulous persuasion in faith is the approbation of feigned ideas or notions; it is credulous belief in the reality of phantoms."

Contemplating the consequences of fear, he said:
"Men, believing in myths, will always fear something terrible, everlasting punishment as certain or probable. They base all these fears not on mature opinions, but on irrational fancies, so that they are more disturbed by fear of the unknown than by facing facts. Peace of mind lies in being delivered from all these fears."

Continuing this theme, he stated:
"A man cannot dispel his fear about the most important matters if he does not know what is the nature of the universe but suspects the truth of some mythical story. So that without natural science, it is not possible to attain our pleasures unalloyed."

The Epicurean paradox, an application of logic and reason, is simple yet thought-provoking:
"Is God willing to prevent evil, but not able? Then he is not omnipotent. Is he able, but not willing? Then he is malevolent. Is he both able and willing? Then whence cometh evil? Is he neither able nor willing? Then why call him God?"

Religion, according to the Greek philosopher and founder of cynicism, Diogenes (ca. 412 BC – 323 BC), had no relevance to his daily life. While cracking a louse on the altar rail of a temple, he exclaimed: "Thus does Diogenes sacrifice to all the gods at once."

His contempt for religion was further revealed when he stated: "When I look upon seamen, men of science, and philosophers, man is the wisest of all things. When I look upon priests, prophets, and interpreters of dreams, nothing is so contemptible as man."

Aristophanes (ca. 448 BC – 380 BC), the Athenian playwright, considered one of the greatest comedy writers in literary history, was also unconvinced by theism. In one of the earliest burden of proof arguments he exhorted: "Shrines! Shrines! Surely you don't believe in the gods. What's your argument? Where's your proof?"

Democritus (ca. 460 BC – 370 BC) was a Greek philosopher, scientist and pupil of Leucippus. He applied a scientific, rationalist philosophy, believing everything to be the result of natural laws without reference to a supernatural prime mover. The theory of Democritus and Leucippus posited that everything was composed of atoms which were physically, though not geometrically, indivisible; that between atoms lay empty space; that atoms were indestructible, had always been and would remain in motion. Also, that there were an infinite number of atoms which differ in shape and size. It is widely considered that the theory of the atomists appears to be more nearly aligned with that of modern science than any other theory of antiquity.

Democritus hypothesised that the Earth was round and that originally the universe was composed of nothing but tiny atoms churning in chaos until, at some point, they collided to form larger units, including Earth. He surmised that there were many worlds, some growing, some decaying, some with no suns or moons and some with several. He held that every world had a beginning and an end, and that it could be destroyed by collision with another world. This was a man of admirable perception and insight who also commented on ethics and politics. Goodness, he believed, came more from practice and discipline than from innate human nature. He suggested that one should distance oneself from the wicked, stating that such association increased a disposition to vice. Anger, while difficult to control, had to be mastered in order for one to be rational. Democritus taught that those who took pleasure from the disasters of their neighbours failed to understand that their fortunes were tied to the society in which they lived and that, consequently, they robbed themselves of any joy of their own. He advocated a life of contentment with as little grief as possible which he said could not be achieved through either idleness or a preoccupation with worldly pleasures. Contentment would be gained, he said, through moderation and a measured life. To be content, one must set one's judgment on the possible and be satisfied with what one has, giving little thought to envy or admiration.

Lucretius (ca. 99 BC – ca. 55 BC) was a Roman poet and philosopher. His only known work is an epic philosophical poem laying out the beliefs of Epicureanism, *De Rerum Natura*, translated into English as *On the Nature of Things*. He followed the same materialistic ideology as Epicurus and by denying that the gods had any way of influencing our world, he declared that mankind had no reason to fear the supernatural:

Fear holds dominion over mortality
Only because, seeing in land and sky
So much the cause whereof no wise they know,
Men think divinities are working there.

Meantime, when once we know from nothing still
Nothing can be create, we shall divine
More clearly what we seek: those elements
From which alone all things created are,
And how accomplished no tool of Gods.

John Lennon would doubtless have approved of Epicurus, Lucretius et al.

In ancient times, natural phenomena were seen as the work of supernatural powers and, for most of human history, gods or God provided the best explanation for the existence of nature and the physical universe. During the last few centuries, however, scientists have developed solutions which are much more logical, more consistent and better supported by evidence. God is being marginalised as never before with a greater proportion of each generation adopting atheistic points of view. In the United Kingdom, for example, in 2012, around 25 percent of the population no longer believed in God, an increase of eight percent in only six years. The European average was higher still. Scandinavians, with their atheist majorities, have traversed much farther than most to the rejection of observant gods and extravagant rituals. They have eschewed religion, for centuries the social glue that bonded people together, in favour of greater cooperation with and between secular institutions such as courts, police and other civic authorities. These institutions have hastened religion's decline by assuming its traditional community-building functions though this could not have happened without contemplative enquiry into religion's role by the people themselves. It has been said that the Scandinavian countries, some of the most advanced, prosperous, peaceful and cooperative in the world, have 'climbed religion's ladder, then kicked it away'. They have found new ways to engender kindness without worrying about a spy in the sky, an ever inquisitive, judgemental God. At the other end of the spectrum comes the United States where, for some reason, the general populace has a greater propensity to unconditionally accept the exhortations of its many preachers.

The opinions of atheists across the world have been moulded by many prominent writers, philosophers and scientists during the modern era. A potent attack on Christianity was levelled by the author, George Eliot (Mary Ann Evans) (1819 – 1880), and her peers who claimed that it was immoral. They contended that it was unethical for God to behave like a 'revengeful tyrant' and wondered why, according to the doctrine of original sin, God was prepared to punish people for a wrong for which they were blameless. What kind of God was it who then absolved them because he had punished his son instead? James Anthony Froude (1818 – 1894), the historian and novelist, wrote in 1849:

"I would sooner perish forever than stoop down before a Being who may have power to crush me, but whom my heart forbids me to reverence."

Expressing doubts about the existence of God, the British philosopher, Professor Anthony Flew (1923 – 2010), wrote:

"If it is to be established that there is a God, then we have to have good grounds for believing this is indeed so. Until and unless some such grounds are produced we have literally no such grounds for believing; and in that situation the only reasonable posture must be that of either the negative atheist or the agnostic. So the onus of proof has to rest on the proposition. It must be up to them: first to give whatever sense they choose to the word 'God', meeting any objection that so defined it would relate only to an incoherent pseudo-concept; and, second, to bring forward sufficient reasons to warrant their claim that, in their present sense of the word 'God', there is a God."

Many people think that religion and belief in God fulfil functions in human society rather than being a direct consequence of the existence of God. Ludwig Feuerbach (1804 – 1872), the German philosopher and anthropologist, proposed that religion was simply a human being's consciousness of the infinite. He stated that mankind's ideas about God were no more than a projection of its ideas onto an imaginary supernatural being. Emile Durkheim (1858 – 1917), a French sociologist, concurred in that he thought religion was constructed by human society, not caused by the supernatural. He stated:
"Religious force is nothing other than the collective and anonymous force of the clan."

He questioned the reality of religion that lay behind the perception. He recognised that religion helped people to develop kinship, find a place in society and that religious ritual created mental states which encouraged group cohesion. Durkheim noted that religion, as perceived, gave a meaning and purpose to life, bound people together and supported moral and social codes. All of these, he posited, sufficed to give people the feeling that the supernatural was at work and, he wrote:

"Since it is in spiritual ways that social pressure exercises itself, it could not fail to give men the idea that outside themselves there exist one or several powers, both moral and, at the same time, efficacious, upon which they depend."

The brilliant British philosopher and economist, John Stuart Mill (1806 – 1873), in his essay on *The Utility of Religion*, argued that:

"Much of the apparent social utility of religion derives not from its dogma and theology but to its inculcation of a widely accepted moral code, and to the force of public opinion guided by that code. The belief in a supernatural power may have had some utility in maintaining that code, but is no longer needed and may indeed be detrimental."

He continued:

"There is an unfortunate tendency in supernatural religion to hinder the development not only of our intellectual, but also our moral nature. Its appeal is to self-interest rather than to disinterested and ideal motives. As with intuitionism in ethics, it stands in the way of the critical evaluation of social norms, and thereby effectively prevents action aimed at social change for the improvement of the human lot in the community. Supernatural religion appeals to the sense of mystery about what lies outside the narrow realm of what we know."

Mill went on to suggest that the power of religion to motivate derives from the human need for some sort of ideal that transcends us. He added:

"To be sure, this ideal is not some supernatural being or standard, as in Christianity or Platonism. It is an idea of the good, but a human idea, a conception of being human that can move us to do our best, a standard beyond our common selfish objects of desire. Such purposes can be achieved, and better achieved, by a religion of humanity than can any supernatural religion. Given the ideal, such a religion of humanity would help us cultivate our feelings and develop our individual capacities, intellectual, moral and emotional, without burdening us with false views about a mysterious Unknowable."

Mill had encapsulated the essence of the atheist's viewpoint; if there has to be a religion, why not replace all those that are based on fantasy, deities and supernatural powers with the religion of humanity? Or preferably, because 'humanity' can have an ambiguous connotation, why not call it the religion of kindness?

Many atheists are also secularist in that they oppose the special treatment afforded organised religion. Secularism is the principle of separation between government and religious institutions to ensure that they are not influenced by each other. In the United Kingdom, for example, a constitutional recognition of an official state religion has been maintained but secularists would prefer the state to be neutral in religious matters (achieved via disestablishment). The two official state-recognised Christian denominations are the Church of England and the Presbyterian Church of Scotland.

Secularists oppose religion or the religious being afforded privileges which, consequently, leave others disadvantaged. The 19th century witnessed a concerted campaign against religion by the secularist movement, its primary target being the highly privileged state church, the

Church of England. The pressure exerted was instrumental in bringing about change; for example, until 1828, nobody could hold public office without signing up to the beliefs of the church; until 1836, only Church of England ministers could conduct marriage ceremonies (excepting a few religious minority cases); until 1871, only members of the Church of England could teach at the universities of Oxford and Cambridge.

In 1842, George Holyoake (1817 – 1906), the British secularist author, became the last person to be convicted of blasphemy because of a public lecture. He was imprisoned for six months. The attendants moved and carried a motion that:

"Free discussion was equally beneficial in the departments of politics, morals and religion."

Charles Bradlaugh (1833 – 1891) was a political activist and, as one of the most famous atheists of his time, the co-founder of the National Secular Society in 1866. He became editor of the secularist newspaper, the *National Reformer*, in 1860 and, in 1868, the paper was prosecuted by the British government for blasphemy and sedition. Bradlaugh was eventually acquitted on all charges and was elected to Parliament in 1880 but, because he would not swear a religious oath, was prevented from taking his seat. The seat fell vacant and a by-election was declared. He was re-elected by Northampton four times in succession as the dispute continued. Supporting Bradlaugh were the great British Prime Minister, William Ewart Gladstone, the Member of Parliament, Thomas Power O'Connor, the Irish playwright, George Bernard Shaw and hundreds of thousands of people who signed a public petition. In opposition were the Conservative Party, the Archbishop of Canterbury and other leading churchmen. He eventually took his seat in 1886 becoming Britain's first openly atheist Member of Parliament. Nowadays, there are, almost certainly, scores of atheists who take their seats in the House of Commons though many are quite likely to maintain a neutral stance in public. Famous political atheists of recent times include Roy Hattersley, Neil Kinnock, Ken Livingstone, Michael Portillo, Alastair Campbell and the Miliband brothers, David and Ed. As the celebrated 20th century American author, Ernest Hemingway, wrote in *A Farewell to Arms*: "All thinking men are atheists."

Secularists believe that the reduced numbers attending places of worship demonstrate that faith itself is in decline and, accordingly, this underlines the unfairness in granting any special privileges or rights to established religion. They have particular concerns about education, seeing religious schools as divisive and in conflict with the interests of a harmonious and diverse society. They oppose special treatment for religious beliefs and organisations whilst respecting the right of individuals to express their faith. Many believe that religion should be regarded as a private matter for the home and place of worship and that the state should favour no denomination over another. As a summary, secularists support the following:

- The complete separation of church and state.

- The disestablishment of the Church of England.

- The repeal of the Act of Settlement (that the crowned heads of the United Kingdom must be Protestants).

- No official representation of religions in Parliament meaning, for example, no bishops in the House of Lords. Britain is the only democracy in the western world with such representation and, in any case, it is questionable whether theological expertise qualifies anyone for high office outside an ecclesiastical environment.

- The banning of prayers from Parliament, council chambers, and so on.
- The ending of religious oaths as a condition of holding public sector jobs.
- The prevention of money donated to religious organisations from public funds being used for missionary work.
- The abolition of any special privileges granted to religious organisations.
- The conversion of faith schools to community schools open to all pupils regardless of faith.
- Non-denominational and multi-faith religious education with no faith being taught either as fact or superior to another. Some secularists believe that Religious Education (RE) should be replaced by citizenship lessons including only brief coverage of the basic tenets of world religions.
- The abolition of blasphemy laws. Secularists support the protection of believers but not the protection of their beliefs and are entirely opposed to religious discrimination. They believe that the law should not restrict reasonable and vigorous criticism of religion but that incitement to religious hatred should, of course, be deemed unlawful.
- Legislation to outlaw discrimination in employment on the grounds of religion.
- The abolition of special treatment given to religious broadcasting.

In the minority, albeit a reducing one, atheists often feel the disdain emanating from intolerant members of the religious community, particularly the ecclesiastical authorities. The atheist stereotype is ungodly and, therefore, considered amoral, a pariah to be kept at arms length from a pious society. A journalist, speaking during a recent BBC TV debate remarked:

"It's not the spread of Islam that I fear; it's the descent into atheism."

This sentiment was allegedly echoed during an electoral campaign by George H. W. Bush when he was Vice-President of the United States. A reporter asked:

"Surely you recognise the equal citizenship and patriotism of Americans who are atheists?"

Astonishingly, Bush replied:

"No, I don't know that atheists should be considered as citizens, nor should they be considered patriots. This is one nation under God."

A highly intelligent man, Bush had expressed an unhealthy intolerance towards others of a different opinion. One explanation, of course, is that it was a calculated response to garner votes. The only other explanation is that his facility for logic and reason was stifled by a mind utterly fettered through religious fervour and emotion. It's what Derren Brown, the famous illusionist and mentalist, referenced as 'bad thinking' in his book, *Tricks of the Mind*. Bush denigrated atheism as if it were some kind of disease but he should have been aware that some of the greatest thinkers, both past and present, have questioned the existence of God. They include: Epicurus, Baruch Spinoza, Thomas Jefferson, Charles

Darwin, Albert Einstein, Andrew Carnegie, David Hume, John Stuart Mill, Percy Bysshe Shelley and, more recently, Bertrand Russell, Carl Sagan, Sir David Attenborough, Professor Richard Dawkins and Professor Brian Cox, to name but a few. Their opinions should not be dismissed lightly as they are worthy of scholarship.

The truth is that atheists are no different, no less virtuous than anyone else; they simply have a different opinion. They are just as likely to appreciate, for example, beautiful scenery, art and music, literature, good cuisine, cinema, sport and charitable work as anyone who attends church services with regularity. It is said that we can judge the heart of a man according to his love of animals. An atheist is just as likely to visit a dog rescue centre, make a donation, take a dog home and treat it with affection for the rest of its life. Moreover, the same person will be just as heart-broken as the faithful, armed as they are with their belief in God, when the beloved pet passes away. It's just that the atheist doesn't believe that he (or she) will be reunited with the dog in another life.

In the western world, religion is inculcated into a child's psyche as early as possible and the received doctrines are borne into adulthood where they remain, frequently unquestioned. It is easier to continue to believe in God than it is to turn to atheism because of the inertia inherent in belief and because to reject the religion of one's formative years does not come naturally. It requires profound thought and a rationality that is derived from prolonged intellectual application; this is not a matter resolved by instant illumination. Because of the continual engagement of thought processes and the consequent control over pure emotion, atheists, in general, are better equipped than most to deal efficaciously with questions of humanity. They have developed a positive view of the universe and the place of humans within it, one which contributes to the progress of human knowledge, individual freedom and human well-being. They are, on balance, less vulnerable to the vast depths of human gullibility. They are less likely to judge fellow human beings according to class, religion, skin colour, race, wealth, politics, education, profession and a host of other defining aspects - which can't be bad. The path leading to their current view of the world and humanity can't be followed without being lubricated by tolerance.

Humanism

Humanism is a way of life based on reason and tolerance and contends that moral values are based on human nature and experience alone. Whilst atheism is merely the absence of belief, humanism is more holistic, a positive attitude to the world centred on experience, thought and realistic hopes. Did Lennon have humanism in mind when he penned 'a brotherhood of man' in *Imagine?* The definition provided by The International Humanist and Ethical Union states:

"Humanism is a democratic and ethical life stance, which affirms that human beings have the right and responsibility to give meaning and shape to their own lives. It stands for the building of a more humane society through an ethic based on human and other natural values in the spirit of reason and free enquiry through human capabilities. It is not theistic, and it does not accept supernatural views of reality."

Humanists believe there are no supernatural beings and, therefore, flatly reject that people receive or have ever received wisdom and instruction from gods by revelation. They believe that science alone provides a source of knowledge about our material universe, beyond which nothing exists. There is no afterlife and no reincarnation and, consequently, human beings do not need the stimulus of these tenuous concepts to lead ethical and fulfilling lives. They believe that mankind is sufficiently evolved to formulate a moral code based on human nature and experience which is in no way contingent on religious beliefs.

The British Humanist Association has developed a number of questions which enable people to determine their humanist tendencies by selecting from multiple choice answers. The questions and possible answers are:

Does God Exist?

A) I am sure there is a God ruling over the universe.

B) It depends what you mean by God, but I think so.

C) I don't know.

D) There is no evidence that any god exists, so I'll assume that there isn't one.

When I die...

A) My soul will go to another place where I will be rewarded if I was good and punished if I was bad.

B) I will survive in some kind of afterlife.

C) That will be the end of me.

D) I will live on in people's memories or because of the work I have done or through my children.

How did the universe begin?

A) God created it.

B) It was set up as an experiment by extremely intelligent aliens from another universe who drop in every now and then to see how we're doing.

C) I don't know.

D) The scientific explanations are the best ones available – no gods were involved.

The theory that life on Earth evolved gradually over billions of years is …

A) Just a theory. My religion tells the true story.

B) Likely to be true, but I think God had a part in it too.

C) Probably true because my science teacher said it was true.

D) True – there is plenty of evidence from fossils, DNA and many other sources showing that this is how it happened.

When I look at a beautiful view I think that …

A) It must have been designed by God.

B) It would be a nice place for a motorway.

C) This is what life is all about – I feel good.

D) We ought to do everything possible to protect this for future generations.

I can tell right from wrong by …

A) Reading a holy book or listening to a religious leader.

B) I don't really think about it much – people should just do as they like.

C) Accepting what my parents and teachers say.

D)   Thinking hard about the possible consequences of actions and their effects on other people.

It's best to be honest because ...

A)   My religion tells me so.

B)   It's usually against the law or the rules to be dishonest.

C)   People respect you more if you're trustworthy.

D)   I'm happier and feel better about myself if I'm honest.

Other people matter and should be treated with respect because ...

A)   God created us all in his image.

B)   They are useful to me.

C)   They are people with feelings like mine.

D)   We will all be happier if we treat each other well.

Animals should be treated ...

A)   With respect because they are part of God's creation.

B)   However we see fit – they don't have souls and were created for us to use.

C)   Kindly because they are sweet and fluffy and kinder than people.

D)   With respect because they can suffer too.

The most important thing in life is ...

A)   To have a good relationship with God.

B)   To make lots of money.

C)   To preserve the planet for future generations.

D)   To increase the general happiness and welfare of humanity.

A humanist would answer 'D' to all, or nearly all, questions with no 'A's and no 'B's. The emphasis on kindness is unmistakable.

The Afterlife

During a recent TV debate on Christianity, one of the participants said:
"I believe in the afterlife because it gives me hope."

When scrutinised, does this statement make much sense? He offered no evidence for his belief and, perhaps, should have said:
"I believe in the afterlife *and* it gives me hope."

By his statement, all he was really portraying was his hope there would be an afterlife. It is likely that most people share his kind of belief in that they fear the finality of death and hope that something (spiritual if not tangible) lies beyond. Of course, had the debate taken place in a region dominated by Buddhist culture, the discourse would have been altogether different as Buddhists reject the monotheistic claim to eternal life preferring their belief in reincarnation. Whilst both cannot be simultaneously true, the impartial observer would probably view each concept as equally implausible. Most religions, however, believe that one's status in another life is a reward or a punishment for one's conduct during life on Earth. During another TV debate, the presenter asked a very pious lady what she thought happened to all those people who were not Christians. She replied that they could only look forward to eternal damnation. The answer was not merely uncharitable but, clearly, logically misguided. According to her skewed dogma, an accident of birth condemns billions of Buddhists, Hindus, Muslims and many other faiths to an afterlife of suffering whilst offering salvation to all those sharing her beliefs. One couldn't help but wonder what kind of partial God she worshipped as she exemplified a paralysis of rational thought, inevitable when the literal truth of biblical texts is accepted unconditionally.

In Abrahamic religions, the view is generally held that one goes to Hell or Heaven depending upon one's deeds and, possibly, faith while on Earth. A contrasting and deeply held view is that one's deeds are irrelevant and one can be delivered to Heaven or Hell according to predestination (a selection according to God alone). Over the centuries, there must have been hundreds, perhaps even thousands, of different afterlife concepts with the most popular persisting. It is as if any idea could be postulated, however preposterous, and if it resonated with the masses it would be retained before becoming enshrined. In the Roman Catholic Church, *limbo* was professed by theologians early in the Middle Ages and, though it never became part of the teaching of the church, it was at times incorporated into its belief. It is a place for those that die with original sin, the general condition of sinfulness into which humans are born as distinct from the actual sins that they commit during their lifetimes. Virtuous individuals who lived before Jesus Christ was born qualified for *limbo* as did those that died before baptism (such as babies). People such as these, it was thought, neither merited the beatific vision nor were they to be subjected to any punishment. However, on the 20th April 2007, Pope Benedict XVI abolished the whole idea of *limbo* when he expressed his doubts about the concept. In other Christian denominations, though, it is still described as some intermediate place of confinement or oblivion. Confused? You will be!

The notion of *purgatory* is particularly aligned with the Latin Rite of the Catholic Church. According to its teachings, all who die in God's grace and friendship, though still impure, are assured of their eternal salvation. After death, they undergo a process of purification to enable them to achieve the level of holiness necessary for entry into the joy of Heaven instead of the punishment of the damned. By reference to the scriptures, the tradition of the church refers to a 'cleansing fire'. Anglicans of the Anglo-Catholic tradition tend to have the same belief. John Wesley (1703 – 1791), the founder of Methodism, also believed in an intermediate state between death and resurrection where holiness could be fostered. Methodism does not officially affirm this belief and denies the possibility of assisting those in *purgatory* by prayer. Is it not at once absurd, incomprehensible and baffling how such speculative notions of belief in a religion become ingrained? In most denominations, Heaven is a place of everlasting reward for the righteous and Hell, in comparison, is a place of eternal torment for the wicked. Similar places of torment and reward can be seen in Greek mythology leading us to suspect that many of its concepts have been adopted by both parallel and succeeding religions. In that case, isn't it curious that the ancient Greek afterlife is regarded as nonsense whilst the eternal life of the Abrahamic religions is deemed to be true and absolute? What is a modern, sophisticated mind to make of it all?

The Greek god Hades is known in Greek mythology as the king of the Underworld, a place where souls continue to live after death. The god Hermes, the messenger of his fellow gods, was responsible for taking a person's dead soul to the Underworld (also known as Hades or the House of Hades). According to ancient Greek religion, Hermes would leave the soul on the banks of the River Styx, the partition between life and death. Charon, the ferryman, would take the soul across the river to Hades providing that the soul had gold for the fare. It was the responsibility of the deceased's family to place a coin, usually an obol, on the mouth or under the tongue of the relative. Once the crossing had taken place, the soul was adjudicated by three wise kings before being directed to Elysium, Tartarus, Asphodel Meadows or the Fields of Punishment. The Elysium Fields were for those that had lived pure lives. It was a place of peace and contentment comprising green fields, valleys and mountains and was in constant sunshine. Tartarus was for those that had blasphemed against the gods, were rebellious or consciously evil. The Asphodel Meadows were the destination for a varied selection of human souls including those whose sins matched their goodness and those who had been indecisive in their lives. The Fields of Punishment were for people that had frequently sinned but not with such gravity so as to be deserving of Tartarus. In Tartarus, the soul would be punished by being burned in lava or stretched on racks.

The ancient Norse religion also referred to several realms in its concept of the afterlife. Valkyries, a host of female goddess-like figures, selected half of the warriors that had died bravely in battle and took them to the Hall of the Slain, Valhalla, ruled by the god Odin. The other half went to the goddess Freya's afterlife field, Folkvangr. The heavenly abodes of Valhalla and Folkvangr were somewhat analogous to the Greek Elysium. In Hel, the Covered Hall, an abode not unlike the Asphodel Meadows could be found. It was the destination for the mediocre, a place where those people who had neither excelled nor disgraced themselves could expect to be reunited with their loved ones. Niflhel, or 'The Dark', was a realm roughly akin to Tartarus. A level deeper than Hel, it was for those who had been guilty of criminal acts including murder, abduction, rape and broken oaths. Severe punishment awaited them.

The afterlife played a very significant role in ancient Egyptian religion, its belief system being one of the earliest known. When the body died, the Egyptians believed, parts of its soul known as the *ka* (body double) and the *ba* (personality) went to the Kingdom of the Dead. While the soul dwelt in the Fields of Aaru, the god Osiris demanded work as recompense for the protection he provided. To reap one's reward in the afterlife was extremely onerous, demanding a pure heart and the ability to recite spells, passwords and formulae from of the Book of the Dead, a funerary text. In the Hall of Two Truths, the deceased's heart was weighed against the Shu feather of truth and justice taken from the headdress of the goddess Ma'at. If the heart was lighter than the feather, the soul could pass on but, if it were heavier, it was devoured by a demon. Egyptians also believed that being mummified and put in a sarcophagus, complete with complex symbols, designs, pictures and hieroglyphs was the only certain way to transcend into the afterlife. Only if the corpse had been properly embalmed and entombed in a mastaba could the dead be resurrected to live again in the Fields of Yalu and accompany the Sun on its daily ride.

Each human, it was believed, consisted of the physical body, the *ka*, the *ba*, and the *akh*. The person's name and shadow were also regarded as living entities and, for an enjoyable afterlife, all of these elements had to be sustained and protected from harm. The *akh* was associated with thought, not as an action of the mind but rather as intellect, a separate living entity. Following death, the *ka* and *ba* were reunited to reanimate the *akh* on the condition that the prescribed funeral rites were executed followed by continual offerings. The *akh*, it was believed, could appropriate good or ill fortune to the living when evoked by prayers or written letters left in the tomb.

It is clear that many cultures see the afterlife as a place of judgement, whereby the way persons conduct themselves in life determines their fate after death. The Aztecs of Mesoamerica did not share this view believing that a person's destination was determined largely by the cause of death. Their warrior culture, much like the Norse, was strongly reinforced by the structure of their afterlife, the most rewarding aspects of which were reserved for warriors, women who died in childbirth and human sacrifices. Some sacrifices were even voluntary on the strength of this belief. Women who died in childbirth were regarded as female warriors who had striven to bring new life to the Aztec Empire. These heroes lived in a celestial paradise where they would aid the Sun god in his journey for part of the day and spend the remaining time sipping moisture from flowers and enjoying themselves. To enter this place of the Sun, one had to live a hero's life or die a hero's death.

The realm of Tlaloc, the rain god, was Tlalocan where those who died by drowning, lightning or water-related diseases such as gout or pustules went when they died. Though less wonderful than the celestial paradise of the warriors, it was a realm of eternal spring and abundance. The least desirable realm was Mictlan, a gloomy, sooty place from which there were no exits. The upper and nether worlds were both thought to be layered. Mictlan had nine layers which were inhabited by different deities and mythical beings. The sky had 13 layers, six more than the layers according to Islam, the highest of which was called Omeyocan where the progenitor dual god, Ometeotl, resided. Mictlan was the destination for those that died from old age, ill health or accident and entailed a long, arduous journey of numerous dangers. Thus, the Aztecs considered death to be an integral part of life and, just as the crops had to be harvested for food, people had to die, they believed, to feed the gods and maintain the cycle of the universe.

The culture of the Incas of Peru had much in common with that of ancient Egypt and held a more optimistic view of the afterlife than the Mesoamerican civilizations. They mummified their dead and respectfully tended the tombs. The bodies of dead rulers often remained in their palaces where they were treated as if they were still alive. Servants offered them gifts and their families consulted them for advice regarding daily affairs. As protective ancestral spirits, dead Incas, in general, continued to play an active role in the world of the living. They disclosed themselves through *huacas* (sacred places or objects) and were revered by their descendants. The Incas, strongly moralistic, believed the souls of virtuous people joined the Sun in Heaven and lived in abundance. They remained connected to their descendants and their lives continued much as they had on Earth whilst the souls of the evil went to an underworld, a cold, barren place where there was nothing to eat but stones.

The belief in an afterlife seems to be globally embedded into all manner of ancient cultures and the characteristics, though variable in detail, have many similarities. It is feasible that these beliefs developed independently with little or no interaction between civilisations but this seems unlikely. It seems far more plausible that an afterlife was conceptualised in the minds of very early humans tens of thousands of years ago and was disseminated across the world by migration. DNA studies have concluded that the first anatomically modern humans, Homo sapiens, evolved in southern Africa up to 200,000 years ago. Though there remains much to be discovered about their origins and dispersal, by about 27,000 years ago Homo sapiens had become the sole human species on planet Earth.

The earliest modern looking skulls yet discovered are about 130,000 years old and come from the Omo basin in Ethiopia and the Klasies River Mouth in South Africa. It appears that about 100,000 years ago, these early populations began to disperse, initially migrating northwards before extending beyond Africa. These migrations were followed by a process known as 'bottlenecking' in which population levels remained relatively static for thousands of years. A contributory factor may have been the eruption of Toba in the northwest of Sumatra 71,000 years ago, an environmental catastrophe of extraordinary magnitude. Parts of India were covered in ash to a depth of up to three metres (10 feet) and global temperatures were lowered for over a thousand years. About 50,000 years ago, according to archaeological and genetic evidence, a further rapid expansion of modern human populations occurred. By this time, Australia had been reached by boat and by 33,000 years ago, the western Pacific islands of Indonesia and New Guinea had been colonised. The Americas were reached 15,000 years ago and were colonised from north to south within 2,000 years. Major expansion into the Arctic began 4,500 years ago as the continental ice sheets retreated and 2,000 years ago, humans began to settle the deep Pacific islands. From there, they reached New Zealand around 850 AD, almost 1,000 years ahead of the great explorer, Captain James Cook.

Homo sapiens was not the only human species in the world of 50,000 years ago. The east and southeast of Asia was inhabited by the descendants of those Homo erectus populations that had colonised the region one million years before. The most well known amongst other human populations are the Neanderthals, distinguished by their distinctive large and low-crowned heads, prominent brows, large teeth and powerful, stocky torsos. They had brains as large as modern man, were skilful, and the burial of their dead was frequently accompanied by some elaboration, signifying a contemporary humanity. We can speculate that the religion of all human species was polytheistic and it is quite likely that some, if not all of them, held beliefs in an afterlife. Of all the human populations, Homo sapiens was the most capable of adapting to its environment. The most notable evidence is provided by the wide variety of artefacts that have been uncovered: engravings, ornaments, primitive figurines, exotic shells, amber and ivory and, most famous of all, cave paintings. These early works of art are an enduring testimony to the humanity of the early hunters. Significantly, Neanderthals had virtually no corresponding cultural traditions and, by approximately 27,000 years ago, they and Homo erectus had become extinct. Any religious beliefs they harboured died with them. Henceforth, Homo sapiens or modern humans were the sole survivors of a human species that had existed for hundreds of thousands of years. Their belief systems, probably adopted from earlier humans, were able to flourish as they migrated to all corners of the globe. The belief in an afterlife, the origin of which was probably a mere spark of aspiration or a tribal superstition, would have been promulgated from one generation to another until it became inherent in a civilisation's religious framework. Once established in the psyche of virtually the whole of humanity, the existence of an afterlife would rarely have been questioned as it offered comfort and hope. By the time Jesus talked about eternal life, he would have found an audience well conditioned and in thrall to the concept.

Chapter 5

The Worst Aspects of Religion

Bloodletting

The shedding of blood during religious rituals was commonplace in civilisations throughout the world for millennia, the primary objective being to appease the gods. We can only assume how these rituals became endemic but it is likely that they had fairly innocuous beginnings with initial offerings of food and flowers. If, as a consequence, a primitive people perceived their lives going well, they would have been readily convinced of the efficacy of their homage. They would have believed that pleasing the gods was both necessary and worthwhile. As soon as their situation worsened, they would have thought that the gods were displeased and sought higher level gifts as compensation. These later offerings probably included the sacrifice of birds and small animals and, afterwards, it is easy to envisage the process of escalation that would have ensued as matters became increasingly grave. It would simply have been a question of time before the sacrificial offerings encompassed humans.

Nowhere in the world was sacrifice observed with greater zeal than in parts of Central and South America. For the most important rites of the Olmec, Maya and Aztecs, only a gift of human blood would suffice. Arms, ears, tongue, thighs, chest or genitals were mutilated and, in many cases, this was deemed as adequate propitiation. At other times, however, the religious rites culminated in the taking of a human life.

Human sacrifice was practised on a vast scale throughout the Aztec Empire although the exact figures are unknown. At Tenochtitlan, the principal Aztec city (now Mexico City), over 10,000 people were sacrificed over the course of four days for the dedication of the Great Pyramid in 1487. Major events such as this demanded mass slaughter. The pyramid was dedicated simultaneously to Huitzilopochtli, the god of war, and Tlaloc, the god of rain and agriculture, each of which had a shrine at the top of the pyramid, accessible by separate staircases. Excavation of the offerings in the main temple has provided some insight regarding the sacrificial process, one of mesmerising complexity. Every sacrifice had to be meticulously planned from the type of victim through to the ceremonies considered appropriate for a specific god. The victims ranged from slaves to high ranking warriors. In a process that could last up to a year, those being offered would be housed, fed and dressed appropriately, with a view to assuming the persona of the god to be pacified. When the sacrificial day arrived, the victims would participate at length in the ceremonies and, drugged and exhausted, would be less likely to struggle before the brutality of the final act. The ritualised murder usually took place at the top of a pyramid, carried out by a number of holy men. The victims were laid upon an altar and held down before a blade was plunged into their breasts, their hearts savagely ripped from their bodies.

Loss of life during war is tragic but it is frequently the price of freedom and, at least, fathomable. The murder of one's own people, however, on the basis of nothing more than a religious belief, a fanciful nonsense, is beyond comprehension. It is estimated that when Genghis Khan and his Mongol hordes swept across vast swathes of Asia during the 12th and 13th centuries, as many as 40,000,000 people died. Most of these did not die on the battlefield but, owing to the sackings of cities and civilian massacres, were counted amongst the collateral damage. The horrors inflicted upon resident populations at the time are almost too difficult for the modern mind to conceive yet they pale in comparison with the sacrificial rites of the Aztecs. How could the perceived value of such unspeakable cruelty have invaded the minds of these people? Though the origins may never become known, Aztec tradition provides some possible clues. It is said that Coatlicue, the mother of the gods, found a ball filled with feathers and placed it in her waistband. This caused her to become pregnant whereupon Coyolxauhqui, her daughter, rallied her mother's 400 children together and goaded them into attacking and decapitating their mother. The instant she was killed, the god Huitzilopochtli emerged from her womb fully grown and armed for battle, analogous to the birth of Athena. He killed many of his brothers and sisters including Coyolxauhqui, whose head he cut off and threw into the sky to become the moon. In one of a number of variations of this story, Huitzilopochtli cut out the heart of his half-sister and threw her body down a mountain. Does the inspiration for the ceremonies of ritualised murder stem from here?

With the emergence of Christianity in Mesomerica, belief in tales such as these was supplanted and consigned to fantasy and mythology. For many centuries, however, the mythology had been a religion which formed a belief system so strong that the sacrifice of innocent victims was not only condoned but encouraged. The priests were always on hand to interpret the desires and demands of the gods. Nowadays, we know that the killings could not make the slightest difference to the well-being of the surviving populace; it was enough that they perceived the rituals to be beneficial.   Surely, nothing throughout history has been more misguided than human sacrifice, supported by religious belief at its most destructive.

It has become clear that children were sacrificed with regularity as they were regarded as the purest of beings. In 2005, a mass grave of child victims less than three years of age was uncovered in the Mayan region of Comalcalco. It appears that the children were sacrificed to consecrate the temples of the Comalcalco acropolis. Mayan art has been discovered depicting the extraction of children's hearts during the ascension to the throne of a new king. Other examples include scenes in which sacrificed boys are discernible on painted jars.   In 2007, archaeologists analysed the remains of 24 children aged between five and 15, buried together with a figurine of the god, Tlaloc. The children were found near the ancient Toltec capital, Tula, and had been decapitated. The remains were dated at around 1050 AD.

Capacocha was the Inca practice of human sacrifice, primarily involving children. It generally applied during or after significant events such as the death of an emperor or during a famine. The children had to be healthy, physically perfect and from six to 15 years old. They were dressed in finery, bejewelled and fattened up for months or even years on the most nutritious diets comprising maize and animal proteins. When the time came for the sacrificial pilgrimage, they were escorted to Cuzco, Peru's capital city, to meet the emperor and enjoy a feast given in their honour. Incan high priests led the children into the mountains, a journey both long and arduous, especially for the younger ones. Coca leaves were offered as an aid to breathing and to ensure that the victims stayed alive. Upon reaching the burial site, the children were given intoxicating drinks to minimise their pain, fear and resistance after which they were killed by ligature strangulation or a severe blow to the head. Sometimes they were, simply, left in extreme mountain temperatures to lose consciousness and die of hypothermia. Sometimes they were buried alive. Archaeologists have found bodies of such victims on Andean mountain tops, naturally mummified due to the low temperatures and dry winds.

The Aztecs believed that if sacrifices were not offered to the god, Tlaloc, it would not rain and their crops would fail. It was believed that Tlaloc demanded the tears of the young should wet the earth. How could such a belief possibly originate? One can but speculate. Perhaps, at a time of severe drought, the holy men prayed to Tlaloc for weeks without success. When the situation seemed hopeless, it may be that one of them noticed a child crying whereupon, coincidentally, the rain began to fall. The link between the child's tears and rainfall would then have been indelibly established and, after that, any occasion that tears failed to produce the desired result would simply have meant that too few tears had been shed. Any perceived success would have reinforced the holy men's belief; any failure would have meant that Tlaloc was displeased and was exhorting them to do more. As a consequence, priests made children cry before a ritual sacrifice, a favoured method being to tear off their finger nails. A smacking would have sufficed but, for the priests, this would have been too mundane, too pusillanimous. In the interests of their religion, they could always be relied upon to conceive something much more elaborate, however unnecessary, and establish another form of ceremonial cruelty.

Religious belief without proof is, paradoxically, the most powerful belief of all in that it requires no verification. Because the religious mind relies on faith, it can willingly accede to a dependence on anything that supports that faith whether it is fiction, rumour, fraud, misinterpretation or error without ever being persuaded to check any sources for veracity. Anything that appears to contradict that faith is excused, eschewed or dismissed as a meaningless distraction. As the great 18th century French writer, philosopher and historian, Voltaire (Francois-Marie Arouet) (1694 – 1778), once said:

"Faith consists in believing when it is beyond the power of reason to believe."

It is estimated that the Aztecs, at their zenith, were sacrificing around 50,000 victims each year. What had God to do with any of this? According to deists, nothing at all, since they believe that, after creating the universe, God has had no involvement in our lives. But, is this in any way plausible? Would God set the universe in motion and then sit on his hands for over 13 billion years. It doesn't make much sense, does it? Nor does it make any sense that, if God exists, he should permit hundreds of thousands of agonising deaths without intervening in some way. Couldn't he have called upon a prophet to help ignorant and superstitious people to change their ways? Or, were all the prophets used up in the Middle East? Surely he, as an omnipotent and merciful God, could have created a new prophet or found some other way of alleviating all the suffering. Instead, the grotesque savagery prevailed for centuries in the name of religious propitiation. The consolation is, if the clerics are to be believed, that as the hearts were being torn out of the bodies of still writhing victims, God loved them, as he loves us all.

Subjugation

The Mesoamerican sacrifices, along with those in Peru, were only terminated when the Spanish conquistadors destroyed the empires of both the Incas and the Aztecs. The assault on the Aztec Empire was led by Hernan Cortes (1485 -1547); that on the Incan empire by his cousin, Francisco Pizarro (ca. 1471 – 1541). Initially, the primary mission of both these men was to save the souls of the heathens and convert them to Christianity but, on discovering the riches (gold and jewellery) available for plunder, this was soon relegated to second place. In April 1519, Hernan Cortes, the chief magistrate of Santiago, Cuba, sailed to the coast of Mexico. He disembarked at a point he called Vera Cruz with 508 soldiers, 100 sailors, 13 horses and 14 small cannon. As he moved inland, he skirmished with some of the native tribes such as the Totonacs and Tlaxcalans but, as they were resentful of Aztec rule, he was able to form alliances with them.

The conquistadors, reinforced by the Tlaxcalans and other indigenous tribes, marched onwards to Cholula, the second largest city in Mexico. Once inside the city, Cortes' forces infamously massacred hundreds of unarmed warriors and nobles as they gathered in the central plaza and then set buildings afire. The motive for the slaughter is uncertain. It may have been because of perceived Cholulan treachery or a premeditated desire to instil fear in the Aztecs and any other hostile native tribes. As Cortes advanced on the capital city, Tenochtitlan, Moctezuma (or Montezuma), the Aztec emperor became increasingly alarmed. He sent a succession of emissaries with gifts of gold and jewellery to persuade Cortes to turn back but to no effect. He could have deployed an overwhelming force against the Spaniards but, for some reason, refrained from doing so. Astride large unfamiliar animals, the Spaniards may have been perceived as gods or, perhaps, reports of the power of their weaponry, particularly the canon and arquebuses (early muskets), induced uncertainty in the minds of the Aztecs and caused them to hesitate. It may have been a tactical ploy to entrap the Spaniards or a deliberate postponement of hostilities until the agricultural season was succeeded by the season for war. Another possibility to have been suggested is that Moctezuma believed that Cortes was a messenger of Quetzalcoatl, the feathered serpent god. So it was that despite advice from some of his military leaders, Moctezuma received Cortes amicably and permitted his forces to be quartered in the city.

Sacrificial rituals had continued during the Spanish advance on Tenochtitlan and when these proved ineffective, the rate of bloodletting increased. When the Spaniards explored the city, they were horrified to encounter the execution slab and piles of newly extracted hearts atop the temple pyramid. Relations between the Spaniards and their hosts became increasingly strained especially when Cortes repeatedly insisted that the Aztecs desist from idol worship and human sacrifice. Cortes, vastly outnumbered, recognised his position in Tenochtitlan was becoming more precarious and, consequently, he ordered that Moctezuma be taken hostage. Moctezuma and other members of the nobility were duly detained at the Axayactal palace and the first Spanish captain assigned to guard the prisoners was none other than Pedro de Alvarado. Alvarado later became the conqueror of most of Central America (El Salvador, Guatemala and Honduras) and, although renowned for his skill as a military leader, is most remembered for his cruelty against humanity. A

Christian, claiming God as his ally, he was responsible for the genocide of the indigenous populations during their subjugation. It is one of the lessons of history that one should beware those who claim to have God on their side and, consequently, believe they have his approval for their ineffable actions.

The highest Spanish authority in the Americas at the time was the Governor of Cuba, Diego Velazquez de Cuellar, who believed that Cortes had exceeded his legitimate powers. Enmity existed between the two men and, consequently, Velazquez mounted an expeditionary force of 1,100 men, commanded by Panfilo de Narvaez, to bring Cortes to justice. Subsequently, Cortes left Tenochtitlan to confront Narvaez, leaving Alvarado in charge. Despite a numerical inferiority, Cortes subdued Narvaez, imprisoned him and incorporated the remainder of the opposing force into his own army. Whilst Cortes was absent, Alvarado gave the Aztecs permission to celebrate the annual festival of Toxcatl, in honour of Huitzilopochtli, on condition that they were unarmed. On the day of the festival, the Aztecs gathered in single file to honour their god of war. Afterwards, they proceeded to the courtyard of the Great Temple to perform the dance of the serpent and while the people were singing and dancing, Alvarado ordered that all escape routes be closed before the Spaniards appeared fully armed. Devoid of any Christian piety, they slaughtered the defenceless Aztecs in an event that became known as 'the Massacre in the Main Temple'. The reasons for the offensive are unclear but it is known that Alvarado was treacherous and had a propensity for extreme brutality. Nearly all of the hundreds of Aztecs present at the ceremony perished, a few escaping over the walls.

On the 24th June, 1520, after an absence of more than 20 days, Cortes returned to Tenochtitlan with 1,300 soldiers, 96 horses, 80 crossbowmen and 80 arquebusiers to find Alvarado under siege. His army, which also comprised 2,000 Tlaxcalan warriors, was able to reoccupy Moctezuma's palace relatively unscathed but, gradually, the Spanish position worsened. The Aztecs closed the roads, raised the causeway bridges and began, systematically, to deplete the Spanish force. Cortes asked Moctezuma to reason with his people but, being regarded as a Cortes puppet, he no longer inspired confidence. It is alleged that, appalled by his complicity, an angry crowd stoned him and he later died from his wounds. Cortes decided, subsequently, that a full retreat from Tenochtitlan was his best tactic and this was put into effect on the 1st July, 1520. A wet, moonless night provided some concealment as the Spanish left first, closely followed by their allies transporting as much treasure as possible. Cortes had hoped to avoid detection by muffling the hooves of his horses and using wooden boards to cross the canals. However, having successfully negotiated three canals, the Spaniards were discovered and sustained heavy losses in the ferocious battle that ensued. Many were taken prisoner and later sacrificed on Aztec alters. This major Aztec victory is known by the Spanish as, 'La Noche Triste' or 'The Night of Sorrows'. It took fully five days for Cortes to reach his haven, Tlaxcala, during which time his remaining forces were continually harrassed by his Aztec adversaries. On the way to Tlaxcala, though heavily outnumbered, he won a battle at the Otumba Valley when his cavalry proved decisive. The Spanish, however, sustained further heavy losses. Estimates vary according to the source but it is likely that by the time Cortes reached his sanctuary, he had lost about 860 of his soldiers and well over 1,000 of his native allies.

Despite his losses, Cortes could not afford to fail. He had defied his superior, Velazquez, so only a successful mission could deflect the wrath of Charles I, King of Spain. He would either be considered a traitor to Spain or its hero. Accordingly, he set about restoring his army by forming further alliances with tribes that were hostile to the Aztecs, assuring them of Spanish protection. As Cortes engendered support, a smallpox epidemic struck Tenochtitlan in October 1520. It is believed to have been introduced by a Spanish slave from the Narvaez expeditionary force who was abandoned in the capital during the retreat. The disease spread beyond the city into local areas with devastating effect, killing around 40 percent of the native population in less than a year. The Aztecs were severely weakened.

By the 22nd May 1521, Cortes had a vast army at his disposal and proceeded to lay siege to Tenochtitlan. His forces comprised 1175 Spanish foot soldiers, 140 horsemen and 175 artillerymen supported by around 75,000 native tribesmen. In addition, his master shipbuilder had constructed 13 brigantines, each of which housed one cannon. When fully manned by soldiers and artillerymen, the brigantines gave Cortes complete domination of the waterways. Gradually, the Spanish severed the city from its food and water supplies and, as the stranglehold continued, famine became inevitable. The debilitated Aztecs fought fiercely to the end as the Spanish forces advanced through the city inch by inch, street by street. Cuauhtemoc, the new Aztec emperor, surrendered on the 13th August, 1521. He was imprisoned, tortured and later executed. Even after the Aztec capitulation, the Spanish forces continued their attack, looting and slaughtering thousands. It is estimated that almost a quarter of a million Aztecs died during the siege of Tenochtitlan which Cortes renamed 'Mexico City'. The nobility was annihilated, the only survivors being young children, and the Aztec

Empire was at an end, never to be resurrected. Cortes was decorated by King Charles I.

The next empire to fall in the New World was that of the Incas though, unlike the demise of the Aztec Empire, it took the Spanish decades of fighting to finally subdue the mightiest civilisation in the Americas. It is estimated that at its zenith, the population of the Inca Empire numbered about 17,000,000. After years of exploration and military skirmishes, the first significant step in the long campaign of subjugation took place in September 1532 when Francisco Pizarro advanced into Peru with a force of only 106 foot soldiers and 62 horsemen. Atahualpa, the Incan Emperor, and his large force confronted the Spanish peaceably at the town of Cajamarca on the 15th November. Rather than meeting with Atahualpa himself, Pizarro sent Hernando de Soto, Friar Vicente de Valverde and a native interpreter instead. Soto read a prepared speech advising Atahualpa that they had come as servants of God to teach them the truth about God's word. He was speaking to them so that they might, he stated:

"Lay the foundation of concord, brotherhood, and perpetual peace that should exist between us, so that you may receive us under your protection and hear the divine law from us and all your people may learn and receive it, for it will be the greatest honour, advantage, and salvation to them all."

Atahualpa was unimpressed but agreed to meet again the next day. The next morning, Pizarro had his men strategically positioned around the town square, the proposed meeting point. Atahualpa arrived with his retinue of lords and over 6,000 men armed only with small battle axes and slingshots to be met by Valverde who attempted to explain the precepts of the Catholic religion. Apparently, he did not go so far as to deliver the *requerimiento*, a speech demanding that the listener submit to the authority of the Spanish Crown and convert to the Christian faith. Instead, the friar presented the emperor with a holy book which, after examining it briefly and realising it was meaningless to him, he threw to the ground. Valverde hurried back towards Pizarro calling on the Spaniards to attack. Pizarro gave the signal for action whereupon the Spaniards unleashed volleys of gunfire at the vulnerable mass of Incas, then surged forward in a unified movement of cavalry and infantrymen. The first target of the Spanish onslaught was Atahualpa and his immediate retinue. The emperor was quickly captured as his guards were slain. The effect of the ambush was so devastating that the shocked Incas were able to offer little more than token resistance. At the end of the massacre, around 2,000 of them were dead whilst the Spaniards emerged virtually unscathed.

After the Battle of Cajamarca, Pizarro demanded a vast ransom in exchange for Atahualpa. The emperor offered to fill a large room with gold and silver which began to arrive in December 1532. By May 1533, Pizarro had received all the treasure he had requested and, shortly afterwards, the Spaniards felt inclined to decide upon Atahualpa's fate, many favouring execution. Soto and Pizarro's brother Hernando, however, were opposed to Atahualpa's execution considering it an injustice. They were of the opinion that Pizzaro had no right to sentence a sovereign prince in his own dominions and that Atahualpa's future should only be decided by the decree of a higher authority, namely, that of King Charles himself. Despite the objections, Pizarro conducted a mock trial and among the charges were polygamy, incestuous marriage and idolatry, all abhorrent in Catholicism but quite common in the religion of the Incas. Atahualpa was pronounced guilty and sentenced to execution by burning, a punishment which horrified him as Incas believed that the soul could not proceed to the afterlife when the body had been burned. Valverde interceded by advising Atahualpa that if he agreed to convert to Catholicism, Pizarro could be convinced to commute the sentence. With only one realistic option, Atahualpa consented to be baptised into the Catholic faith and was given the name Juan Santos Atahualpa. In accordance with his request and Valverde's pledge, he was garroted instead of being burned on the 26th July, 1533. It would have been more Christian to return Atahualpa to his people as a vassal ruler whereby he could have been instrumental in promoting the Catholic faith throughout the empire. This would have saved many thousands of lives. Indeed, after Atahualpa's death, his brother was installed as such a leader. It might as well have been Atahualpa but, for reasons known only to Pizarro, the Christian way was so often subordinate to his way.

Having deprived the Inca Empire of its leadership, Pizarro and Soto moved south towards the Peruvian capital, Cuzco, which they conquered in November 1533. They then led their forces in an orgy of looting, pillaging and torture as they searched for more treasure. Pizarro's treachery at Cajamarca, driven by the dual motives of heathen conversion to Christianity and the acquisition of great wealth in the form of gold, silver and emeralds was the beginning of the end for the empire of the Incas. Today, Catholicism is the dominant religion of the people in Central and South America but, for the privilege, their forebears paid a heavy price. On the 26th June 1541, Pizarro was assassinated in his palace in Lima, the city he had founded. Approaching 70 years of age, he was stabbed in the throat and fell to the floor where he suffered a frenzy of further stab wounds. As he was dying, he painted a cross on the floor in his own blood and cried out for Jesus Christ.

Other Religious Atrocities

Religious dogma and bigotry have the capacity to first distort and then pervert the mind. People who have appeared normal in every respect, who have been kind to their families, friends and their animals have, when influenced by religious fervour of any persuasion, been capable of acts of extreme barbarity. History has confirmed unequivocally the poignancy of Thomas Jefferson's words stated thus:

"Millions of innocent men, women, and children, since the introduction of Christianity, have been burnt, tortured, fined, and imprisoned; yet we have not advanced one inch toward uniformity. What has been the effect of coercion? To make one half the world fools and the other half hypocrites. To support roguery and error all over the earth."

In 1488, Bartolomeu Dias (ca. 1451 – 1500), a Portuguese nobleman and explorer, became the first European to sail around the southernmost tip of Africa. He wished to continue sailing to find a route to India but was forced to turn back when his crew, tired and afraid, refused to proceed. The way was then clear for his countryman, Vasco da Gama (ca. 1460 – 1524), to sail around the Cape of Good Hope and land at Kappad, near Calicut, India on the 20th May 1498. A passage to India had been found which obviated the need to travel through Muslim controlled territory. He returned to Portugal more than two years after the start of his journey to be richly rewarded, decorated and feted as a hero. He had travelled a distance greater than the circumference of the world and is rightly regarded as one of the greatest explorers in history. Less well known, however, is that throughout his life he was capable of the most extraordinary cruelty to his fellow man. On his orders, some of his captives had their hands, ears and noses hacked off but it was during his second voyage to India that one of the most barbaric incidents of his life took place. In September 1502, Dom (Lord) da Gama, with a small fleet under his command, encountered a ship returning to India from a pilgrimage to Mecca. The ship, named Meri, had over 300 men, women and children on board. The Meri surrendered without a fight and, once its stores had been looted, da Gama had all the passengers and crew secured in the hold before setting the ship on fire. As the Meri burned, it was bombarded by the Portuguese ships. Passengers occasionally escaped onto the deck, beseeching Allah for deliverance and pleading for mercy, the women even tossing their babies into the sea. Anyone who escaped into the water was ordered to be slain. As the flames subsided, da Gama commanded his men aboard to relight the fires. This passage of events went on for four days and nights, the fires being relit repeatedly before the Meri disappeared without trace.

The heinous crime was but a prelude to da Gama's deeds at Calicut. Capturing some 30 Hindu fishermen who had sailed out in small boats to sell fish to his crews, he had them all hanged. That night, he ordered that the bodies be dismembered and thrown into the sea from where they drifted ashore. Grief stricken families were left to try to identify their relatives from the few rags that still clung to mutilated flesh. On another occasion, a Hindu priest acting as an envoy of the King of Calicut visited da Gama for talks. It is reputed that he disliked the priest and accused him of being a spy before ordering that his lips and ears be sliced off. Da Gama became feared and hated in equal measure and, in 1524, made his last voyage eastwards as Governor of Portuguese India. His initial voyage to India had been the forerunner to a new epoch in Portugal's history. A poor country of fishermen and peasants had been elevated into one which was able to capitalise on its trading supremacy in the Indian Ocean to create a rich, burgeoning Portuguese Empire. Vasco da Gama died on Christmas Eve, 1524, in Cochin (now Kochi), India. Dressed in the mantle of the Order of Christ, his body was carried on the shoulders of the monks of The Brotherhood of Mercy without anyone being aware of the irony of it all.

In his book entitled, *Vasco da Gama and his Successors 1460 – 1580*, K.G. Jayne wrote:

"There can be little doubt that the burning of the Meri and similar achievements were regarded in Europe as laudable manifestations of zeal for religion. D. Vasco, had his conduct been challenged, would assuredly have answered, with honest and indignant surprise, that he was only doing his duty as a Christian in exterminating the vile brood of Muhammad; that his acts of piracy and pillage were authorized by 'letters of marque from God'."

Vasco da Gama's atrocities provide confirmation, yet again, that the tyrants to be most feared are those who believe they are doing God's work. Compared to his great predecessor, the virtuous Henry the Navigator, Dom Vasco was a psychopathic killer, yet he appears to have led a charmed existence. Isn't this one of the great conundrums of life? Why is it that some of the most barbaric people in history lead relatively comfortable lives whilst inflicting immense suffering on innocent victims? At the same time, many good natured people with a respect for humanity and exuding kindness die at a young age after leading wretched lives. Why does God in his supervision not curb the evil ones and their

unfettered savagery?   How can it possibly benefit God to bestow
untimely ends on decent people whilst allowing others that inflict pain
and sorrow to live full lives? The answer, as always it seems, is that we
cannot hope to understand God and that he moves in mysterious ways.

The First Crusade took place between 1096 and 1099 culminating in
the recapture of Jerusalem.   The city had not been under Christian
dominion for 461 years, ever since the period of the 7th century Muslim
conquests. Whilst the crusade had causes deeply rooted in the social and
political features of 11th century Europe, the ultimate event initiating it
was a plea for assistance from the Byzantine Emperor, Alexios I
Komnenos. Alexios was deeply worried about the advances made by the
Seljuq Turks who had reached a territory near Constantinople and, in
March 1095, he sent envoys to Pope Urban II to ask for aid.   Urban
responded positively, perhaps hoping to repair the rift established some
40 years earlier between the eastern (Greek) and western (Latin)
branches of the State Church of the Roman Empire. These later became
known as the Eastern Orthodox Church and the Roman Catholic Church,
respectively. He may have seen this as an opportunity to reunite his
church under papal primacy by helping the eastern Christians in their
time of need. So it was that at the Council of Clermont in November
1095, he gave an impassioned sermon to a large audience of French
nobles and clergy which graphically detailed the atrocities, though
largely apocryphal, being committed against pilgrims and indigenous
Christians. He was able to inspire his audience in a way that could not
have been achieved had he been exhorting merely political, economic or
territorial gain.   Urban was able to summon a force which inevitably
arouses heightened passions, namely that of religion, and which once

aroused can behave erratically and unpredictably. Part of what he said was:

"From the confines of Jerusalem and the city of Constantinople a horrible tale has gone forth and very frequently has been brought to our ears: namely, that a race from the kingdom of the Persians, an accursed race, a race utterly alienated from God, a generation, forsooth, which has neither directed its heart nor entrusted its spirit to God, has invaded the lands of those Christians and has depopulated them by sword, pillage, and fire; it has led away a part of the captives into its own country, and a part it has destroyed by cruel torture; it has either entirely destroyed the churches of God or appropriated them for the rites of its own religion. They destroy the altars, after having defiled them with their uncleanness. They circumcise the Christians, and the blood of the circumcision they either spread upon the altars or pour into the vases of the baptismal font. When they wish to torture people by a base death, they perforate their navels, and, dragging forth the end of the intestines, bind it to a stake; then with flogging they lead the victim around until his viscera have gushed forth, and he falls prostrate upon the ground. Others they bind to a post and pierce with arrows. Others they compel to extend their necks, and then, attacking them with naked swords, they attempt to cut through the neck with a single blow. What shall I say of the abominable rape of the women? To speak of it is worse than to be silent. The kingdom of the Greeks is now dismembered by them, and deprived of territory so vast in extent that it can not be traversed in a march of two months. On whom, therefore, is the task of avenging those wrongs and of recovering this territory incumbent, if not upon you? You, upon whom above other nations God has conferred remarkable glory in arms, great courage, bodily energy, and the strength to humble the hairy scalp of those who resist you."

Given the content of Urban's speech, it is hardly surprising that his address had the desired effect. With passions heightened, armies of knights and peasants were gathered in 1096, primarily from France and Germany, to begin their journey eastwards. However, Urban, not to be blamed for a lack of prescience, whilst successfully mobilising Christian forces, unintentionally unleashed a vicious side effect of anti-Semitism. Subsequent preaching during the First Crusade inspired an outbreak of anti-Jewish violence which resulted in the deaths of large numbers of innocent victims. If a holy war was to be fought against the Muslims, why not extend it to all unbelievers? In the minds of many, Jews were considered the Christ-killers and an enemy on equal footing with the advocates of Islam. Even some priests leading bands of Crusaders were sympathetic to this point of view and persecuted Jews on the way to the Holy Land. Godfrey de Bouillon was a Frankish knight and one of the leaders of the First Crusade. He was regarded as both honourable and chivalrous and, later, after the successful siege of the holy city, he became the first ruler of the Kingdom of Jerusalem, eschewing a kingly title. Yet, even he could not rationalise his feelings as he succumbed to prejudice saying:

"...to go on this journey only after avenging the blood of the crucified one by shedding Jewish blood and completely eradicating any trace of those bearing the name 'Jew'."

There is no evidence, however, that he fulfilled this pledge; indeed, he was known to have accepted payment from Jewish communities to ensure their protection. The hierarchy of the Catholic Church as a whole condemned Jewish persecution and the Holy Roman Emperor, Henry IV, issued a proclamation prohibiting violence against Jewish enclaves. The protestations had little effect. In the spring of 1096, a large army of Crusaders numbering around 10,000 was raised by Count Emicho of Flonheim, a German noble, and proceeded to march through the Rhine valley. After some 22 Jews had been killed in Metz, Bishop John of Speyer restrained Emicho's Crusaders from slaying his town's Jewish inhabitants who had sought refuge in the synagogue. Despite his brave attempts, 11 more innocents were murdered. On the 18th May, the Bishop of Worms, Adalbert II, also tried to shelter Jewish inhabitants but all were slain save a few who were forcibly baptised. Estimates of the dead run as high as 800 men, women and children, massacred when they refused Christian baptism. A week later, Emicho was persuaded not to enter the city of Mainz by Bishop Ruthard, accepting an offer of gold donated by Jewish citizens in exchange for their safety. However, despite his acceptance of the tribute, he did little to prevent his ill-disciplined rabble from entering the city on the 27th May. Bishop Ruthard tried to protect the Jews by hiding them in his lightly fortified palace and many among the Christian burghers (mercantile class members) also offered them shelter. The burghers joined with the bishop's militia and the forces of the military governor in repelling the first waves of Crusaders but, in the end, their brave stand was subdued. Hopelessly outnumbered, Bishop Ruthard and his guardians fled to leave the Jews to their fate and, despite the fine example shown by the burghers, many ordinary citizens, fuelled by frenzy, joined in the persecution and pillage.

The Jews, fortified by their faith, showed extraordinary courage. They believed that it was the will of God that they must die, that their souls would live on in the afterlife. Some bowed their heads before their executioners and, stoically, faced decapitation. Husbands slew their wives rather than have them face the wrath of the mob, before falling on their swords. Mothers cut the throats of their children and faced the hysterical rabble on their own, only to be slaughtered on refusing conversion to Christianity. A few Jews accepted the faith of their tormentors and were spared. One of these men, later consumed by guilt, killed his family and burned himself alive. Mainz was the scene of the greatest violence with at least 1,100 Jews being killed but the pogroms did not end there. The Jews of the Rhineland were decimated, an estimated 4,000 losing their lives. They had been killed by a juggernaut, incapable of rational thought and blinded by a malformed religious belief, destroying everything alien in its path.

Entirely innocent people had been butchered because they had been unfairly labelled as Christ-killers. It had been more than a millennium since the death of Jesus meaning that the Jews of the time of the First Crusade were no more culpable of his crucifixion than were the Crusaders themselves. Do people have to die simply because they are descendants of a particular race? It makes no sense, does it? In a different setting, any Crusader on his own meeting a Jewish child would have been no threat to that child. However, as an integral part of a mob driven by religious hatred and mass hysteria, his behaviour was unspeakable. With his ability to reason suspended, he adopted the psychology of the mob. Crazed and adrenalin fuelled, he would have been capable of slaughtering a child without a moment's hesitation. It seems that as a mob increases in size, its rationality declines proportionately and, in the absence of an overwhelming opposing force, nothing can quell its voracious appetite before it has been sated. Afterwards, would any of the Crusaders involved in the murderous acts have felt any remorse? Individual members of mobs, after quiet reflection, are frequently regretful, ashamed or even mortified by having allowed themselves to be carried away in a tide of violence. In the case of the Crusaders, however, because of their religious motivation, remorse is unlikely to have been felt. Religious conviction seems to have the greatest propensity to distort otherwise normal human minds and induce unimaginable levels of depravity. They did, after all, have God on their side didn't they? Where was God, by the way, when the slaughters were taking place in the townships? Once again, he seems to have been looking the other way.

The Tribunal of the Holy Office of the Inquisition, more generally known as the Spanish Inquisition, was established in 1480 by the Catholic monarchs, Ferdinand II of Aragon and Isabella I of Castille. The Inquisition was originally intended to verify the orthodoxy of those who converted to Christianity from Judaism and Islam (known as *conversos*). This regulation of the newly converted was intensified in 1492 and 1501 after royal decrees were issued ordering the expulsion of any Jews and Muslims who were unwilling to embrace Catholicism. Various motives have been suggested for the decision of the monarchy to fund the Inquisition including the reduction of social tensions, the weakening of opposition, the increase of political authority, the dissuasion of conspirators and the profit to be gained from the sequestration of the assets of convicted heretics. The Inquisition was under the formal control of the Spanish monarchy and was not definitively abolished until 1834, during the reign of Queen Isabella II.

In many ways, the Inquisition can be seen as the corollary of the multi-religious nature of Spanish society following the reconquest of the Iberian Peninsula.   The Muslim Moors had dominated most of the peninsula for almost 600 years until the gradual re-establishment of Christian rule following victory at the Battle of Las Navas de Tolosa (1212) and the recapture of Cordoba (1236) and Seville (1248).   The region of Granada remained under Muslim dominion until the final Christian victory in 1492.   The *Reconquista*, however, did not initially result in the total expulsion of Muslims from Spain since they, along with the Jews, had been tolerated by the Catholic elite. Large cities, including Seville, Valladolid and Barcelona had substantial Jewish populations. Gradually, however, the Muslims became increasingly oppressed, initially by alienation and then torture.   Soon afterwards, the Jews became the target for similar maltreatment. Towards the end of the 14th century there was, in some Spanish cities, a wave of violent anti-Semitism culminating in the pogroms of June 1391. Hundreds of Jews were killed in Seville where the synagogue was burned down. The loss of life was also high in Cordoba, Valencia and Barcelona.

One of the consequences of the violence was the mass conversion of Jews to Catholicism.   Forced baptism was contrary to the law of the Catholic Church and, theoretically, any Jew who had been forcibly baptised could legally return to Judaism. This was, however, somewhat incongruously interpreted. Legal definitions of the time acknowledged that a forced baptism was not a valid sacrament but confined this to cases where it was administered by torture or, at least, some form of physical violence. A person who had consented to baptism merely under the threat of death or serious injury was, curiously, still regarded as a voluntary convert and, accordingly, forbidden to revert to the former faith. After the public violence, many of the converted felt it prudent to remain in their new religion.

During her stay in Seville in 1478, Queen Isabella I was convinced by Alonso de Hojeda, a Dominican friar, of the existence of crypto-Judaism (an adherence to Judaism whilst professing Christianity) among Andalusian *conversos*. Jews insincere in their new faith were known as *Marranos* whilst their Muslim counterparts were called *Moriscos*. A report produced by Pedro Gonzalez de Mendoza, Archbishop of Seville, and by the Segovian Dominican, Tomas de Torquemada, supported this assertion. Consequently, Queen Isabella and her husband, Ferdinand, resolved to implement the Inquisition in Castille to expose and punish *Marranos*. Pope Sixtus IV was disinclined to support the Inquisition but, even so, on the 6th February 1481, six people were convicted and burned alive in Seville. From that point, the Inquisition gathered pace and soon there were eight tribunals in the Castillian kingdom. Uneasy with the spread of the Inquisition, Sixtus IV issued a papal bull proscribing any extension into Aragon stating:

"Many true and faithful Christians, because of the testimony of enemies, rivals, slaves and other low people, and still less appropriate, without tests of any kind, have been locked up in secular prisons, tortured and condemned like relapsed heretics, deprived of their goods and properties, and given over to the secular arm to be executed, at great danger to their souls, giving a pernicious example and causing scandal to many."

In 1483, however, after persuasion by Ferdinand, Sixtus IV conceded and issued a second edict naming Tomas de Torquemada as the first

Inquisitor General of Aragon, Valencia and Catalonia. Torquemada wasted no time in establishing procedures for the Inquisition. A new court would allow a 30-day grace period for confessions and the gathering of accusations by neighbours. Evidence that was used to identify a *Marrano* was arbitrary, even risible, and included the absence of chimney smoke on Saturdays (signifying that a family might secretly be honouring the Sabbath) or the buying of substantially more vegetables before Passover. The court employed physical torture to extract confessions. Crypto-Jews were allowed to confess and do penance whilst those who refused to confess and were subsequently found guilty of relapsing were burned at the stake. During Torquemada's 15-year reign of terror, hundreds of Jews were put to death and thousands were falsely imprisoned. In later years, the Inquisition turned its attention to *Moriscos* and Protestants who met the same fate as the Jews. By the time the Inquisition was eventually abolished, it is estimated that around 5,000 people had been burned alive.

The victims didn't attempt to subvert the monarchy, they didn't kill anybody, didn't commit grievous bodily harm or steal from anyone. On the contrary, it was *their* assets that were sequestrated, so why were they put to death? Incredulously, it was simply because, though worshipping the same God, they were perceived to be exercising the 'wrong' faith. In 1540, the first Protestant was burned at the stake in Spain. Francisco de San Roman was a rich merchant and, during his travels to Germany and the Netherlands, he was influenced by Lutheranism. He became a disciple of Jacobo Spreng, a former prior of the Augustian monks in Antwerp. On journeying through Flanders, he was apprehended by the authorities of the Catholic Church who discovered books by the Protestant theologians, Luther, Melanchthon and Oecolampadius, in his luggage. San Roman was interrogated by the Dominicans to whom he confessed the reformed doctrines which included salvation by faith alone and the claim that the pope was the antichrist. He was imprisoned for six months, set free and arrested again for preaching Protestantism. After being handed over to the Spanish Inquisition, he condemned the Catholic doctrines of the mass, auricular confession, purgatory and prayers to the saints. No matter what the provocation, the friars were unable to convince him to retract. San Roman was duly burned at the stake, the proceedings being orchestrated by the friars, the men of God. During the early part of the burning, he made an involuntary movement of the head which was mistakenly taken as a sign of repentance. The friars quickly removed him from the flames and, as he recovered, he calmly asked them:

"Do you envy my happiness?"

He was returned to the flames, his courage undiminished, as resolute and unerring in support of his ideology as his accusers were misguided and unbending in upholding theirs. In 1565, 26 English sailors were burned at the stake and many more were given prison sentences. They had committed no crimes; they were simply Protestants serving on merchant vessels visiting Spanish ports. The legalised murder of innocents continued for many years though somewhat less avidly than during the time that Torquemada strode upon his doctrinal stage as a vengeful colossus.

Tomas de Torquemada wasn't the first of the Spanish inquisitors but he was by far the most notorious. He was a Dominican friar, a holy man, who saw no irony in the conflict between his enforcement of Catholicism and his violation of the moral teachings of Christ. Religious dogma had, at first, infiltrated then imprisoned his mind which, in turn, became anaesthetised from his actions. He was described by a Spanish chronicler as:

"The hammer of heretics, the light of Spain, the saviour of his country, the honour of his order."

Is it not truly astonishing just how misguided people of the 15th century could be when concerned with matters of religion? Torquemada was immensely cruel, an aberration of humanity acting in the name of God. Is there anything more reprehensible than a man of God condoning and presiding over murder, banishing from his distorted mind the recognition of the sanctity of life? Torquemada's name became a byword for fanaticism in the service of Catholicism. In 1832, his tomb was desecrated, his bones stolen and burnt to ashes.

The Thirty Years' War (1618 – 1648) was fought primarily in the area now comprising Germany and, at various times, involved most of the countries in Europe. It was one of the most destructive conflicts in European history. Initially, the war was fought largely as a religious dispute between Protestants and Catholics in the Holy Roman Empire although disagreements over the internal politics and balance of power within the empire also played their part. Gradually, the war developed into a more general conflict involving most of the European powers but, at its core, was the aspiration for political pre-eminence between France and the House of Habsburg. The religious imperatives evident at the start of the war were less important at its end by which time the power and influence of the Catholic Church had substantially declined. Once again, the warring factions worshipped the same God and, ostensibly, followed the same teachings of Jesus yet they were prepared to kill each other because of different ways of expressing their faith.

The siege of Magdeburg, a prominent city in the northern part of central Germany, took place between November 1630 and May 1631. The largely Protestant inhabitants were confronted by the forces of the Holy Roman Empire and the Catholic League led, respectively, by Field Marshall Pappenheim and Johann Tserclaes, Count of Tilly. The city fell on the 20th May when the Catholic armies put the garrison to the sword and then, despite Tilly's efforts, ran completely out of control. The imperial soldiers, Walloons and Croats in particular, set fire to the city and began a wholesale slaughter of the inhabitants. It was an orgy of murder, rape, looting and destruction. Of 30,000 citizens, a mere 5,000 survived and for a fortnight in the aftermath, charred bodies were dumped into the River Elbe to prevent the spread of disease. The German writer, Friedrich Schiller, described the massacre as:

"A scene of horrors for which history has no language – poetry no pencil."

In a letter, Field Marshall Pappenheim later wrote:

"I believe that over twenty thousand souls were lost. It is certain that no more terrible work and divine punishment has been seen since the Destruction of Jerusalem. All of our soldiers became rich. God with us."

It is clear from Pappenheim's words that he believed God sanctioned the massacre and, in this case, favoured the Catholics over the Protestants. Otto von Gericke, Burgomeister in 1631, graphically and chillingly recorded the destruction of the city by imperial troops thus:

"Then was there naught but beating and burning, plundering, torture, rape and murder. Most especially was every enemy bent on securing much booty. When a marauding party entered a house, if its master had anything to give he might thereby purchase respite and protection for himself and his family till the next man, who also wanted something should come along. It was only when everything had been brought forth and there was nothing left to give that the real trouble commenced. Then, what with blows and threats of shooting, stabbing and hanging, the poor people were so terrified that if they had had anything left they would have brought it forth if it had been buried in the earth or hidden away. In this frenzied rage, the great and splendid city that had stood like a fair princess in the land was now, in its hour of direst need and unutterable distress and woe, given over to flames, and thousands of innocent men, women and children, in the midst of a horrible din of heartrending shrieks and cries, were tortured and put to death in so cruel and shameful a manner that no words would suffice to describe, nor no tears to bewail it. Thus in a single day this noble and famous city, the pride of the whole country, went up in fire and smoke; and the remnant of its citizens, with their wives and children, were taken prisoners and driven away by the enemy with a noise of weeping and wailing that could be heard from afar, while the cinders and ashes from the town were carried by the wind to Wanzleben, Egeln, and still more distant places."

By the end of the war and the signing of the Peace of Westphalia in 1648, the city's population had fallen even further and only 450 inhabitants remained. The devastation was of such a magnitude that, for decades, 'magdeburgisation' became a well used term for total destruction, rape and pillage. Additionally, the terms 'Magdeburg justice', 'Magdeburg mercy' and 'Magdeburg quarter' came into circulation, being used originally by vengeful Protestants when executing Catholics who begged for their lives. It is difficult to comprehend that these were Christians in combat with Christians who were quite prepared to murder each other for the sake of relatively insignificant differences in their beliefs. Sadly, Magdeburg was no isolated atrocity; in 125 years from 1524, religious wars in Europe accounted for the loss of over 11 million lives. All of the dead had believed in the love of the same God.

It was not only in mainland Europe that Catholics and Protestants were so intransigent in their views that dissent was punishable by death. Under the reign of Queen Mary I, in particular, from July 1553 until her passing in November 1558, England was very much the same. Mary was the only surviving child of King Henry VIII and his first wife, Catherine of Aragon. Disappointed by the lack of a male heir after his wife had suffered several miscarriages, Henry became anxious to re-marry. He appealed to Pope Clement VII to annul his marriage but his requests were rejected. Undeterred, in 1533, Henry married Anne Boleyn who was pregnant with his child and shortly afterwards, Thomas Cranmer (1489 – 1556), the Archbishop of Canterbury, formally declared the marriage to Catherine null and void. Without Pope Clement's sanction, Henry felt he had little choice but to break with the Roman Catholic Church and declare himself Head of the Church of England, which he duly did. Thomas Cranmer was entrusted with the task of implementing the first doctrinal and liturgical structures of the reformed Church of England. Under Henry's rule, he did not make any radical changes due to the conflict that existed between religious conservatives and reformers. Though Henry had severed his relationship with The Church of Rome, he had no enthusiasm for the pursuit of an agenda of religious reform akin to the Protestantism sweeping through Europe. In 1521, Pope Leo X had conferred on Henry the title of Defender of the Faith in recognition of his treatise against the Protestant leader, Martin Luther. Protestant reformers faced persecution until the later years of Henry's reign when there was an amelioration in his views. Talented academics such as John Frith (1503 – 1533), an English Protestant priest and writer, and William Tyndale (1492 – 1536), a theologian and scholar, held and published opinions considered heretical and, consequently, both were burned at the stake. Tyndale was a man of outstanding intellect. He was born in Gloucestershire, studied at Oxford University and gained his Master of Arts Degree in 1515, when 21 years old. He later proved to be a gifted linguist. One of Tyndale's associates commented that he was:

"So skilled in eight languages – Hebrew, Greek, Latin, Spanish, French, Italian, English, and German, that whichever he speaks, you might think it his native tongue."

Around 1520, Tyndale became a tutor in the family of Sir John Walsh at Little Sodbury, Gloucestershire. Having become attracted to reforming doctrines, he devoted himself to the study of the scriptures. The open affirmation of his sentiments in the house of Walsh and his preaching led to disputes with Roman Catholic dignitaries. In consequence, he travelled to London where Sir Humphrey Monmouth and other friends financially aided him to translate the scriptures into the commonly spoken English of the day. One cleric, entrenched in Roman Catholic dogma, once taunted Tyndale with the statement:

"We are better to be without God's laws than the Pope's."

An infuriated Tyndale replied:

"I defy the Pope and all his laws. If God spare my life ere many years, I will cause the boy that drives the plow to know more of the scriptures than you!"

Tyndale fled to Germany in 1524 so that he might enjoy greater freedom to carry out his work. There he lived a frugal existence, ever watchful to evade the Catholic authorities. He was influenced by the work of Desiderius Erasmus (ca. 1466 – 1536), the Dutch theologian who made the Greek New Testament available in Europe, and also by Martin Luther. Tyndale was the first to translate considerable parts of the Bible from the original languages of Greek and Hebrew into English. While a number of translations had been made from the seventh century onward, particularly during the 14th century, Tyndale's was the first English translation to be extracted directly from Hebrew and Greek texts, rather than Latin. It was also the first to take advantage of Johannes Gutenberg's moveable type printing press which facilitated a wide distribution. This was construed as a direct challenge to the hegemony of both the Roman Catholic Church and the Church of England. Tyndale also wrote, perhaps unwisely in 1530, *The Practyse of Prelates*, opposing Henry VIII's divorce on the grounds that it contravened scriptural law. In 1535, Tyndale was betrayed in Antwerp, arrested and imprisoned in the castle of Vilvoorde, near Brussels, for over a year. He was tried for heresy, strangled and burned at the stake in 1536 when his last words were:

"Oh Lord! Open the King of England's eyes."

Had Tyndale been able to evade capture for a few more years, he would have been able to return to his native land in relative safety, a mark of the turbulence and capriciousness of the times. The Tyndale Bible, as it was known, continued to play a key role in spreading Reformation ideology across the English-speaking world. The Great Bible, published in 1539 and authorised by Henry VIII, was the first English translation to be read aloud in the services of the Church of England. It was largely based on the Tyndale Bible. Later, the 54 independent scholars who created the King James Bible in 1611 drew substantially on Tyndale's translations. Estimates suggest that the New Testament in the King James Bible comprises 83 percent Tyndale with the Old Testament comprising around 76 percent.

After her divorce, Catherine was demoted to Dowager Princess of Wales and dismissed from court. Her daughter, Mary, was deemed illegitimate, removed from the line of succession (later restored) and also dismissed. She did not speak to her father for three years until Jane Seymour, Henry's third wife, was the arbiter of a peace between them. Like her mother, Mary was a devout Catholic and remained so steadfastly throughout her life despite Henry's attempts to dissuade her. When Henry insisted that she recognise him as Head of the Church of England, renounce papal authority, acknowledge that her parents' marriage was illicit and accept her illegitimacy, she reluctantly, though tactfully, signed a settlement to that effect. Her younger half-brother, Edward VI, succeeded Henry in 1547. Since Edward was only nine years old at the time, governance was held by a regency council dominated by Protestants who hastily fostered their faith throughout the country. The 1549 Act of Uniformity, for example, prescribed Protestant rites for church services using Thomas Cranmer's new *Book of Common*

Prayer. It was not until Edward's reign that Cranmer began to introduce major reform by establishing an English Protestant church structure. Mary, however, remained resolute in her Roman Catholicism. She even appealed to her cousin, the Holy Roman Emperor, Charles V, to enable her to practise her religion in her own chapel. As Edward extended his father's religious reforms, he remained in discord with his half-sister. When Mary was in her thirties, she attended a celebration with Edward and their mutual half-sister, Elizabeth, for the Christmas of 1550. Both the 13-year old Edward and Mary were reduced to tears when he reproached her in front of the court for flouting his laws of worship. Even so, Mary repeatedly ignored Edward's demands that she abandon her faith.

By 1553, Edward was mortally ill and, because he believed Mary would restore Catholicism, he resolved to remove her from the line of succession. To make good his plan he also had to disinherit Elizabeth even though she was, most definitely, not a Catholic. Edward and his advisers resolved that his cousin, Lady Jane Grey, should succeed him as monarch. On the 6th July 1553, Edward VI died from a lung infection, possibly tuberculosis, and four days later, a bewildered Lady Jane was proclaimed queen. In response, Mary garnered a military force at Framlingham Castle, Suffolk, and successfully deposed Jane on the 19th July. The hapless Lady Jane, also known as 'The Nine Days Queen', an innocent bystander entangled in a web of political intrigue, was imprisoned in the Tower of London and was later beheaded. She was barely 17 years old. Mary rode triumphantly into London on the 3rd August 1553 accompanied by her half-sister Elizabeth and a procession of over 800 gentlemen and nobles.

One of Mary's first actions as queen was to order the release of notable Catholics from the Tower of London and, shortly afterwards, she issued a proclamation that she would not compel any of her subjects to adopt her religion. By the end of September, however, leading reforming clergymen such as John Bradford, John Rogers, John Hooper, Hugh Latimer and Thomas Cranmer had been imprisoned. Mary's first Parliament, assembled in early October 1553, pronounced the marriage of Henry and Catherine legitimate and abolished Edward's religious laws. Church doctrine was restored to the form of 1539. Mary had always regretted the fissure with Rome instituted by her father and the establishment of Protestantism by her half-brother, Edward. She reverted the English church to Roman jurisdiction in 1554 and revived the Heresy Acts in the same year. As a consequence, numerous Protestants were executed during the Marian Persecutions whilst around 800 were exiled. The first executions, including those of John Rogers and John Hooper, occurred over a period of five days in early February 1555. The imprisoned Archbishop of Canterbury, Thomas Cranmer, was compelled to watch Bishops Ridley and Latimer being burned at the stake. As a consequence of this trauma, Cranmer renounced Protestant theology and rejoined the Catholic faith. According to the normal interpretation of the law, he should have been pardoned as a repentant but Mary refused to acquit him. On the day of his burning, he unexpectedly withdrew his recantation stating:

"And as for the pope, I refuse him, as Christ's enemy, and Antichrist with all his false doctrine."

In all, during Mary's five-year reign, 283 people were executed, earning her the sobriquet, 'Bloody Mary' from her Protestant opponents. Her re-establishment of Catholicism was reversed after her death, in 1558, by her successor and half-sister, Queen Elizabeth I. In the end, all those killings were for nothing. Mary had ordered the deaths of people who worshipped the same Jesus and the same God; the only difference was the way in which they worshipped and expressed their faith. Not once did it seem to cause her any consternation that Jesus might not approve of her actions. Her mind had become distorted by her hatred of Protestantism, a movement she believed had to be eradicated by force rather than persuasion.

When Elizabeth I acceded to the throne of England and Ireland, another reversal took place and the Catholics, once again, were persecuted by the law of the land. The measures imposed became even harsher after the Rising of the North, in 1569, when Catholic nobles failed in their attempt to depose Elizabeth in favour of her cousin, Mary, Queen of Scots. An act was passed prohibiting any member of the Catholic Church from conducting the rites of his faith. Forfeiture was the penalty for the first offence, a year's imprisonment for the second and life imprisonment for the third. All those who refused to swear allegiance to Elizabeth by taking the Oath of Supremacy were called *Recusants* and deemed guilty of high treason. A further law of high treason was enacted providing that the death penalty would be applied to any Papist found guilty of converting an Anglican or Protestant to Catholicism. The convert was also to be put to death. A priest was hanged after simply conducting Mass and the religious laws were enforced with even greater zeal after the Gunpowder Plot of 1605, occurring during the reign of Elizabeth's successor, James I. These were the days of the priest holes (hiding places for priests) built into many of the principal Catholic houses of England. It was quite common for castles and country houses to have means of concealment or escape to be used in the event of hostility or surprise. However, during the time of legalised persecution, the number of secret chambers increased markedly within the houses of many Catholic families. These were often secluded apartments or chapels, sometimes in the roof space, enabling Mass to be undertaken in the utmost privacy. In close proximity, there was usually a cleverly designed hiding place to accommodate the officiating priest and religious artefacts in case of emergency. Priest holes frequently left the priest hunters perplexed as they conducted exhaustive searches in the houses of suspects. Search parties would frequently include expert carpenters and stonemasons who would try every possible technique in their search for evidence including systematic measurements, soundings, removal of panelling and excavation. It was not uncommon for a rigorous search to last up to a fortnight without anyone being uncovered. All the while, the fugitive may have been concealed within a wall's thickness of his pursuers, in extreme discomfort because of the prolonged confinement. Immured in this way, priests were known to have died from starvation or from a lack of air.

Elizabeth established an English church that shaped a national identity which remains to this day. She elevated England's standing abroad as can be seen from the comment of Pope Sixtus V:
"She is only a woman, only mistress of half an island, and yet she makes herself feared by Spain, by France, by the Empire, by all."

Her views on religion were much more tolerant than others in her government and, considering faith to be a personal matter, she did not wish, as Francis Bacon (1561 – 1626), the famous Elizabethan statesman and philosopher, put it:

"To make windows into men's hearts and secret thoughts."

One cannot help wondering what God was thinking as he witnessed one group of ideologues murdering another in his name, without intervening to give them any form of divine guidance. How can any person capable of logic and reason make sense of it all, apart from concluding it makes no sense?

A witch-hunt is a search for witches or evidence of witchcraft, often synonymous with moral panic, mass hysteria and lynching. Even so, in many cases, witch-hunts were legally sanctioned resulting in countless official witchcraft trials throughout both Europe and North America. During the period of the 14th to the 17th centuries, the persecution of witches led to the torture of tens of thousands of innocent women, men and even children. In hindsight, there can be no question that the victims were wrongly accused because their professed crimes were not just implausible but usually impossible. Nevertheless, under the provocation of extreme physical torture, many of the hapless confessed which served to add credence to the barbaric practice of witch-finding. The penalty for being convicted of witchcraft was death, usually by burning at the stake.

As so often in the past, ecclesiastical authorities were, in their misguided, distorted view of the world about them, the prime movers sanctioning the death of innocent people. In 1486, the *Malleus Maleficarum* (translated as *Hammer of Witches*) was written by two Dominican Inquisitors, Heinrich Kramer and James Sprenger, who had for a decade been prosecuting witches in southern Germany. During that time, faced with resistance from the local clergy, Kramer sought support from the papacy and, in 1484, he obtained a declaration from Pope

Innocent VIII directing the local church authorities to give the Dominican duo every possible assistance. Part of the declaration stated:

"It has indeed lately come to Our ears, not without afflicting Us with bitter sorrow, that in some parts of Northern Germany, as well as in the provinces, townships, territories, districts, and dioceses of Mainz, Cologne, Treves, Salzburg, and Bremen, many persons of both sexes, unmindful of their own salvation and straying from the Catholic faith, have abandoned themselves to devils, incubi and succubi, and by their incantations, spells, conjurations, and other accursed charms and crafts, enormities and horrid offences, have slain infants yet in the mother's womb, as also of the offspring of cattle, and blasted the produce of the earth, the grapes of the vine, the fruits of the trees ..."

The *Malleus* had an inflammatory style, authored with a view to transmitting fear and anxiety. In the first section, a concise and well-considered thesis was expounded which included the argument that witchcraft was a crime against the church, was female and diabolical. In the second section, the writers defined all the tricks of witchcraft and suggestions as to how to guard against them. Finally, in section three, they presented guidance for the courts, how to prosecute and obtain convictions. In Part 1, Kramer and Sprenger claimed that the majority of witches were women saying:

"What else is a woman but a foe to friendship, an inescapable punishment, a necessary evil, a natural temptation, a desirable calamity, a domestic danger, a delectable detriment, an evil of nature, painted with fair colours? Cicero in his second book of *The Rhetorics* says:

"The many lusts of men lead them into one sin, but the one lust of women leads them into all sins; for the root of all woman's vices is avarice."

And Seneca says in his *Tragedies*:

"A woman either loves or hates; there is no third grade."

And the tears of a woman are a deception, for they may spring from true grief, or they may be a snare. When a woman thinks alone, she thinks evil. But the natural reason is that she is more carnal than a man, as is clear from her many carnal abominations. And it should be noted that there was a defect in the formation of the first woman, since she was formed from a bent rib, that is, a rib of the breast, which is bent as it were in a contrary direction to a man. And since through this defect she is an imperfect animal, she always deceives."

Given the extreme misogynistic bias of the *Malleus* and the profound superstition and gullibility of the general populace, it is not difficult to understand why 80 percent of the thousands of witches executed were women. Contrary to an environment in which they should have been afforded protection by a Christian Church, their persecution was actually condoned and compounded by the priesthood, the disciples of God.

If any more proof were needed with regard to the destructive power of religious belief, one needs to look no further than the fervently misguided Hindu custom of *sati* (also known as *suttee*). It was a ritualised funeral practice among some Indian communities in which a recently widowed woman would be burned to death on her husband's funeral pyre. The tradition, which took place over centuries, originated with the goddess, Sati, later known as Dakshayani, who self-immolated because she could not bear the disdain her father, Daksha, felt for her husband, Shiva.

A number of Mughal emperors had tried to outlaw *sati* but achieved only partial success and on the 4th December 1829, during the rule of the British Raj, the practice was formally banned in the lands of the Bengal Presidency by the governor, Lord William Bentinck (1774 – 1839). At the time, the number of widows being sacrificed was down to around 400 each year. When priests of the Hindu community protested to General Sir Charles James Napier (1782 – 1853) that it was their custom, he replied:

"Be it so. This burning of widows is your custom; prepare the funeral pile. But my nation has also a custom. When men burn women alive we hang them, and confiscate all their property. My carpenters shall therefore erect gibbets on which to hang all concerned when the widow is consumed. Let us all act according to national customs."

It seems Sir Charles succeeded in bringing minds, warped by religious dogma, to their senses. The 1829 ban, though it was formally challenged subsequently, survives to this day.

The persecution of the Jewish people did not end with the Crusades; indeed, it continued throughout history culminating in the Holocaust of World War II. Jews, however, have also been capable of acts of great atrocity though not, it would seem, on overtly religious grounds. Forcible conversion to their faith was never seriously part of their agenda. To their credit, unlike Christians and Muslims, they considered it meaningless for anyone to adopt their faith involuntarily. Under the auspices of the Ottoman Empire, the Muslim, Christian, and Jewish communities of Palestine were allowed to exercise jurisdiction over their own people. Zionism, a political faction supporting the self-determination of the Jewish people in a sovereign homeland in Palestine, began in the late 19th century. The first wave of Zionist immigration to Palestine started in 1881 and lasted until 1903. During this time, the Jews arrived primarily from Eastern Europe and Yemen. The first mass immigration of Jews to the Land of Israel, the First Aliyah as it was known, laid the foundation for Jewish settlement in Palestine. The arrival of thousands of immigrants caused unease amongst the indigenous population and, in 1891, a group of Jerusalem notables sent a petition to the central Ottoman government in Constantinople dissenting against the immigration and the sale of land to Jews. Nevertheless, the immigration continued such that, under the First Aliyah, around 30,000 Jews settled in Palestine. The Second Aliyah took place between 1904 and 1914 during which time approximately 40,000 Jews immigrated, largely from Russia and Poland. This second wave of immigrants comprised, primarily, idealists inspired by the revolutionary changes then sweeping the Russian Empire. They aspired to create a communal agricultural settlement system in Palestine and thus became the founders of the kibbutz movement.

Ottoman rule over the eastern Mediterranean lasted until World War I when the Ottomans sided with Germany and were driven from much of the region by the British. The British-led Egyptian Expeditionary Force, commanded by General Edmund Allenby (1861 – 1936), captured Jerusalem on the 9th December 1917. By that time, it occupied the whole of the Levant having defeated the Turkish forces in Palestine at the Battle of Megiddo (September 1918). The capitulation of Turkey took place on the 31st October. As a mark of respect, Allenby famously dismounted from his horse when he entered Jerusalem to be greeted by Christian, Jewish and Islamic leaders.

The Palestine Mandate was a legal commission for the administration of Palestine, the draft of which was formally confirmed by the Council of the League of Nations on the 24th July, 1922 and which came into effect on the 26th September, 1923. The Mandate formalised British rule in the southern part of Ottoman Syria from 1923 - 1948. With the consent of the League of Nations, Britain divided the Mandate territory into two administrative areas: Palestine, under direct British rule, and the autonomous Transjordan (now Jordan). The Mandate, referring to the Balfour Declaration of 1917 issued by Arthur Balfour, the British Foreign Minister, was:

"… in favour of the establishment in Palestine of a national home for the Jewish people, it being clearly understood that nothing should be done which might prejudice the civil and religious rights of existing non-Jewish communities in Palestine, or the rights and political status enjoyed by Jews in any other country."

Tensions, frequently erupting into violence, continued between the Arabs and Jews throughout the period of the Mandate. The Third (1919 – 1923) and Fourth Aliyahs (1924 – 1929) attracted an additional 100,000 Jews to Palestine. Finally, the rise of Nazism and the increasing persecution of Jews in the 1930s led to the Fifth Aliyah and an influx of a quarter of a million Jews. The Arab revolt or Great Uprising of 1936 – 1939 was a violent remonstration against British colonial rule and the implications of mass Jewish immigration. Thousands were killed or injured and, consequently, the British felt compelled to issue the White Paper of 1939. This introduced restrictions on Jewish immigration and renounced Britain's intention of forming a Jewish national home in Palestine as originally asserted in the 1917 Balfour Declaration. With countries around the world rejecting Jewish refugees fleeing the Holocaust, a clandestine movement known as Aliyah Bet was founded to transport Jews to Palestine. By the end of World War II, the Jewish inhabitants of Palestine had increased to 33 percent of the total population. The religious tensions which had encumbered relations between Muslims and Jews for centuries continued to simmer but, by this time, aspirations of nationhood had assumed a higher priority.

During the aftermath of World War II, as the British prevaricated, the Jews became increasingly impatient and terrorist organisations turned against a war weary establishment. Even after several attempts, Britain had been unable to construct a solution which was acceptable to both sides. From October 1946, the Conservative opposition leader, Winston Churchill, began calling for the 'poisoned chalice' that was Palestine to be referred to the United Nations but it was not until April 1947 that this formally occurred. Leading up to the referral, on the 29th June 1946, the British authorities initiated a military operation known as Operation Agatha or Black Saturday. As over 10,000 soldiers and police searched for arms, arrests were made in Jerusalem, Tel-Aviv, Haifa and dozens of settlements. The objectives of the raids included dissuading terrorists from carrying out further attacks against British troops and officials as well as inhibiting the unilateral declaration of a Jewish state. Significant caches of weaponry were confiscated and around 2,700 people were arrested. Subsequently, some terrorist activities were discouraged but those of the more extreme groups continued and even intensified.

In response to Operation Agatha, the Irgun, a militant Zionist underground organisation, bombed the King David Hotel in Jerusalem on the 22nd July, 1946.   The hotel was the headquarters of the British government in Palestine including, principally, the Secretariat of the Government of Palestine and the Headquarters of the British Forces in Palestine and Transjordan. The explosives were smuggled into the hotel inside milk cans and placed by the main columns supporting the wing most used by the British authorities. The blast caused the collapse of the western half of the southern wing and, soon after, the Royal Engineers employed heavy lifting equipment to begin the rescue operation. Over then next three days, six survivors were extracted from the debris and 2,000 lorry loads of rubble were removed. Of the 91 fatalities, 21 were first-ranking government officials and 49 were office workers, hotel staff and junior members of the Secretariat.   The remainder comprised soldiers, police and members of the public. The death toll included 41 Arabs, 28 British citizens and 17 Jews. In addition, 46 people were injured.

It was a devastating assault with more people killed than by any bombing carried out during the subsequent Arab-Israeli conflict.   The British Prime Minister, Clement Attlee, commented in the House of Commons:

"Honourable Members will have learned with horror of the brutal and murderous crime committed yesterday in Jerusalem. Of all the outrages which have occurred in Palestine, and they have been many and horrible in the last few months, this is the worst. By this insane act of terrorism 93 innocent people have been killed or are missing in the ruins. The latest figures of casualties are 41 dead, 52 missing and 53 injured."

The United Nations (UN) Partition Plan for Palestine was adopted by the UN General Assembly on the 29th November 1947. It replaced the

British Mandate with independent Arab and Jewish States and a Special International Regime for the City of Jerusalem, administered by the UN. The Partition Plan endeavoured to address the divergent objectives and claims of two competing movements, Jewish nationalism (Zionism) and Arab nationalism, and included a detailed description of the boundaries for each proposed state. The plan was accepted by leaders of the Jewish community but was rejected by the Arab leadership who claimed the whole of Palestine. The Arabs argued that it violated the rights of the majority of the people in Palestine which at the time was 67 percent non-Jewish. Britain reluctantly announced that it would accept the plan but refused to implement it by force on the basis that it was not acceptable to both parties. The British favoured a single state inhabited by both Jews and Arabs, believing that partition was unworkable. They stipulated that the Mandate for Palestine would end on the 14th May 1948. Britain refused to share the administration of Palestine with the UN Palestine Commission during the transitional period or to assist in an orderly handover of authority to any successor. It was clear that the British did not intend to remain on Palestinian soil for a moment longer than necessary.

As soon as the UN Partition Plan was adopted, civil war broke out in Palestine. The British, who were still under an obligation to maintain order, planned their withdrawal and rarely intervened. The Deir Yassin massacre took place on the 9th April 1948 when around 120 fighters from Jewish paramilitary groups attacked a Palestinian Arab village. The residents, all Muslims, numbered roughly 600 and they had lived peaceably with their Jewish neighbours from nearby villages. In the opinion of the paramilitaries, the attack on the village was strategically necessary because it threatened Jewish neighbourhoods and the main road to the coastal plain. Also, and more pertinently, an assault would convey a message to the Arabs that the Jews intended to fight for Jerusalem. Up to 200 villagers were killed including women and children; some were shot, whilst others died when hand grenades were tossed into their homes. Around 25 prisoners were executed after the event and their corpses were thrown into quarries. The killings were censured by the leadership of Haganah, the primary Jewish paramilitary force, and by two of the district's rabbis.

The Deir Yassin massacre, however, was by no means an isolated event. It is considered that Jewish troops murdered over 800 civilians and prisoners of war. Most of the killings took place as Arab villages were vanquished during the civil war and the subsequent Arab – Israeli war. One historian termed the atrocities as ethnic cleansing that:

"… carried with it atrocious acts of mass killing and butchering of thousands. Palestinians were killed ruthlessly and savagely by Israeli troops of all backgrounds, ranks and ages."

It is alleged that the Israelis were responsible for at least 24 massacres; that acts of indiscriminate killing of civilians and prisoners, in up to 68 villages, transpired despite no threat being levelled at Israeli soldiers. Though actual numbers are uncertain, both Israeli archives and testimonies from Palestinians confirm that atrocities occurred in numerous villages. Besides Deir Yassin, the worst of these took place in Saliha, Lydda, Abu Shusha and Al-Dawayima. In Al-Dawayima, it is believed that 455 people were killed including 170 women and children.

On the 14th May 1948, David Ben-Gurion, the leader of the Jewish community in Palestine, formally announced the establishment of the State of Israel. The next day, Israel was invaded by the armies of Egypt,

Jordan, Syria, Lebanon and Iraq. Following initial reversals, Israel began to gain the ascendency and, by the time the armistice agreements of 1949 had been signed, Israel had control of 78 percent of the territory comprising former Mandatory Palestine, about one-third more than its original allocation under the Partition Plan. After the first four or five months of the war, an Israeli objective emerged which aimed, by aggression and expulsion, to reduce the size of the new state's large, hostile and potentially subversive Arab minority. Archives and diaries provide circumstantial evidence of a deliberate intent by Haganah, and later by the Israel Defence Forces (IDF), to minimise the number of Arabs in the Jewish state and seize their property for the benefit of masses of Jewish immigrants.

The 1948 Palestinian Exodus, also known as the *Nakba*, occurred when over 700,000 Palestinian Arabs fled or were expelled from their homes. The first to leave did so in anticipation that their lives would be threatened. Others fled with only the few possessions they could carry when they learned of the village massacres. The thousands who remained were forcibly expelled and those who resisted were savagely treated. Many left with the aspiration of being able to return to their homes when the war ended but, when the time came, they were actively discouraged by the Israeli hierarchy. Those that managed to return found that their homes had been razed to the ground or, if they were still intact, were occupied by Israeli families. The nationalistic aims of the Palestinians and the Israelis had exacted a heavy price in human tragedy, the repercussions of which are in evidence to this day. On the 3rd February 1970, in a statement to the International Conference of Parliamentarians, Bertrand Russell wrote:

"The tragedy of the people of Palestine is that their country was 'given' by a foreign power to another people for the creation of a new state. The result was that many hundreds of thousands of innocent people were made permanently homeless. With every new conflict their numbers increased. How much longer is the world willing to endure this spectacle of wanton cruelty? It is abundantly clear that the refugees have every right to the homeland from which they were driven, and the denial of this right is at the heart of the continuing conflict. No people anywhere in the world would accept being expelled en masse from their country; how can anyone require the people of Palestine to accept a punishment which nobody else would tolerate?"

Perhaps, the British government of 1948 was right all along, that the Partition Plan was unworkable. Would a Palestinian state governed by democratically elected representatives of both the Arab and Jewish communities have been a better option? We'll never know. What is certain, however, is that had all the inhabitants of Palestine, whether Arab or Jew, been of the same religion, partition would have been an irrelevance.

Chapter 6

Corruption in the Church

Paedophilia

Corruption is prevalent in all walks of life: politics, business and commerce, the press, police force, local government, charitable organisations, sports governing bodies (e.g. the Federation Internationale de Football Association (FIFA)); in fact, almost anywhere that human traits and frailties are not restrained by means of adequate regulation. Causes of corruption are manifold but are likely to include, for example, avarice, envy, vengeance, hatred and a desire to evade or conceal. The last place we would expect, or at least should expect, to find corruption is in ecclesiastical circles but, disappointingly, this is not borne out in practice. The vast majority of the righteous, benevolent clergymen we all know are in no way implicated but we cannot escape the fact that wrongful acts, such as paedophilia, have been perpetrated by clerics and these have, almost certainly, prevailed for centuries. With its requirement for the celibacy of its priests, it is the Catholic Church which, almost exclusively, shoulders the burden of responsibility for child sex abuse. Very few crimes would have been reported. Those that were would have been suppressed by inclination lest the whole edifice of the church became contaminated causing it to lose influence. Most of the crimes would have been undetected because no mechanisms were ever put in place to unearth them.

In March 2010, Pope Benedict XVI became embroiled in a child sex abuse scandal which required his considered response as head of the Catholic Church. Historically, the significant events are as follows:

- In 1975, two young victims in Ireland signed declarations avowing their silence over allegations that they were sexually abused by Father Brendan Smyth. It subsequently emerged that Sean Brady (later a cardinal) witnessed the proceedings.

- In 1986, Father Peter Hullerman was convicted in Germany of the sexual abuse of minors and was given an 18-month suspended sentence. He continued to work in the church. It was alleged that he had been suspected of abuse on an earlier occasion but had avoided being exposed by transferring to another diocese. It is suspected Joseph Ratzinger, Archbishop of Munich and Freising before he became Pope Benedict XVI, was responsible for the transfer.

- In 1997, Smyth admitted to an astonishing 74 cases of sexual abuse over a period of 35 years. He was sentenced to 12 years in prison but died of a heart attack after only one month in confinement.

- In 2000, the Commission to Inquire into Child Abuse was initiated by the Irish government to report on the extent of child sex abuse in Roman Catholic institutions since 1936. The following year, Pope John Paul II, directed bishops to inform the Vatican of any case of abuse and to prevent the accused from having any further contact with children.

- In 2002, Cardinal Bernard Law, Archbishop of Boston, resigned in the midst of allegations that he failed to act on known cases of abuse within his diocese. He found employment in the Vatican following his resignation.

- In 2004, the Christian Brothers, a Catholic religious order with ties to boys' schools in Ireland, obtained an injunction which prevented the commission from revealing the identity of any of its members, past and present.

- In 2009, the Commission to Inquire into Child Abuse published the results of its investigation. Known as the Ryan Report, it detailed the findings garnered from 2,000 victims and the extent of the institutional cover-up.

- On the 20th March 2010, Pope Benedict XVI responded to the findings in a letter addressed to Irish Catholics as further abuse cases emerged in Germany, Switzerland, Austria, the Netherlands, Italy, Mexico and Brazil.

In his pastoral letter, he condemned the child sex abuse scandal that had overwhelmed the Irish Catholic Church but, whilst there was plenty of 'hand wringing', he was criticised for failing to institute a programme of reforms. He failed to abate the increasing pressure demanding the resignation of bishops who were in any way implicated when in positions of authority during the paedophile priest cover-up.

The head of the German bishops' conference, Archbishop Robert Zollitsch of Freiburg, admitted that the Roman Catholic Church had

deliberately concealed cases of sexual abuse by priests.   While he
believed most abuses happened outside the church, he stated:
"Assaults that took place in such numbers within our institutions shame
and frighten me.   Every single case darkens the face of the entire
church."

Zollitsch apologised for a sexual abuse cover-up that occcurred in a
Black Forest community while he was responsible for human resources
at the Freiburg diocese 20 years earlier.   In Ireland, Father Brian D'Arcy,
an influential author and broadcaster, said he was disappointed that the
pope had failed to reference a major reform programme for the Catholic
Church in the pastoral letter. He said:
"Those reforms should include priestly celibacy, canon law and
unquestioning authority.   All those questions need to be asked in the
reform of the institution. His letter is only one step on the way."

D'Arcy also criticised the pontiff for professing a link between a decline
in churchgoing and sexual abuse. He added:
"He seems to be linking a decline in faith to this abuse and that is wholly
incorrect."

In his article in the Observer on the 21st March 2010, Fintan O'Toole
commented that the cover-up of child sex abuse by the Catholic Church
was not about sex and not about Catholicism.   Also, it was not about
priestly celibacy.   On this point, he agreed with Pope Benedict's
'distressingly bland pastoral letter'. O'Toole felt that it was about power
as he wrote:

"The urge to prey on children is not confined to the supposedly celibate clergy and exists in all walks of life. We know that it can become systemic in state and voluntary, as well as in religious, institutions. We know that all kinds of organisations – from banks to political movements – can generate a culture of perverted loyalty in which otherwise decent people will collude in crimes 'for the greater good'."

The Catholic Church, he asserted, was not unique in these respects. He went on to state:

"What makes it different – and what gives this crisis its depth – is the church's power. It had the authority, indeed the majesty, to compel victims and their families to collude in their own abuse and to keep hideous crimes secret for decades. It is that system of authority that is at the heart of the corruption. And that is why Benedict's pastoral letter, for all its expressions of 'shame and remorse', is unable to deal with the central issue. The only adequate response to the crisis is a fundamental questioning of the closed, hierarchical power system of which the pope himself is the apex and the embodiment. It was never remotely likely that Benedict would be able to understand those questions, let alone answer them. It is this contradiction that explains why the church has been trying, and failing, to put the abuse crisis behind it for well over a decade now."

Fintan O'Toole commented that it was symbolically apt that the grotesque figure of the dead paedophile, Father Brendan Smyth, had returned to threaten the position of the head of the Irish Church, Cardinal Sean Brady. Smyth had almost destroyed the reputation of Brady's predecessor, Cahal Daly. It could be considered a kind of poetic justice that Smyth's horrific career and the church's failure to curtail his activities had re-emerged to haunt another cardinal. O'Toole wrote:

"For the shock that Smyth's exposure delivered to Irish Catholicism has not yet been absorbed by the hierarchy. Both in Ireland and worldwide, the institution's all-male leadership refuses to face the fact that its own existence is at the heart of the problem. A closed system of authority in which democracy is a dirty word, secrecy is a virtue and unaccountable individuals combine spiritual prestige and temporal power is a breeding ground for abuse and cover-up. The universal nature of the church's response to abuse, from Belfast to Brazil and Australia to Austria, tells us the institution itself is the problem. Much of the criticism has focused, understandably, on the actions of individuals such as Brady when he investigated Smyth in 1975 or Benedict (Joseph Ratzinger as he then was) who sent an abuser in his Munich archdiocese for 'therapy' in 1980. But the system for dealing with these crimes was the same everywhere: swear the victims to secrecy; send the abuser to be 'cleansed' in a clinic; shift him to another parish (or in extreme cases like Smyth's to another country); and, above all, do not tell the police."

O'Toole mentioned the Murphy Report, so named because it was Judge Yvonne Murphy, a circuit court judge, who headed an inquiry carried out by the Irish government into the sexual abuse scandal of the Catholic archdiocese of Dublin. The report was released on the 26th November 2009, a few months after the Ryan Report. It concluded that:

"The Dublin Archdiocese's preoccupations in dealing with cases of child sexual abuse, at least until the mid 1990's, were the maintenance of secrecy, the avoidance of scandal, the protection of the reputation of the Church, and the preservation of its assets. All other considerations, including the welfare of children and justice for victims, were subordinated to these priorities. The Archdiocese did not implement its own canon law rules and did its best to avoid any application of the law of the State."

The 720-page report stated that there was no doubt that clerical child sexual abuse was concealed from January 1975 to May 2004. As documented by the Murphy commission, the complaints of parents and their children were ignored and, furthermore, other families were placed in immediate danger as prelates suppressed scandals, taking refuge in canon law to shield offenders at the expense of children. It was claimed by complainants that most uninvolved priests turned a blind eye to their allegations. It was even unearthed that some acts of abuse had actually taken place inside St Mary's Pro-Cathedral, the episcopal seat of the Archbishop of Dublin since 1825. The report also concluded that, as a consequence of the fixation with secrecy and the avoidance of scandal, successive senior clergymen failed to report complaints to the Garda (the Irish police force) prior to 1996. The archbishops, bishops and other officials could not claim they were unaware that paedophilia is a crime and that they have the same obligations as everyone else to uphold the law and report serious crimes to the authorities. Subsequently, a number of bishops resigned.

The findings of the Ryan Report were appallingly similar concluding that sexual abuse was endemic in boys' institutions. The schools investigated revealed a substantial level of abuse of boys in care extending in severity from improper fondling to rape with violence. Perpetrators of the abuse were able to carry on undetected for long periods. However, when confronted with evidence of sexual abuse, the inclination of the religious authorities was to transfer the offender to another location where, in many instances, he was free to abuse a different set of victims. The safety of the children did not appear to have been taken into consideration. The situation in girls' institutions was different. Although girls were subjected to predatory sexual abuse by male employees or visitors, this was regarded as opportunistic rather than systemic.

Describing the Murphy Report as 'devastating', O'Toole continued in his article to comment:

"Why did bishops, who were not monsters and who presumably believed themselves to be exemplars of goodness, choose to send child rapists out into parishes rather than bring the institution into disrepute? The brutally truthful answer is: because they could. There is no starker illustration of the corrupting influence of excessive power."

He noted that this power was all-encompassing, deluding the Catholic hierarchy and their priests into believing they belonged to a special caste which was not subject to the civil law. Indeed, one of Ireland's leading canon lawyers had insisted on a radio programme that priests do not have to report child abuse. He added:

"Priests are not auxiliary policemen ... they do not have an obligation to go down to the police."

He claimed that, on the contrary, when Brady learned of Smyth's crimes: "He was dealing with a particular in camera investigation within the church. It would be a violation of his obligations if he went to the police."

O'Toole continued by stating:

"That appalling arrogance was bolstered by an even more sinister knowledge. Bishops and priests knew that, because of their spiritual authority, they could manipulate the victims into feeling guilty. Kindly priests would offer those who disclosed abuse absolution of their sins, as if they were the ones who had stains on their souls. And parents who reported the violation of their children were often fearful lest they themselves be seen to be damaging the church they loved."

A previous Archbishop of Dublin, Dermot Ryan, wrote in internal case notes:

"The parents involved have, for the most part, reacted with what can only be described as incredible charity. In several cases, they were quite apologetic about having to discuss the matter and were as much concerned for the priest's welfare as for their child and other children."

"It is that capacity," Fintan O'Toole observed, "to place yourself above the law and to make those who have been wronged feel 'quite apologetic', that is peculiar to the church. These are the factors that explain, not just why the institution put its own interests above those of children but also, why it succeeded for so long. The church is not alone in believing that evil could be tolerated for a 'good cause'. But it was unique in the democratic world in its ability to get away with doing so in case after case and for decade after decade."

The Ryan and Murphy Reports covered only a short period in the history of the Catholic Church. To contemplate the number of children that must have been sexually abused by Catholic clerics over a period stretching back as far as the Middle Ages and beyond is as distressing as it is inestimable. No child should have to endure such suffering but to have to do so without any chance of refuge is abhorrent in the extreme.

Papal Wrongdoing

Beyond paedophilia, all manner of corruption in the Catholic Church has been prevalent for centuries. In 1810, Thomas Jefferson, as perceptive as ever, summed up the general malaise when he stated:

"A short time elapsed after the death of the great reformer of the Jewish religion, before his principles were departed from by those who professed to be his special servants, and perverted into an engine for enslaving mankind, and aggrandising their oppressors in Church and State; that the purest system of morals ever before preached to man, has been adulterated and sophisticated by artificial constructions, into a mere contrivance to filch wealth and power to themselves; that rational men not being able to swallow their impious heresies, in order to force them down their throats, they raise the hue and cry of infidelity, while themselves are the greatest obstacles to the advancement of the real doctrines of Jesus, and do in fact constitute the real Anti-Christ."

The church had lost its true sense of purpose and, with the primary objective of its continued preservation, had become an industry. Near the end of the Middle Ages, corruption in the Catholic Church was a serious issue. Some priests and nuns, despite taking vows of chastity, engaged in sexual relationships. Even popes fathered and raised illegitimate children. Pope Innocent VIII (1432 – 1492) was pope from 1484 until his death and is alleged to have had 16 children. He was succeeded by Pope Alexander VI (1431 – 1503) who had many mistresses and several children, some of whom he openly acknowledged as his own. His surname, Borgia, became a byword for the depravity of the papacy of that era. On the 30th October 1501, a banquet was organised in the papal palace by Don Cesare Borgia, the son of Alexander VI, which became known as the Banquet of Chestnuts. Fifty prostitutes attended for the entertainment of the guests and, after a sumptuous feast, chestnuts were strewn onto the floor around candle lit lamp stands. The clothes of the prostitutes were auctioned after which everyone crawled naked to pick up the chestnuts. Following this spectacle, members of the clergy and guests engaged with the prostitutes in an orgy of sexual activity.

It seems murder might also have been on a papal agenda as a number of historians believe that Pope Boniface VIII is implicated in the assassination of his predecessor, Pope Celestine V. When he was 17 years old, Pietro Angelerio became a Benedictine monk and began a life of solitude. In 1240, aged 25, he occupied a cave on Mount Morrone from which he derived his surname and, five years later, he moved to Mount Majella with two other companions. Whilst there, he fasted for six days a week, prayed for long periods and suffered extreme discomfort by wearing hair shirts and iron chains. He founded the Order of the Celestines and became famous throughout most of Italy. People came from far and wide to hear him speak and he maintained this way of life for the next 50 years. After the death of Pope Nicholas IV in 1292, there was no clear successor causing a dilemma unsolved for two years. It was then that Pietro del Morrone felt compelled to warn the cardinals that unless the issue was soon resolved, they would all suffer God's punishment. Pietro had inadvertently turned the spotlight on himself and the cardinals, suitably impressed, unanimously decided that he should be the next pope, a proposition which he fervently declined. He changed his mind to become Pope Celestine V only after lengthy negotiations with a deputation of cardinals accompanied by the kings of Naples and Hungary.

It soon became apparent to the 80-year old Celestine that he was no match for the corrupt individuals that beset him and, after demonstrating little competence during his five months in office, he abdicated on the 13th December 1294. In explanation, he cited the causes as:

"The desire for humility, for a purer life, for a stainless conscience, the deficiencies of his own physical strength, his ignorance, the perverseness of the people, his longing for the tranquility of his former life."

Cardinal Benedetto Caetano was proclaimed Pope Boniface VIII and he did not hesitate to begin enriching himself and his family. Furthermore, Celestine's return to solitude didn't last long before Boniface, regarding him as a potential threat, captured and imprisoned him. Celestine died in prison several months later on the 19th May 1296. Many scholars believe that Boniface had ordered his murder as a nail-sized hole was discovered in his skull.

Many abbots and bishops exploited their positions to lead lives of luxury and leisure, more akin to princes than humble servants of God. The cardinals of Rome lived in magnificent palaces and wore exquisite, jewel-encrusted robes. To pay for these lavish lifestyles the church hierarchy formulated several methods, both imaginative and corrupt. For example, the populace was advised to undertake pilgrimages to sites of holy relics and shrines to gain absolution for their sins. In general, they paid for the privilege. The artifice became, as Jefferson put it, 'a mere contrivance to filch wealth' from gullible people conditioned to believe in the integrity of the clergy.   Simony, the selling of ecclesiastical preferment, became widespread as positions in the church were sold to the highest bidder.   Also included was the selling of spiritual benefits such as supposed, though largely bogus, holy relics.   However, the most profitable and controversial of all the corrupt practices was the selling of indulgences.   These replaced the severe and considerably more painful penances of the early church such as the wearing of hair shirts or walking on hot embers.   At first, an indulgence was simply a certificate underwritten by the church for the full or partial remission of temporal punishment due for sins already forgiven, the sinner having confessed to a priest and received absolution.   Later, however, the faithful asked that indulgences be given for saying their prayers, carrying out acts of devotion, attending church services and going on pilgrimages. Confraternities requested indulgences for presenting performances and processions before going further and expecting them as reward for holding meetings.   It did not take long before greedy commissioners saw an opportunity too good to turn down as they sought to maximise the price of each indulgence.   Professional pardoners (*quaestores* in Latin) promised salvation from eternal damnation as they vigorously sold indulgences to collect monies for specific projects.   With the permission of the church, indulgences even became a way for Catholic rulers to raise funds for their own purposes.   Before long, the certificates were being forged as the scope of their forgiveness was ingeniously and continually enhanced.   In 1392, even the papacy became alarmed and Pope Boniface IX wrote to the Bishop of Ferrera condemning those religious orders who falsely claimed they had his authorisation to forgive all manner of sins. Boniface accused the clerics of exacting money from the simple-minded by promising them perpetual happiness in this world and eternal glory in the next. Authentic indulgences, though still a deception on a grand scale, required papal approval.

Dissension

One of the first to object to the corruption in the Catholic Church was John Wycliffe (1328 – 1384), an English philosopher, theologian, lay preacher, reformer and Oxford University doctor of divinity. His followers were known as Lollards, a somewhat rebellious movement that preached anti-Catholic and biblically-centric reforms. The Lollard movement preceded the Protestant Reformation by more than a century and, hence, Wycliffe has been called 'The Morning Star of the Reformation'. In the 14th century, the Bible was available only in Latin and Greek so its contents had to be interpreted by clerics for the benefit of the general population. The church preferred it this way, fearing that if the Bible became freely available in common languages, dissension might be aroused to threaten papal power. Wycliffe was an early advocate for translation and worked directly from the Latin Vulgate to produce Wycliffe's Bible in English. He commented:

"Englishmen learn Christ's law best in English. Moses heard God's law in his own tongue; so did Christ's apostles."

Referring to Wycliffe's Bible, the Catholic Church authorities stated:

"By this translation, the Scriptures have become vulgar, and they are more available to lay, and even to women who can read, than they were to learned scholars, who have a high intelligence. So the pearl of the gospel is scattered and trodden underfoot by swine."

It is probable that Wycliffe personally translated the Gospels of Matthew, Mark, Luke, and John and, possibly, the entire New Testament while his associates translated the Old Testament. Wycliffe's Bible is believed to have been completed by 1384 with updated versions being made available by John Purvey and his assistants in 1388 and 1395.

Wycliffe was allied to John of Gaunt, the head of government, who was vehemently opposed to ecclesiastical influence at court. At these times, the power of the papacy was immense with monarchs genuflecting and seeking papal approval. Popes have excommunicated kings and emperors and, on the occasions when two or three popes simultaneously held office, have excommunicated each other. From the 11th century, the papacy had assumed a position of leadership in western Europe which included presiding over the mobilisation of the crusades. Innocent III (in office from 1198 – 1216) was probably the most powerful pope of the Middle Ages and papal pretensions to superiority over secular rulers often led to political conflicts, particularly when the rulers were less than compliant. In 1302, Pope Boniface VIII propounded the theory of the 'two swords' which held that both temporal and spiritual leadership should be under the direct control of the papacy. He stated:

"We learn from the words of the Gospel that in this Church and in her power are two swords, the spiritual and the temporal."

Ambitious popes quoting the scriptures were a formidable force. Wycliffe attacked the abuses in the church and its vast wealth, maintaining that the Bible was the supreme authority, not the Catholic hierarchy. He commented:

"Let us see how such prelates are infected by the splendour of the world and by avarice … so they become rich men in the world's eye."

He was one of the earliest opponents of papal authority and its influence on secular power, fervently believing that the church's domain should be limited to religious matters. In his book, *De officio regis,* he states:

"One should be instructed with reference to the obligations in regard to the kingdom - to see how the two powers, royal and ecclesiastical, may support each other in harmony in the body corporate of the Church. The royal power is consecrated through the testimony of Holy Scripture and the Fathers. Christ and the apostles rendered tribute to the emperor. It is a sin to oppose the power of the king, which is derived immediately from God. Subjects, above all the clergy, should pay him dutiful tribute. The honours which attach to temporal power hark back to the king; those which belong to precedence in the priestly office, to the priest. The king must apply his power with wisdom, his laws are to be in unison with those of God. From God, laws derive their authority including those which royalty has over the clergy. If one of the clergy neglects his office, he is a traitor to the king who calls him to answer for it. It follows from this that the king has an 'evangelical' control. Those in the service of the Church must have regard for the laws of the State. In confirmation of this fundamental principle the archbishops in England make sworn submission to the king and receive their temporalities. The king is to protect his vassals against damage to their possessions; in case the clergy through their misuse of the temporalities cause injury, the king must offer protection. When the king turns over temporalities to the clergy, he places them under his jurisdiction, from which later pronouncements of the popes cannot release them. If the clergy relies on papal pronouncements, it must be subjected to obedience to the king."

It is clear Wycliffe believed that papal power in temporal matters should be restricted, if necessary reclaimed, and held under the auspices of the monarch. No doubt he felt that, under such a system, there would less chance of abuse and corruption. Convinced that the church had lost its way, Wycliffe was determined to usurp the existing structure and replace it with priests who lived in poverty, were bound by no vows, had received no formal consecration and preached the Gospel to the people. These itinerant preachers spread his teachings. They went in pairs, barefoot, wearing long dark-red robes and carrying a staff. The books and treatises of Wycliffe's last six years included continual attacks upon the papacy until, in the end, the pope and the antichrist seemed to him to be equivalent concepts. While he was saying Roman Catholic Mass in the parish church on the 28th December 1384, he suffered a stroke and died on the last day of the month. He was buried in Lutterworth. On the 4th May 1415, the Council of Constance declared Wycliffe a heretic and, by order of the Catholic Church, it was decreed that his books be burned and his vestiges exhumed. The exhumation did not take place until 1428 when, at the command of Pope Martin V, his skeleton was burned and the ashes cast into the River Swift. Wycliffe's followers, the Lollards, were subsequently outlawed and persecuted though they remained an irritant to English Catholic authorities until the English Reformation, a century later.

Jan Hus (1369 – 1415), was a Czech priest, philosopher, reformer, rector at Charles University in Prague and a great admirer of Wycliffe. Although many of Wycliffe's works were proscribed by the Catholic Church, Hus translated *Trialogus* into Czech and aided its distribution. He took an active role in the movement for church reform by criticising the morals of the clergy, episcopate and papacy from his pulpit. On the 20th December 1409, Pope Alexander V issued a papal bull which empowered the Archbishop of Prague to eradicate Wycliffism. All books authored by Wycliffe were to be ceded, his doctrines rescinded and free preaching discontinued. The books and manuscripts were subsequently burned and Hus and his followers were excommunicated. As a consequence, riots ensued in parts of Bohemia (now largely the Czech Republic) and as the government supported Hus, the power of his adherents (the Hussites) increased from day to day.

Hus spoke out against the sale of indulgences stating that man can only be granted forgiveness for sins by true repentance, not money. He objected to popes or bishops having the power to exhort others to go to war in the name of the church arguing that they should rather pray for their enemies and bless them. As the conflict with the established church continued, three men who openly described indulgences as fraudulent were beheaded to become the first Hussite martyrs. Propositions were made to restore peace as Hus argued that Bohemia should have the same religious freedom as other countries and that condemnation should be subject to the sanction of the state. The Council of Constance was convened on the 1st November 1414 with the primary objective of resolving the papal schism of 1378 (in which two men claimed to be the true pope). Hus was asked to attend by Sigismund, King of Hungary and heir to the Bohemian crown, in an attempt to end the religious dissension within the church. With Sigismund's promise of safe passage, Hus agreed to go. Initially, all was well, but after a few weeks he was imprisoned by his opponents. As the guarantor of Hus's safety, a greatly angered Sigismund tried to intercede but was placated by the church prelates. They convinced him that he could not be bound by promises to a heretic so, feeling absolved, he capitulated and took no further part in the matter. This was an example, so abhorrent to Wycliffe, of papal power being exercised over temporal authority. Initially, Hus was in constant communication with his friends but, afterwards, he was conveyed into the hands of the Archbishop of Constance who imprisoned him in his castle. There he remained for 73 days, poorly fed, chained day and night. His trial began on the 5th June 1415 and ended three days later. He refused to recant his views and conceded his continued veneration of Wycliffe, saying that he wished his soul might at some time occupy the same place as his mentor. Afraid to be seen offering support to a heretic, King Wenceslaus of Bohemia declined to give Hus any help and so, on the 6th July 1415, he was condemned to death. The executioners undressed him and tied his hands behind his back. They chained his neck to a stake around which wood and straw had been piled to shoulder height. At the last moment, he was again asked to recant his views and save his life but he declined with the words:

"God is my witness that the things charged against me I never preached. In the same truth of the Gospel which I have written, taught, and preached, drawing upon the sayings and positions of the holy doctors, I am ready to die today."

He was then burned and his ashes were thrown into the River Rhine. To some observers, Hus's efforts were predominantly designed to rid the church of its ethical abuses rather than a more ambitious campaign of sweeping theological change. To others, however, the seeds of the reformation are clear in Hus's and Wycliffe's writings. In explaining the plight of the average Christian in Bohemia, Hus wrote:

"One pays for confession, for mass, for the sacrament, for indulgences, for churching a woman, for a blessing, for burials, for funeral services and prayers. The very last penny which an old woman has hidden in her bundle for fear of thieves or robbery will not be saved. The villainous priest will grab it."

Between 1420 and 1431, Hussite forces defeated the armies of five consecutive papal crusades in a conflict known as the Hussite Wars. A century later, as many as 90 percent of the inhabitants of Czech lands were non-Catholic and followed the teachings of Hus and his successors. In 1999, nearly six centuries after the Hussite Wars, Pope John Paul II expressed his deep regret for the cruel death inflicted on Jan Hus.

Martin Luther (1483 – 1546) was a German priest, professor of theology and the iconic figure of the Protestant Reformation. Almost 150 years after the death of John Wycliffe, indulgences were still being vigorously sold by the Catholic Church and it was Luther's vehemently outspoken opposition to this fraudulent practice that sparked the flame of independence. In 1501, aged 17 years, Luther entered the University of Erfurt and one year later received his Bachelor's degree. This was followed by a Master's degree in 1505 and, in accordance with his father's wishes, he enrolled into the law school of his university. After a short time, he left the faculty of law in favour of theology and philosophy, expressing a particular interest in the works of Aristotle (384 BC – 322 BC), the great Greek philosopher and polymath. However, philosophy also proved unsatisfactory, teaching him to apply logic and reason but including no guidance about the love of God. He felt reason could not show the path to God and, thereafter, he developed an ambivalent relationship with Aristotle, railing against his emphasis on rationality. Whilst reason could be applied to life in general, he felt, it was irrelevant in matters relating to God. Mankind, Luther believed, could only learn about God by divine revelation and by studying the scriptures. As he eschewed reason and logic, his commitment to the absolute truth of the scriptures became fanatical and, consequently, he claimed:

"No good work happens as the result of one's own wisdom; but everything must happen in a stupor . . . Reason must be left behind for it is the enemy of faith."

He also said:

"Reason is the devil's handmaid and does nothing but blaspheme and dishonour all that God says or does" and "Reason is directly opposed to faith, and one ought to let it be; in believers it should be killed and buried."

To explain his mistrust of philosophy, he stated:

"One should learn philosophy only as one learns witchcraft, that is to destroy it; as one finds out about errors, in order to refute them."

On the 2nd July 1505, he was on horseback during a thunderstorm when a lightning bolt almost struck him. Terrified of death and divine judgment, he cried out:

"Help! Saint Anna, I will become a monk!"

Unable to break his vow, he left the university and entered an Augustinian friary in Erfurt on the 17th July 1505. Luther lived in austerity, dedicating himself to long periods of fasting and prayer. In 1507, he was ordained into the priesthood and in 1508 began teaching theology at the University of Wittenberg. He gained a Bachelor's degree in Biblical Studies in 1508 followed by another Bachelor's degree, a year later, in the *Sentences* by Peter Lombard (the main textbook of theology in the Middle Ages). On the 19th October 1512, he was awarded his doctorate of theology and, shortly afterwards, was received into the prestigious position of Doctor in Bible. He retained this post for the remainder of his career.

In 1516, Johann Tetzel, a Dominican friar and papal commissioner for indulgences was sent to Germany by the Roman Catholic Church on a money raising mission to aid the rebuilding of St Peter's Basilica in Rome. Roman Catholic theology stated that faith alone was insufficient to justify man; that more was required such as donating money to the church. On the 31st October 1517, Luther wrote to Albert, Archbishop of Mainz and Magdeburg in protest against the sale of indulgences. He enclosed with his letter a copy of the *Disputation of Martin Luther on the Power and Efficacy of Indulgences* which came to be known as *The Ninety-Five Theses* (see the Addendum). It is possible that, initially, he was not seeking a confrontation with the church but was simply raising a scholar's objection to disingenuous practices. Some of the theses were, however, overtly challenging, particularly Thesis 86 which asks:
"Since the pope's income today is larger than that of the wealthiest of wealthy men, why does he not build this one church of St. Peter with his own money, rather than with the money of indigent believers?"

It is a question that resonates even today. The Catholic Church has vast wealth but when does it ever contribute to save the victims of famine in the continent of Africa?   It could proactively ensure, by funding preventative measures, that famine is consigned to a rarity.   Instead, it safeguards its wealth and relies on the general public to generously respond to each catastrophe.   It is a lesson of history that some things never change.

Luther insisted that, since forgiveness could be granted only by God, the church's claim for the efficacy of indulgences was mistaken; a false assurance.   The enduring, iconic image of Luther nailing his theses to the church door at Wittenberg is, almost certainly, apocryphal but the offence he caused the church was real and was to reverberate around Europe.   In January 1518, some of Luther's friends translated the theses from Latin into German, had them printed by printing press and widely distributed.   Ironically, in the previous century, one of the first items to be printed on Gutenberg's invention had been certificates of indulgences. Within a couple of weeks, copies of the theses had spread throughout Germany and, within two months, they were available throughout the continent.   As Luther's fame grew, people thronged to Wittenberg to listen to his oratory.   A prolific writer, he published a commentary on *Galatians* and his *Work on the Psalms*.   These were followed by three of his most notable works, published in 1520, namely, *To the Christian Nobility of the German Nation, On the Babylonian Captivity of the Church* and *On the Freedom of a Christian*.

Archbishop Albert decided not to reply to Luther's letter and forwarded the theses to Rome after having had them scrutinised for heresy.   In debt to the papacy, he was himself in need of the revenue generated by the sale of indulgences and, as Luther later pointed out:

"The pope had a finger in the pie as well, because one half was to go to the building of St Peter's Church in Rome."

Pope Leo X was well-versed in dealing with reformers and heretics and over the next three years he deployed a number of theologians and envoys against Luther in an attempt to persuade him to retract his views. One of the theologians referred to Luther as the new Jan Hus. On the 15th June 1520, Pope Leo warned Luther via a papal edict that he would be excommunicated unless he recanted 41 specific sentences from his works within a 60-day period. Luther responded by publicly setting fire to the edict at Wittenberg on the 10th December 1520 and, to explain his actions, he penned *Why the Pope and his Recent Book are Burned* and *Assertions Concerning All Articles*. Consequently, he was excommunicated by Pope Leo X on the 3rd January 1521 in the papal bull, *Decet Romanum Pontificem*.

On the 18th April 1521, Luther appeared as ordered before the Diet of Worms, a commission dealing with matters of concern to the Holy Roman Empire. It took place in Worms, a town on the River Rhine, and was conducted from the 28th January to the 25th May 1521 under the auspices of Emperor Charles V. Prince Frederick III, Elector of Saxony, was the guarantor of Luther's safety, essential after the treacherous treatment of Jan Hus. The elector was to prove a staunch ally, a man of integrity, unlike the pusillanimous Sigismund.

Johann Eck, a German scholastic theologian, speaking on behalf of the Holy Roman Empire presented Luther with copies of his works, asking if he had written them and upheld their content. Luther confirmed his authorship but requested more time to think about the second part of the question. He thought profoundly, consulted his friends and prayed. He responded to the tribunal the following day, saying:

"Unless I am convinced by the testimony of the Scriptures or by clear reason (for I do not trust either in the pope or in councils alone, since it is well known that they have often erred and contradicted themselves), I am bound by the Scriptures I have quoted and my conscience is captive to the Word of God. I cannot and will not recant anything, since it is neither safe nor right to go against conscience. May God help me, Amen."

Over the next five days, a number of private meetings were held to establish Luther's fate. On the 25th May 1521, he was declared an outlaw when Emperor Charles V announced the commission's conclusions (the Edict of Worms) and stated:

"For this reason we forbid anyone from this time forward to dare, either by words or by deeds, to receive, defend, sustain, or favour the said Martin Luther. On the contrary, we want him to be apprehended and punished as a notorious heretic, as he deserves, to be brought personally before us, or to be securely guarded until those who have captured him inform us, whereupon we will order the appropriate manner of proceeding against the said Luther. Those who will help in his capture will be rewarded generously for their good work."

As a consequence of the edict, it was a criminal act for anyone in Germany to provide Luther with food or shelter and, moreover, his life was threatened as he could be killed with impunity. However, he had left Worms for home before the verdict and, on the 4th May 1521, he was intercepted by some of Frederick III's horsemen who escorted him to the security of Wartburg Castle at Eisenach. Perhaps Frederick had anticipated the potential danger to Luther's life had he remained unprotected.   During his stay at Wartburg, Luther worked on his translation of the New Testament from Greek into vernacular German and issued a plethora of doctrinal and polemical manuscripts. A renewed offensive on Archbishop Albert, for example, caused the cessation of the sale of indulgences in his episcopates.

Luther returned to Wittenberg on the 6th March 1522 to help quell the rioting that had broken out at the behest of a number of extremists. He worked alongside the authorities to restore public order reminding citizens of the primacy of core Christian values. He urged them to trust in God rather than violence in order to promote the necessary reforms and change. At this time, he was in conflict not only with the established church but also against radical reformers who provoked social unrest and hostility.

Luther was successful in Wittenberg but was unable to suppress radicalism further afield which led to the German Peasants' War (1524 – 25).   The war was Europe's largest and most widespread popular uprising prior to the French Revolution of 1789. It involved the hoi polloi, upper classes and aristocrats and embodied rhetoric from the fledging religious reform movement (Protestantism) through which the peasants aspired to legitimacy. They thought Luther might offer them his support but, though he had sympathy with some of the peasants' grievances, he urged them to obey the temporal authorities. He became incandescent with rage at the widespread destruction, the burning of convents, monasteries, palaces and libraries. His language could be inflammatory and uncompromising.   In his *Against the Murderous, Thieving Hordes of Peasants,* he explained the gospel's attitude to wealth, censured the violence as the work of the devil and called for the nobles to exterminate the rebels like mad dogs. He wrote:

"Therefore let everyone who can, smite, slay, and stab, secretly or openly, remembering that nothing can be more poisonous, hurtful, or devilish than a rebel ... For baptism does not make men free in body and property, but in soul; and the gospel does not make goods common, except in the case of those who, of their own free will, do what the apostles and disciples did in Acts 4:32–37. They did not demand, as do our insane peasants in their raging, that the goods of others—of Pilate and Herod—should be common, but only their own goods. Our peasants, however, want to make the goods of other men common, and keep their own for themselves. Fine Christians they are! I think there is not a devil left in hell; they have all gone into the peasants. Their raving has gone beyond all measure."

Luther felt justified in his opposition to the rebels for three reasons. Firstly, by behaving violently instead of submitting to the secular government, they were shunning Christ's counsel to, 'render unto Caesar the things that are Caesar's'. Saint Paul had stated in his Epistle to the Romans 13:1–7 that all authorities are God's appointees and, as such, should not be defied. Secondly, the violence of rebellion, robbery and plunder placed the peasants 'outside the law of God and Empire' so they deserved 'death in body and soul, if only as highwaymen and murderers'. Lastly, he claimed the rebels were guilty of blasphemy for calling themselves *Christian brethren* and perpetrating their sinful acts under the banner of the gospel. Without Luther's support, many rebels disarmed voluntarily. Others, feeling betrayed, continued the fight before finally succumbing at the Battle of Frankenhausen on the 15th May 1525. It is clear that Luther disagreed with change being achieved by violent means. He was an early advocate of the metonymic adage coined over three centuries later by the author, Edward Bulwer-Lytton, 'The pen is mightier than the sword'.

On the 13th June 1525, Luther married Katharina von Bora, a former nun and 15 years his junior. Though some priests and former monks had already married, it was Luther's wedding which, despite Melanchthon's disapproval, set the seal of respectability on clerical marriage. Protestant priests have been allowed to marry ever since. The pair embarked on a happy and successful marriage, Katharina bearing six children. Though frequently quite poor, Luther once confided to a friend:

"My Katie is in all things so obliging and pleasing to me that I would not exchange my poverty for the riches of Croesus."

He became increasingly involved in reorganising church services and was a prolific hymn writer. His hymns influenced the development of singing in churches and provided the inspiration for composers such as Johann Sebastian Bach to write music. Luther published his German translation of the New Testament in 1522 and he and his associates completed the translation of the Old Testament in 1534, enabling the full Bible to be printed. His translation into the language of the people made the Bible more accessible, comprehensively influencing the church, German culture and a standard version of the German language. He continued to work on refinements of his translations until the end of his life.

From the 1530's, printed images of Luther that depicted his monumental size were critical to the acceptance of Protestantism. In contrast to the images of delicate Catholic saints, Luther was corpulent and double-chinned with a fleshy face and piercing deep-set eyes. He was of imposing stature, the equal of the German princes who became his allies in the proliferation of Lutheranism. It was evident that he did not shy away from earthly pleasures whether it be drinking beer or having conjugal relations with his wife, behaviour that was the antithesis of the ascetic values of the Catholic Church.

Luther expressed his opinions about Jews throughout his career, though relatively few of his works commented on them directly. Even though he rarely encountered Jews during his life, his attitudes were conditioned by a theological and cultural tradition which regarded Jews as a rejected people, guilty of the murder of Christ. He lived within a community that had orchestrated the expulsion of Jews some 90 years earlier and he considered them blasphemers and liars because they had repudiated the divinity of Jesus. With conflicting sympathy, however, he wrote in 1516:

"Many people are proud with marvellous stupidity when they call the Jews dogs, evil-doers, or whatever they like, while they too, and equally, do not realise who or what they are in the sight of God."

In 1523, Luther advised kindness toward the Jews in his work *That Jesus Christ was Born a Jew*, though it was suspected that his motivation was to convert them to Christianity. When he realised that his efforts had failed, his antipathy towards them grew increasingly bitter. His other major works were his 60,000-word treatise, *On the Jews and Their Lies* and *On the Holy Name and the Lineage of Christ*, both published in 1543 only three years before his death. He posited that the Jews were not the chosen people but 'the devil's people' and he referred to them with vile and violent language, unbecoming of a priest. Luther advocated the burning down of synagogues, trashing Jewish prayer-books, prohibiting rabbis from preaching, seizing Jewish property and money, and demolishing their homes. He described them as 'poisonous, envenomed worms' that should be forced into labour or expelled for all time. In what amounted to an incitement to murder, he stated:

"We are at fault in not slaying them."

Luther railed against the Jews in Saxony, Brandenburg, and Silesia. Josel of Rosenheim, a Jewish spokesman who tried to protect the Jews of Saxony in 1537, later blamed their troubles on Luther and explained:

"That priest whose name was Martin Luther - may his body and soul be bound up in hell! - who wrote and issued many heretical books in which he said that whoever would help the Jews was doomed to perdition."

Josel asked the city of Strasbourg to prohibit the sale of Luther's anti-Semitic works. His request was initially rejected, then agreed when a Lutheran pastor in Hochfelden used a sermon to urge his parishioners to murder Jews. Luther's influence continued long after his death and, throughout the 1580's, riots led to Jews being expelled from several German states. He was the most widely read author of his time and acquired the status of a prophet within his country. In the view of many historians, his inflammatory rhetoric was a significant factor in the development of anti-Semitism in Germany and the horrifying events of the 1930s and 1940s.

Luther suffered ill health for a number of years in the latter part of his life and, on the 15th February 1546, presented his last sermon at Eisleben, his birthplace. It was dedicated, almost entirely, to the Jews whom he fervently believed should be expelled from Germany. In his rant against them, he orated:

"We want to practise Christian love toward them and pray that they convert ... they are our public enemies and if they could kill us all, they would gladly do so; and so often they do."

Three days later, an apoplectic stroke divested him of his speech and he died shortly afterwards, aged 62 years. Luther was buried beneath the pulpit in the Castle Church in Wittenberg, his long-standing friends Johannes Bugenhagen and Philipp Melanchthon officiating at the funeral. A year later, the troops of his former adversary, the Holy Roman Emperor Charles V, entered the town but, on the emperor's express and magnanimous order, his grave was not defiled.

Luther was a complex man, entirely focused and single-minded. When commenting on political issues (such as the Peasants' Revolt), he would advocate non-violence, peaceful protest and negotiation. Only if peaceful means were rejected would he exhort the secular powers to ruthlessly repress anarchy. When it came to matters of religion, however, there was no room for compromise, particularly in his attitude towards the Jews. As a young man he had eschewed philosophy and reason believing that complete truth was to be found only in the scriptures. To these, and God, he submitted in total and unconditional obeisance, never contemplating that much of the content on which he relied might be errant, replete with fabrication, myth and fable. He knew that Jesus was Jewish, yet he vehemently asserted that the Jews should be persecuted, even murdered. Totally in thrall to the scriptures, emotionally consumed and captivated by them, he was incapable of recognising any incongruity or irony in his exhortations. Here was a learned, intelligent, holy man who lost the ability to reason. He condemned all Jews as Christ-killers but was unable to see that the subjects of his rants were completely innocent of Christ's death. Having shunned reason at an early age, in later life his mind was inhabited by bigotry and hatred as he increasingly resembled the caricature of a mad priest.

Luther was, clearly, a controversial and uncompromising figure and one of the most influential men in history. For all his imperfections, it may be that it was his unwavering single-mindedness that underpinned his success and that, had he been more inclined to flexibility, he may not have so doggedly pursued reform in the face of an exceedingly powerful adversary, the Catholic Church. It is also worth noting that, unlike John Wycliffe and Jan Hus, he had powerful friends in the form of a number of German princes who ensured his protection throughout his theological struggle.

Thomas Aquinas, a paragon of Catholicism, was not just a holy man but a saint. He belonged to the Dominican Order whose foundation was dedicated to the conversion of the Albigenses (inhabitants of the town of Albi, near Toulouse, France) and other heretical factions, initially by peaceful means but later by the use of force. The Albigenses believed in the duality of good and evil and, curiously, regarded Jesus as a rebel against God. In the *Summa Theologica*, Aquinas wrote:

"With regard to heretics two points must be observed: one, on their own side; the other, on the side of the Church. On their own side there is the sin, whereby they deserve not only to be separated from the Church by excommunication, but also to be severed from the world by death. For it is a much graver matter to corrupt the faith which quickens the soul, than to forge money, which supports temporal life. Wherefore if forgers of money and other evil-doers are forthwith condemned to death by the secular authority, much more reason is there for heretics, as soon as they are convicted of heresy, to be not only excommunicated but even put to death. On the part of the Church, however, there is mercy which looks to the conversion of the wanderer, wherefore she condemns not at once, but 'after the first and second admonition', as the Apostle (Paul) directs: after that, if he is yet stubborn, the Church no longer hoping for his conversion, looks to the salvation of others, by excommunicating him and separating him from the Church, and furthermore delivers him to the secular tribunal to be exterminated thereby from the world by death."

Under the direction of the church, heresy was considered a capital offence by the secular law of most European countries in the 13th century. Aquinas preferred that heretics be dealt with by a secular tribunal rather than by a magisterial authority. He specifically stated that heretics deserved to be killed, consistent with his theology according to which those who sinned had no intrinsic right to life. He believed that heretics should be executed by the state and elaborated thus:

"In God's tribunal, those who return are always received, because God is a searcher of hearts, and knows those who return in sincerity. But the Church cannot imitate God in this, for she presumes that those who relapse after being once received, are not sincere in their return; hence she does not debar them from the way of salvation, but neither does she protect them from the sentence of death."

Here was a future saint advocating death when, one would have presumed, his aim should have been to affirm the sanctity of life. Did it never occur to him what Jesus would have thought? He was totally convinced that anyone who ventured an opinion which was at variance with church doctrine should be killed; excommunication lacked the severity to be commensurate with the sin. A true holy man might have been expected to say:

"I regret that I'm going to have to excommunicate you but I will pray for you and hope that you will see the error of your ways."

No doubt, he was concerned that a more lenient approach would have caused others to become infected with the same malady and threaten the stranglehold of the church. This anathema could not be tolerated; better to kill than take the risk. Even the intelligent mind can lose sight of human decency when it becomes deformed by religious dogma. There can be little more dangerous than a holy man who, because of a difference of opinion, states:

"Poor unbeliever, I'm going to save you from yourself and have you put to death."

Is it not a preposterous notion to believe that morality depends on religion when churchmen like Thomas Aquinas abandon their duty of care to their fellow man in favour of their interpretation of the scriptures?

Aberrant though they were, Luther and Aquinas were as choirboys when compared to John Calvin (1509 – 1564), the influential French theologian and pastor during the Protestant Reformation. To many, he was a deranged tyrant, persecutor and murderer. Originally trained as a lawyer, he was intelligent and talented but, in common with many religious maniacs, he was totally self-absorbed, self-righteous and convinced he was involved in God's work. His sacerdotal claims brought him to the leadership of a malevolent theocracy in Geneva,

Switzerland, and over a five-year period from 1542 he sanctioned 57 executions and 76 expulsions from a city of only 16,000 inhabitants. Calvin's draconian regulations referred not simply to theological matters but also to features of daily life such as dancing, singing, clothing, hair styles and confectionery.   Punishments frequently resulted in the confiscation of property and banishment from the city. Adultery under Calvin's stewardship, once a custodial offence, was punishable by death. One woman was drowned in the River Rhone after having been brutally tortured whilst her partner was decapitated. The harshest punishments, however, were reserved for those that challenged Calvin's writings or his doctrine.   Jacques Gruet was tortured and executed for expressing atheistic views and admonishing Calvin as a hypocrite. A book printer who repudiated Calvin's theory of predestination (all events have been willed by God) had his tongue perforated with a red hot iron and was subsequently expelled. French historian, Audin, described Calvin's reign in Geneva as follows:

"There is but one word heard or read: Death. Death to every one guilty of high treason against God; death to every one guilty of high treason against the State; death to the son that strikes or curses his father; death to the adulterer; death to heretics. During the space of twenty years, commencing from the date of Calvin's recall, the history of Geneva is a bloody drama, in which pity, dread, terror, indignation, and tears, by turns, appear to seize upon the soul. At each step we encounter chains, thongs, a stake, pincers, melted pitch, fire, and sulphur. And throughout the whole there is blood. One imagines himself in Dante's Hell, where sighs, groans, and lamentations continually resound."

Michael Servetus (1511 – 1553) had the misfortune to incur Calvin's wrath and ultimately paid with his life. He was a Spanish theologian, physician and cartographer and was the first European to accurately describe the function of pulmonary circulation. During correspondence, he disputed Calvin by advocating a non-trinitarian Christology and rejecting the predestination concept that souls are condemned to Hell regardless of desert. Servetus fervently believed that there was no foundation in the scriptures for the trinity of God the Father, Son and Holy Spirit and this sparked censure and recrimination from both Catholics and Protestants. As their letters continued, Calvin wrote to Servetus:

"I neither hate you nor despise you; nor do I wish to persecute you; but I would be as hard as iron when I behold you insulting sound doctrine with so great audacity."

In time, their correspondence became more heated until Calvin, highly frustrated, confided in a friend by saying:

"Servetus has just sent me a long volume of his ravings. If I consent he will come here, but I will not give my word; for if he comes here, if my authority is worth anything, I will never permit him to depart alive."

Servetus had underestimated Calvin's megalomania and continued to write even after his correspondent's letters had ceased. On the 4th April 1553, Servetus was arrested by the Catholic establishment and imprisoned in Vienne, France. He escaped three days later but, with Calvin's co-operation, the French Inquisition convicted Servetus of heresy. Later, in an attempt to flee to Italy, Servetus inexplicably rested in Geneva where he was recognised and imprisoned. Calvin refused

Servetus even the most basic human needs. He was chained in a dark, flea-ridden room and was left to sleep amongst his own excrement without any change of clothing. Treated more badly than a common felon, he petitioned the city councillors for improved conditions, writing: "Fleas are devouring me; my shoes are torn to pieces; I have nothing clean to wear. I beg of you, for the love of Christ, not to refuse me what you would give to a Turk or a criminal. Nothing has been done for to fulfill your orders that I should be kept clean. I am in more pitiful condition than ever. It is abominably cruel I should be given no chance of attending to my bodily needs."

At his trial, Servetus was condemned on the counts of preaching non-trinitarianism and for his views against infant baptism. On the 27th October 1553, he was burned alive at the stake just outside Geneva. His last words were:
"Jesus, Son of the Eternal God, have mercy on me."

With as much 'compassion' as he could muster, Calvin had requested that the sentence be commuted. He recommended decapitation, the familiar sentence for a traitor, instead of a heretic's burning but his plea was dismissed. As Servetus was not a citizen of Geneva, he could not be legitimately executed and historical evidence supports the fact that Calvin was guilty of premeditated murder. Proof, if proof were needed, that religious dogma has the power to corrupt even a most intelligent mind.

Sebastian Castellio (1515 – 1563), was a French preacher and theologian and one of the first Reformed Christian advocates of religious tolerance and freedom of conscience and thought. He was a man of outstanding intellect and integrity and, in 1543, after the plague struck Geneva, he was the only cleric in the city to visit the sick and administer the last rites. The clerics of the Geneva Consistory and Calvin himself refused to do likewise. To be absolved from his duty, Calvin directed his servants to declare him 'indispensable' and, later, writing in his own defence, he stated:

"It would not do to weaken the whole Church in order to help a part of it."

Initially a friend and pupil of Calvin, Castellio's relationship with his master deteriorated and he had to endure a lifetime of persecution at Calvin's behest. Along with a number of other scholars, Castellio was outraged by the execution of Servetus which he viewed as a blatant murder and, speaking of Calvin, he referred to his 'hands dripping with the blood of Servetus'. He wrote:

"To kill a man is not to protect a doctrine, but it is to kill a man."

Admonishing Calvin further, he stated:

"When Servetus fought with reasons and writings, he should have been repulsed by reasons and writings."

He cited the words of Church Fathers such as Augustine and Chrysostom, advancing freedom of thought, and even turned Calvin's own words against him from a time when he (Calvin) was being persecuted by the Catholic Church. Calvin had written:

"It is unchristian to use arms against those who have been expelled from the Church, and to deny them rights common to all mankind."

Castellio eloquently debated the question, 'What is a heretic?' He contended that to view one man's interpretation of Christian scripture as inerrant was fallacious and pointed out that a heretic is anyone who disagrees with another regarding the meaning of scripture. It was, therefore, a relative term and a relative charge. He stated:

"When I reflect on what a heretic really is, I can find no other criterion than that we are all heretics in the eyes of those who do not share our views."

One can scarcely imagine the lives that would have been saved had those in power been able to dilute their bigotry with doses of Castellio vision and intellect. Castellio is also to be credited with advanced thinking about the concept of limited government. He repeatedly argued for a separation of state and church and was fervidly opposed to theocracy. Positing that no one has the right to direct and control another person's thoughts, he asserted that authorities should have 'no concern with matters of opinion' and concluded:

"We can live together peacefully only when we control our intolerance. Even though there will always be differences of opinion from time to time, we can at any rate come to general understandings, can love one another, and can enter the bonds of peace, pending the day when we shall attain unity of faith."

How brilliant, not only of his time, but of any time. Sebastian Castellio was an outstanding human being with a maturity of thought well in advance of the age; he and John Lennon would have made amiable companions.

Thomas Jefferson and his presidential predecessor, John Adams, both men of great learning and scholarship, detested Calvinism. Three years before his death, Jefferson wrote to Adams:

"His religion was a demonism. If ever a man worshipped a false God, he did. The being described in his five points is … a demon of malignant spirit. It would be more pardonable to believe in no God at all, than to blaspheme him by the atrocious attributes of Calvin."

He never ceased to denounce the 'blasphemous absurdity of the five points of Calvin' and one observer noted:

"It is hard to say which surpassed the other in boiling hatred of Calvinism, Jefferson or Adams."

The five points to which Jefferson referred are:

1. Total depravity. This doctrine asserts that as a consequence of man's fall into sin, every person is enslaved to the service of sin. People are not naturally inclined to love God with all their strength but are inclined to serve their own interests ahead of their neighbour's interests, rejecting God's rules.

2. Unconditional election. This asserts that God has chosen those whom he will bring to himself though not based on foreseen virtue, merit, or faith; rather, it depends on God's mercy alone. God has decided to extend mercy to those chosen and to withhold mercy from those not chosen. Those chosen receive salvation through Christ whilst those not chosen receive the just wrath for their sins against God.

3. Limited atonement. This doctrine asserts that the substitutional atonement of Jesus was definite in its purpose and in what it accomplished. It is implied that only the sins of the elect were atoned for by Jesus' death. Calvinists believe that the atonement is not limited in its value or power but it is limited in the sense that it is designed for some and not all.

4. Irresistible grace. This asserts that the saving grace of God is applied to those whom he has determined to save. The doctrine holds that the influence of God's Holy Spirit cannot be resisted and that the Holy Spirit 'graciously causes the elect sinner to co-operate, to believe, to repent, to come freely and willingly to Christ'.

5. Perseverance of the saints. This refers to the preservation of those that are set apart by God (called saints), and not particularly, those who are very holy, canonised or in Heaven. The doctrine asserts that since God is sovereign and his will cannot be frustrated by humans or anything else, those whom God has called into communion with himself will continue in faith until the end.

How could Calvin have derived such depressing theological concepts, obsessed as they are with sin, absolution, salvation and eternal damnation? Aside from an interpretation of some spurious scriptural text, where is his evidence? Lest we forget, of course, faith doesn't require evidence. Any attempt to replicate his thought processes would be psychologically bewildering but then, how can you make sense of mumbo-jumbo and outlandish piffle? Had there been any justice, Calvinism would have withered and been displaced by *Castellionism*.

Instead, the brilliant, benign Castellio has been consigned to a mere footnote in history whilst the name of Calvin lives on in infamy and the numerous religious sects he spawned. It is estimated that, today, around one-third of the world's Protestants are Calvinists. How can this be? Well, in the 16th century, the laity's ignorance and fear of malignant despots (and their God) would always hold sway over the benevolence, reason and common sense of men like Castellio. The 18th century statesman, Edmund Burke, once said:

"The only thing necessary for evil to flourish is for good men to do nothing."

But confrontation was barely an option. To dispute the doctrines of a Calvin could spell death; to disagree with a Castellio would simply invite debate. God must have been looking the other way again or taking some more time off.

Chapter 7

By Chance

A Garden Party

The master of ceremonies requested quiet at a garden party held in the beautiful surroundings of a Worcestershire country house. The party was being held in aid of a number of charities and the local vicar wished to address the attendees. He started by asking everyone to close their eyes and, after 10 seconds or so, he declared it was time to open them again and look around. He said:

"Aren't we lucky that God has given us the opportunity to live amongst all this beauty?"

He was quite right; it *was* just a matter of luck. The people present might easily have been born into famine-ridden Ethiopia. What would he have said, though, had he been standing in the aftermath of a severe earthquake? It would, surely, not have been:

"We thank God for all this devastation."

In common with many of the people present, the vicar's inclination was to thank God for all the beauty in the world but, no doubt, to absolve him from any blame when confronted with its ugliness. It's easy to thank God for hummingbirds and butterflies but not so easy to thank God for mosquitoes, especially when one of them has just caused a child to die from malaria. Clearly, if God is responsible for all that happens in the universe, he must be responsible for all situations and events whether good or bad. Most people don't see it that way, however, perhaps because to do so might invite some form of divine retribution. Then again, even Sir Cliff Richard has been known to blame God.

In 1999, Jill Dando, a friend of Sir Cliff's, was the most popular female presenter on BBC television. A lovely young woman, seemingly in every respect, she had already been awarded the BBC Personality of the Year award. In the prime of her life, she was engaged to be married and, as the saying goes, 'the world was her oyster'. On the 26th April, she was inexplicably murdered by a single gunshot to the head outside her home in Fulham, West London. There seemed to be no motive and, with the nation in shock, Sir Cliff said that he was angry with God. For a time, at least, he felt that God was responsible for permitting her murder but, no doubt eventually, he was consoled by the usual platitudes:
'God needed her more than we did' or, 'She's gone to a better place' or the reliable catch-all, 'God moves in mysterious ways'.

Well, with all God's power he surely didn't need any help from Jill and, therefore, one would have thought he could have waited a little longer before taking her from this world to the next. Or, perhaps God had nothing to do with it and the cruellest of blows was delivered purely by chance, a most rare component of ill fortune.

If God had nothing to do with the murder of Jill Dando and since we are never, because of interactions with our environment, in full control, our lives must be subject to randomness or pure chance. In other words, life is very much about good luck and bad luck. We do have an element of control in that we can, for example, reduce the chances of injury by being careful but whether or not we die in a road accident or a plane crash is simply a matter of chance. Some people die in plane crashes and some, thankfully most, don't. Consider the case of three comrades who spent most of their time during World War I in battle trenches. They survived the cold, damp, trench foot and the rats but towards the end of the war were ordered 'over the top' with the rest of their unit. Pressing forwards towards their target, they could sense the enemy bullets whistling by them when one of the three was hit and died instantly. The other two, undeterred, continued to advance when one of them was hit below the collar bone putting him out of action. The remaining soldier was part of a successful raid with the rest of his unit and the two friends were later re-united. The wounded soldier took no further part in the war whilst his friend returned home unhurt when the hostilities were over. The wounded man lived to the ripe old age of 103 but his good friend died as the victim of a stroke when he was only 37 years old. Their fallen comrade was barely 19 years of age. How can one begin to explain all of this? If God were involved, it would be as if he were playing some gigantic chess game, moving people around and deciding their fate on the basis of his rule book or, simply, on a whim. As this seems unlikely and not particularly merciful, there are two possibilities; either God relaxed after having set randomness in motion, or pure chance was at play all along without the need for God.

A recent television documentary introduced survivors of the Holocaust of World War II. One of the people interviewed was a grandfather of seven who had spent time in the Belsen death camp, liberated by the British 11th Armoured Division on the 15th April 1945. His father, mother and sister had perished in the camp and he praised God for sparing him, seemingly unaware of the paradox. So, if God saved him, who was responsible for the death of his family? He blamed the Nazis for this but, if that's the case, it must have been the British that saved his life. He believed that God must have sent the British but he couldn't explain why God failed to save his family and thousands of other Jews in the camp. He could not understand that of the many thousands that were incarcerated, there was a likelihood that a few would be lucky enough to survive without God's involvement. That's the nature of randomness.

On the 6th February 1958, the great Manchester United football team, known as the Busby Babes, was returning from Belgrade after having reached the semi-final of the European Cup for the second consecutive year. Travelling in a BEA Elizabethan class plane, they landed at Munich airport for a planned refuelling. Two take-off attempts had to be aborted because of an uncharacteristic surge in the port engine and the passengers disembarked as the pilot sought engineering expertise. It was snowing lightly by the time the air crew were ready to try again. During the third attempt, the plane just failed to reach take-off speed (119 knots) and crashed through a perimeter fence before its port wing was torn off as it hit a house, home to a family of six. The family survived but most of the occupants of the plane were not so fortunate. In the end, 23 lost their lives, most of them instantly, and 21 survived. The wonderful young team with an average age of but 22 were decimated and it took the club several years to recover from its loss. Duncan Edwards, the star of the team even though he was only 21 years old, survived the crash and fought for his life for 15 days in a Munich hospital before succumbing to the inevitable. His injuries were so severe that, had he lived, he would never have played football again.

Bobby Charlton, knight of the realm, was 20 years old at the time of the crash. Just before the fatal take-off, he and Denis Violett swapped places with two of their team mates, Tommy Taylor and David Pegg, who preferred to sit at the back of the plane. Bobby and Denis survived the crash with relatively minor injuries whilst Tommy and David perished. Bobby Charlton went on to establish a most distinguished career with Manchester United and England yet he often looked back to that fateful day when so many of his friends were lost. He wondered why, for example, he was spared but his great friend Duncan Edwards was not. It appears that had he not changed seats, he would have been among the deceased. God's unseen hand may have selected Bobby and guided him to change his seat but then, Tommy Taylor was also an exceptional footballer and an exceptional man. Did God play a part in the crash? If he did, the reason is unfathomable. The answer is probably not; if he had played a part he could easily have prevented the final take-off attempt by calling up a snow blizzard, a tyre puncture or some other inhibiting condition. God in his mercy wouldn't have let Duncan suffer for 15 days to no avail. No, it looks like pure tragic chance was at play once again.

If God didn't select Bobby Charlton to survive in February 1958, did he choose Sir Terry Wogan, that most popular of broadcasters, for his undoubted success? Well, not according to Sir Terry. He was asked this question at the end of his excellent documentary, *Terry Wogan's Ireland*, during which he travelled to every major city in his Irish homeland. It was clear from the programme that he had little affection for the Catholic Church whose vagaries he suffered during his formative years and was firmly of the opinion that his success was attributable, primarily, to luck. Undeterred, the interviewer tried again asking:

"But if, when your life is over, you meet Saint Peter standing at the Pearly Gates, what would you say then?"

Wogan replied resolutely that he would say:

"Oh, go on with you, you're pulling my leg."

He had shown the courage to match his conviction by not courting popularity with his answer even though he must have known that some people might have found it disappointing, if not offensive, particularly in Ireland. Aside from the programme, Terry Wogan has spoken about the grief of losing his first daughter and that, despite a Catholic upbringing, he was actually an atheist. He explained:

"I'm afraid I don't believe in God. My mother was devout and so is my wife. But I have the intellectual arrogance that makes it very hard to believe in him. I don't have the gift of faith. I remember at school I used to make up sins at confession; what priests told us were sins were not sins at all."

He made a valid point; atheism does require a degree of intellectual introspection. Unlike Sir Terry, Nick Clegg, leader of the Liberal Democrats and admitted atheist, was inclined to shift ground to the less controversial position of agnostic when challenged during an election campaign. A politician, unless inured with unwavering commitment, will always be inclined to adopt the least risk option having identified the potential for lost votes, real or imagined. Putting that to one side, he has demonstrated his religious tolerance by bringing up his children as

Roman Catholics, the religion of his wife. One supposes that his children will learn of his views when they reach an appropriate age and take their own considered path thereafter. By his approach, Nick Clegg exemplified what free thinking people do.

Millions of people throughout the world die from various forms of cancer though with the advances made by medical science, mortality rates will continue to decline. As a hypothesis, suppose there are 1,000 cancer patients throughout the country who are diagnosed as terminally ill with less than three months to live. After a period of two months, one of the male patients makes a remarkable recovery and, to the astonishment of the doctors, seems to be free of the cancer that had assailed him. It is hailed as a miracle in the local newspapers even though the doctors take a more pragmatic view, namely, that the treatment and drugs were successful against fearful odds. It also seems like a miracle to the patient and he thanks God for sparing him. This is hardly surprising given that he was told that he had only weeks to live, that he should make preparations for leaving this world and then, subsequently, he was told he was cured. Within a few more weeks, everyone else died, so there were no miracles for them. In fact, the chances of one person out of 1000 being cured are reasonably high. The chances against any individual winning the British national lottery are about 14 million to one but the chances that *someone* will win are a near certainty. The lottery winner wouldn't call the win a miracle (at least not in the spiritual sense) even though the chances of success for an individual are far less than the likelihood of just one out of 1,000 terminally ill cancer patients making a recovery. Miracles tend to be reserved for matters of life and death but whether we consider the case of the cured cancer patient or the lottery winner, the probability of witnessing either is too high to warrant being called a miracle. A more apt description would be 'pure chance'.

On the 20th March 1993, two bombs concealed in cast iron litter bins were detonated in Bridge Street, Warrington, in the county of Cheshire, England. The bombs had been planted by the Irish Republican Army (IRA) and large amounts of shrapnel caused immense damage. Three-year old Jonathan Ball died at the scene whilst his nanny somehow survived. The second victim was 12-year old Tim Parry who received the full force of the blast and was gravely injured. He died a few days later on the 25th March when doctors switched off his life support machine, having been granted permission from his family. Over 50 other people were injured, four of them seriously. Can any sense be made of anything as harrowing as this? The lives of two innocent children were cut short because of extremists and their misguided dogma. Was God involved in some way and, if so, why didn't he save the children? Or, was it just randomness and chance at work once again? Colin Parry, Tim's father, despite his unimaginable heartbreak, always acted with great dignity and, subsequently, became a prominent peace campaigner. When asked if the death of his beloved son had made him more religious, he replied:

"If you mean have I found God, the answer is 'No'."

Natural Disasters

On the 12th January 2010, a catastrophic earthquake measuring 7.0 on the Richter scale struck Haiti, the poorest country in the western hemisphere. The earthquake's epicentre was 16 miles to the west of the capital, Port-au-Prince, and by the 24th January, at least 52 aftershocks measuring 4.5 and upwards had been recorded. The Haitian government announced that an estimated 316,000 people had died, 300,000 had been injured and 1,000,000 made homeless. Communications systems, air, land and sea transport facilities, hospitals and electrical networks were damaged, severely inhibiting rescue and aid efforts. On the 23rd January, the government officially abandoned the search for survivors. Those rescued amounted to around 70 and comprised people from all ages, from babies to the very old. Some had managed to survive for several days in air pockets within tons of rubble. As each of the rescued was pulled to safety, often through small apertures, the event was declared a miracle. Tens of thousands of victims must have died instantly. Thankfully, we never saw the trauma and suffering of many hundreds that were left injured and barely alive, amidst choking dust, trapped by fallen masonry. Aftershocks will have disturbed and shifted the rubble, further restricting movement and causing the victims even greater pain as the pressure increased on broken limbs and torsos. Mercifully, many will have had the life crushed out of them. There was no miracle for them, rather the antithesis, and no miracle for the tens of thousands who died or were badly injured. We might think of these as *unmiracles*. It seems that for every miracle for which we give thanks to God, there are many thousands of *unmiracles* which have nothing to do with God. Doesn't this defy logic and reason? Were there really any miracles in Haiti or was it just a question of good or ill fortune; chance in all its capriciousness?

The Chilean mining accident began in the afternoon of Thursday, the 5th August 2010 as a significant cave-in at the troubled 121-year old San Jose copper and gold mine. The mine was located deep in the Atacama Desert, one of the driest and most hostile regions on Earth, about 28 miles north of Copiapo in northern Chile. As a consequence of the subsidence, 33 men ('Los 33') became trapped 700 metres (2,300 feet) underground and about three miles from the entrance to the mine. The mixed crew of experienced miners and technical support personnel, subsequently, survived for a record 69 days before they were rescued. A mixture of previous geological instability at the old mine and inadequate safety precautions had resulted in a series of accidents, including eight deaths, during the 12 years immediately before the incident. Consequently, it was initially feared that the workers could not have survived the collapse or, if they had survived, would starve to death before a rescue operation could be mounted.

The people of Chile had just emerged from a devastating earthquake and tsunami less than six months before the cave-in. The nation's outpouring of concern for the plight of the miners and the strong empathy for their grief-stricken families led the national government to take over the faltering rescue attempt from the mine's financially embarrassed owners, the San Esteban Mining Company. Eight exploratory boreholes were hurriedly drilled. On the 22nd August, 17 days after the accident, a note written in bold red letters was delivered to the surface. It had been taped to a drill bit which had penetrated an area considered accessible to the trapped workers. It read, simply:

"We are well in the shelter, the 33."

The whole nation erupted in a wave of euphoria and demanded that the country's leaders find a way of safely extricating the trapped workers from their confinement. Accordingly, a comprehensive plan was implemented to nurture the workers during their entrapment and elevate them to the surface one by one. It included the deployment of three large international drilling rig teams, nearly every government department, the expertise of the United States NASA agency and more than a dozen multi-national corporations. A rescue shaft was drilled which was used, initially, to deliver supplies and, later, to transport paramedics below. On the 13th October, all 33 men were brought safely to the surface over a period of almost 24 hours. After winching the last trapped miner to daylight, the paramedics, all still underground, held up a sign for the TV cameras reading:

"Mission accomplished Chile."

The sign was seen by an estimated one billion viewers around the world who were witnessing the rescue live. During the time of their confinement, the miners, most of whom were Roman Catholic, asked for religious items including Bibles, crucifixes, rosaries, statues of the Virgin Mary and other saints to be sent down to them. After Pope Benedict XVI had bequeathed each man a rosary, the gifts were brought to the mine in person by the Archbishop of Santiago. A number of miners attributed religious significance to the events. Mario Sepulveda said:

"I was with God and with the Devil and God took me."

Monica Araya, the wife of the first man rescued, stated:

"We are really religious, both my husband and I, so God was always present. It is a miracle, this rescue was so difficult, it's a grand miracle."

As one story in the UK Daily Mail reported:

"A deep religious faith powered this rescue; miners and families and rescuers alike believe their prayers were answered."

Both government representatives and the Chilean public have repeatedly credited divine providence with keeping the miners alive and their subsequent rescue was viewed as a miracle. Chile's president Sebastian Pinera stated:

"When the first miner emerges safe and sound, I hope all the bells of all the churches of Chile ring out forcefully, with joy and hope. Faith has moved mountains."

It is truly astonishing, isn't it? A religious people give thanks to God for saving the miners but blank their minds to the fact that God must have visited the miners' predicament on them in the first place. It makes no sense to credit God with the recovery and assume that he was looking the other way when a geological fault occurred. Either God is to blame for the accident and is to be praised for changing his mind and saving the miners or the accident was caused by geological instability and the miners were recovered because of the efforts of the highly skilled rescue teams. If God did save the miners, wouldn't it have been a lot less trouble if he'd made sure that they'd all completed their shift and returned safely home before he destabilised the mine? Chance, of course, knows no such logic and dictates that when instability occurs in a mine, it can happen when miners are present and, at other times, when they are not.

Little more than a month later, New Zealand witnessed a mining disaster of its own. It occurred on the 19th November, 2010 in the Pike River Mine and was the country's worst mining disaster since 1914. An explosion transpired when 31 miners and contractors were present. Two miners, some distance from the explosion, managed to walk free and were treated for minor injuries. The 29 men remaining never emerged. There wasn't much to thank God for this time.

On the 11th March 2011, a massive undersea earthquake hit Japan. It was the most powerful known Japanese earthquake and one of the five most powerful in the world since modern record keeping began in 1900. It triggered extremely destructive tsunami waves of up to 40.5 metres (133 feet). Around 20,000 people died and, in a demonstration of blatant ignorance, some observers assigned the catastrophic events to divine retribution for the atrocities committed by the Japanese during World War II. Clearly, for some, the atomic bombs dropped on the cities of Hiroshima and Nagasaki in August, 1945, killing more than a quarter of a million inhabitants, exacted insufficient compensation. Death and destruction had to be wreaked on the innocent great grandchildren of the perpetrators too.

Others thought that maybe, Shinto, the indigenous religion of Japan was somehow to blame, being polytheistic with no room for God. However, no credence can be attached to this either. The population of Haiti is largely Roman Catholic and, undoubtedly, prays frequently to God, yet over 15 times more Haitians died in their earthquake than did the Japanese. Unless people think clearly and objectively, it has been repeatedly proven that they will believe almost anything.

What Difference Does Prayer Make?

The Battle of Kursk took place when German and Soviet forces confronted each other on the eastern front during July and August, 1943. It remains both the largest series of armoured clashes and the costliest single day of aerial warfare in history. Before the commencement of hostilities, an 18-year old private of the Wehrmacht called Heinrich Brandt wrote a letter to his parents. It began:

"My dear Mother and Father. A great battle is soon to start between ourselves and the Soviets. My friends and I are very frightened and pray every waking moment for our deliverance though our commanding officers seem confident. Perhaps if you also pray to God for me, it might help. If I do not return, please know that I have always loved you."

At Kursk, Dmitri Vlasov, an 18-year old recruit of the Red Army penned a similar letter. He wrote:

"Mama, I have not known such fear in all my 18 years. Please pray to God that I live. When I was at home, I did not believe in God but now I think about him 40 times a day. We are all so scared, I don't know where to hide my head. Papa and Mama, farewell, I will never see you again, farewell, farewell, farewell."

One million men were killed or wounded in the battle and the Wehrmacht were, subsequently, forced into a prolonged retreat. The two boys never saw their homes again. Their prayers and those of their anxious parents made no difference. Millions of prayers before and during the battle went unanswered; billions, no doubt, during the whole of World War II. Parents prayed every waking hour of every day but millions of sons never returned and, in the harshest of cases, some parents outlived all of their sons, suffering the multiple traumas of successive killed in action (KIA) notifications. Does God choose who lives and who dies or does he, simply, set a roulette wheel in motion? Perhaps, this is close to the answer; the most influential aspect is chance.

The transatlantic slave trade took place between the sixteenth and nineteenth centuries during which time Africans from the central and western parts of the continent were transported to North and South America. It is estimated that about 12 million people were shipped across the Atlantic in support of this abhorrent commercial practice. The conditions for the slaves aboard ship were an abomination. Millions of prayers would have been offered for deliverance but, for many, life on the plantations would have been equally harsh. Tens of thousands died without ever experiencing freedom again, having led wretched lives. Under the circumstances, all they could do was pray and, although virtually all of them must have felt that their prayers were not being answered, it was the act of prayer that provided them with a semblance of comfort. Prayer inspired hope and although the hope was largely an illusion, it was all they had. Did God single out those to be captured and live in misery or was randomness to blame?

A simple experiment was performed to determine whether prayers are actually answered, whether they make any difference at all. The experiment required only the most elementary knowledge of probability theory and a dice game. Three players threw a die 960 times hoping for a six. It would be expected that, on average, each player would succeed with one sixth of the throws though in a relatively small sample of 960, there could be some small variation. As the sample gets larger, the deviation from the expected number of successes would be reduced. Taking part in the experiment was a devout Christian, a devout Muslim and an atheist and, before each throw, the believers prayed for a six. The atheist, without the encumbrance of prayer, completed the experiment well before the others and when all had finished, the final scores were:

atheist – 163, Christian – 159, Muslim – 161. No doubt, in denigration of the experiment, the believers would claim that God would not waste his time on such banalities. However, you can be sure that if the results had been favourable to them, they would have voiced their claims of proof to high Heaven. The experiment, of course, does not prove that prayer actually had a negative effect but it strongly suggests that it had no effect whatsoever. Pure chance had determined the outcome as it so frequently does and will continue to do until the end of time. As Victor Hugo, the famous French writer, statesman and human rights activist once said:

"Prayer is an august avowal of ignorance."

Chapter 8

Heaven and Paradise

Where is Heaven?

One of the great bulwarks of religion is the promise of an afterlife, of eternal life. Jesus referred to a Kingdom of God or a Kingdom of Heaven whilst Muhammad's equivalent was a place he called Paradise. There is not a shred of evidence that either place exists but the mere thought that they might is most beguiling. Almost certainly, religion would not exist as the force it is today if it were not for the concept of the hereafter. The great Muslim polymath of the Middle Ages, Ibn Rushd (also known as Averroes) went so far as to say that it is the Muslim doctrine of the afterlife that best motivates people to live ethical lives. He noted that the Christian and Jewish doctrines were too focused on the spiritual elements of the afterlife while the Muslim description of the physical pleasures was more enticing. Why is there a different point of view here? After all, the prophets are supposed to have communed with God and one would have thought that he would have given them a consistent description of the afterlife. Not only that, were not Jesus and Muhammad supposed to have met and conversed during the *Isra*? It may be, of course, they didn't consider it necessary to discuss the afterlife on the assumption of sheer bliss and, perhaps, God thought it best to leave the description to their imaginations.

Averroes had a tendency to accept everything in the Quran as true but, interestingly, whilst not completely rejecting the idea of a physical afterlife, felt it was unlikely. Many people agree that an afterlife is most improbable and to believe it exists is, simply, a triumph of hope over reason and logic. Carl Sagan (1934 – 1996) was an American astronomer, astrophysicist and cosmologist of outstanding intellect. According to his wife, Ann Druyan, he was not a believer in an afterlife stating:

"When my husband died, because he was so famous and known for not being a believer, many people would come up to me, it still sometimes happens, and ask me if Carl changed at the end and converted to a belief in an afterlife. They also frequently ask me if I think I will see him again. Carl faced his death with unflagging courage and never sought refuge in illusions. The tragedy was that we knew we would never see each other again. I don't ever expect to be reunited with Carl."

Alternatively, there are those that have such a fervent belief that they are prepared to commit suicide, having lived but a short time, to indulge in the pleasures offered in the next life. Only extremists would sacrifice the certainty of this life for the potential of another one but, if completely indoctrinated by their mentors, their doubts can be diffused. On the 11th September 2001, members of Al-Qaeda, a Sunni Islamist militant group founded by Osama bin Laden, chose certain death when, as human projectiles, they attacked the twin towers of the World Trade Centre in New York and the Pentagon in Arlington County, Virginia. It seems that each terrorist was lured by the promise of 24 virgins to satisfy innate desires, a bargain which tends to endorse the physical, and predominantly Muslim, view of the afterlife as expressed by Averroes. They were probably so keen to meet their concubines that they didn't bother to ask about their physical attributes, making the assumption that they were all nubile, beautiful young women. For all anyone knows, they might have been like the hags from Shakespeare's *Macbeth*, perhaps virginal but not that desirable. Also, one wonders whether there is a never-ending conveyor belt of virgins in Paradise bearing in mind that their virginity would be a transient state. Or, maybe things are different there in that a mystical regeneration continually takes place ensuring that virginity is perpetuated – once a virgin in Paradise, always a virgin. All of this, of course, is mere conjecture; the most likely scenario is that the terrorists, having been incinerated, are just atoms floating about in the atmosphere.

In the 2007 comedy-drama film, *The Bucket List*, starring Jack Nicholson and Morgan Freeman, there is a scene during which Edward Cole (Nicholson) discusses the afterlife with Carter Chambers (Freeman). Edward Cole is a billionaire philanthropist and Carter Chambers is a car mechanic. Both men have been diagnosed with terminal lung cancer and, with this in common, they strike up a firm friendship despite being from completely different backgrounds. Furthermore, Cole is an atheist whilst Chambers is a devout Christian and, consequently, a believer in eternal life. During a plane journey, the topic of their beliefs is raised. Implying that there is nothing else, Cole said:

"When you die, you die" to which Chambers asked:

"But what if you're wrong?"

"Then I win," replied Cole and Chambers retorted, smiling:
"I'm not sure it works that way."

Of course, nobody knows how it works but would Cole, having done so
much good in the world, be barred from Heaven simply because it was
beyond his belief? Wouldn't that be a little unfair to him and to millions
of other kind, generous people?

Jesus and Muhammad told us that we should aspire to get to Heaven
(or Paradise) but never told us where it can be found. Perhaps God
didn't tell them because we don't need to know; we are, simply,
transported there when the time comes. The nearest star outside our solar
system is Proxima Centauri which is 4.2 light years (approximately
25,000 billion miles) away. Heaven could be situated there but it is
unlikely to be so close to Earth. What about all the inhabitants of other
worlds, millions of light years away, who might also want to spend
eternal life there? The most obvious, most equitable place for Heaven to
be situated would be at the centre of the universe some millions of
billions of miles away. This would be fair to all civilisations but, even at
the speed of light, it would take us a virtual eternity to get there. The
journey to Heaven, therefore, must be spiritual rather than physical.
With spiritual travel, anything is possible so it may be assumed that the
journey is completed in an instant. On that basis, Heaven doesn't have to
be at the centre of the universe after all; it could be anywhere.

What Happens in Heaven?

Apart from failing to tell us Heaven's location, Jesus never explained
what life is like there; what actually happens. Nobody seems to give the

slightest consideration to the quality of life in the afterlife as long as it exists; they make the assumption that everything about it is wondrous. Muhammad, at least, gave us a glimpse of Paradise when he described seeing the angel singing Allah's praises in 24 billion billion languages. One would be hard pressed to think of anything worse than this; all that praising, day and night for millennia. Is God's vanity so colossal that his appetite for praise cannot be sated? It seems he's ensuring that he has some fun but what about everyone else? Whatever's in store, it's eternal and that's a very long time so one would hope there might be some form of enjoyment, at least in part. If life there is entirely monastic, an eternity of prayer, hymn singing and praising God, then the majority of the inhabitants are likely to be a little downcast. Greater drudgery is impossible to imagine and whilst the prophets might be pleased with that kind of existence, most people would yearn for some greater variety and interest.

There might, of course, be football matches played during the afterlife. Football is, after all, a kind of religion and as Bill Shankly, the great manager of Liverpool Football Club, once remarked:

"Football isn't a matter of life and death; it's more important than that."

All manner of questions could be answered. Would the great Arsenal team of the 1930's under Herbert Chapman be capable of beating the Busby Babes? Imagine the number of spectators for that game. It could run into several million. Would the Magical Magyars, the wonderful Hungarian team of the 1950's beat the 1970 Brazilians? Was the great England team from the golden age of football during the late 1940's, better than the World Cup winners of 1966? Would Duncan Edwards have become universally acknowledged as even better than Pele? There are so many questions that it would take an eternity to answer them all. We could even ask God if he had a favourite football team and, who knows, some of the prophets might even be half decent players. Of course, they'd have to swap their robes for something more aerodynamic even though Bill Shankly once remarked about a former teammate:

"Tom Finney would have been great in any team, in any match and in any age, even if he had been wearing an overcoat."

Tom, however, of Preston North End and England was one of the greatest footballers in the history of the game and it would be just too much to expect the prophets to match his standards. One can just imagine Muhammad, ever the warrior, kicking lumps out of Moses; and Jesus, picking himself up after some extremely rough treatment, saying: "Now kick the other one!"

Hopefully, Muhammad's team would win most of the time because he doesn't appear to have been a particularly good sport. Once he'd achieved pre-eminence, those who offended him were quickly dispatched which may, at least in part, explain the Islamic hyper-sensitivity to criticism prevalent to this day. If Islam could, somehow, develop a sense of humour, greater tolerance would surely follow.

The possibilities are endless. What about the tennis matches to be seen? Was the majestic Pancho Gonzales, world number one during the 1950's, as good as Rod Laver or Roger Federer? All the great players from different eras could be matched up. In the world of athletics, Jesse Owens could race against Usain Bolt in both the 100 and 200 metres. They would be the greatest human races ever seen but what about horse racing? How would champion racehorse Frankel have fared against some of the equine marvels of yesteryear like Shergar, Sea Bird II, Mill Reef, Brigadier Gerard and Secretariat? It really is a most intriguing prospect isn't it? If this is what we can expect from the afterlife, most people would be content and millions of years would pass, seemingly, in the blink of an eye. Football might not be allowed, of course, but there might be weekly rock concerts or classical spectaculars which would certainly help to pass the time. Disinterested parties would be free to worship and pray every day for millions of years instead.

You wonder whether you're expected to have an occupation in Heaven, don't you? Are you expected to keep your previous occupation or are you able to easily diversify? Heaven is unlikely to need accountants but teachers are always in short supply so, perhaps, any accountants could retrain as teachers. Nor would there be any need for clerics because everyone would be so much closer to God and, presumably, his expectations of us would, at last, be made clear by personal address. Imagine a world without priests, imams, bishops, archbishops, cardinals and popes. If the clerics are redundant in the afterlife, what is to become of them? Whatever it is, it's liable to involve dressing up. On Earth, their costumes always added a touch of authenticity and gravitas to the rituals they discharged, conferring on the wearer a sense of aggrandisement.

You might wonder what would happen if Heaven turns out to be a disappointment. What if you don't fit in? You might want to go to a football match but are reminded by the rest of your group (spoilsports) that you haven't reached your daily quota of prayers. What if you don't like the food or the chef, or both? There are millions of reasons over the course of eternity why you might become disillusioned or, simply, bored. That's were reincarnation comes in. You may be able to apply to leave

Heaven but your new life form cannot be predetermined. You might return to Earth as a golden eagle or, equally, you might return as a slug. If it's the latter, you'd better be prepared to dodge all the blackbirds and slug pellets. Moreover, if you do happen to return as a slug or a worm, it might take millions of years before you are able to adopt a human life form again. This is because your destiny is determined by the number of good deeds you perform whilst on Earth. Lots of good deeds might, eventually, elevate you to another level in a subsequent rebirth, perhaps as a newt or a crab. The problem is that there can't be much scope for anyone to become a great or heroic slug. In *The Bucket List*, Edward Cole, misunderstanding reincarnation, asks:

"What does a snail have to do to reincarnate? Leave a perfect trail of slime?"

You may not even return to Earth because it will have disappeared long before we get anywhere near to eternity. You may have to go to a different planet, presumably one that closely resembles Earth. However, if reincarnation is not that appealing and you've tired of singing God's praises, you may be permitted to spend the rest of your time in a deep sleep, in which case you needn't have bothered going to Heaven in the first place. With so many possible outcomes, perhaps Saint Peter interviews everyone at the Pearly Gates to determine in advance whether they are likely to give the afterlife their full commitment. Any rejects could be selected for reincarnation at that juncture, that is, sooner rather than later.

One of the primary reasons that people on Earth hope for an afterlife is that they can be given the opportunity to see their loved ones once again. Were it not for this single fact, most people would be happy to turn to dust when their time came to depart. However, meeting up again is not as elementary as it first appears. It seems reasonable to assume that nobody would wish to proceed through eternal life as an 80-year old; people would wish to be in their prime. Suppose when you reach the Pearly Gates, Saint Peter asks what age you would like to be when you go through into Heaven. You might reply that you'd like to be 35 years old because by that time you had acquired some wisdom and were in reasonably good physical condition. Footballers might opt to be around 28 years old. Al-Qaeda terrorists would almost certainly be refused entry but if they were disguised and managed to fool Saint Peter (or an Islamic equivalent), they'd probably target their mid-twenties. Your father might decide that he'd like to be 30 years old so, in Heaven, you'd be older than your father. It's rather confusing isn't it? When your grandmother met Saint Peter, suppose she'd also opted to be 35 years old. On Earth, she was 50 years older than you so that when you meet her, she'd be more like your best friend than your grandmother.

It may be, of course, that since Heaven is a spiritual, ethereal place adjustments can take place instantaneously. Perhaps when you meet your grandmother, though her nominal age is 35, she assumes a temporary age of 85. If she hadn't actually lived that long, the system employed might give you a temporary age of 15 as she becomes 65 for the duration of your get-together. If you think this is complicated, imagine what would happen if you, your wife and son were having a picnic and your uncle brought your grandparents over to join you. Your son would have to disappear until his great-grandparents left. With so many unforeseen problems, it might just be better if we keep our memories while we can and live a respectable life disregarding the inducement of another one. John Lennon wrote:

Imagine there's no Heaven
It's easy if you try

It's easier to imagine no Heaven than it is to imagine what life would be like in Heaven. There are just too many complications and far too many questions one would like to ask. Will our pets be able to join us? Will we all have to wear the same clothes? Is there some way we could meet people we never knew like Winston Churchill, William the Conqueror and Napoleon? Perhaps there are Time Machines in Heaven; if not, that's definitely one for the celestial suggestion box. It may be that all these questions are answered as an integral part of Saint Peter's interview but until that point we have no choice but to take everything on trust. Jesus offers us eternal life in a, seemingly, sublime place without ever explaining what it entails but, when you come to think about it, who really wants to live forever, anyway? Afterlife enthusiasts are liable to aspire to longer lives than others but even they would probably succumb to exhaustion after a million years or so.

When he was 88 years old, the famous and popular, if somewhat eccentric, Sir Patrick Moore (1923 – 2012), said:

"My eyes, ears and what passes as a brain are alright but my body isn't. I am near the end of my life now but I don't think it ends here. If it did, the entire thing would be pointless, but the universe is not pointless. No, we go on to the next stage."

For a scientist, isn't this a most unscientific appraisal? He was right when he asserted that the universe is not pointless; indeed, it will endure virtually ad infinitum so it can hardly be pointless. But, in terms of the universe, Earth is insignificant and, as Sir Patrick knew better than most, will disappear altogether one day, many billions of years before the universe reaches a state of maximum entropy (complete disorder). Therefore, to use the integrity of the universe as a pretext for an afterlife seems an oblique extrapolation to say the least.

Professor Brian Cox, the particle physicist and broadcaster, disagreed with Sir Patrick when he declared:

"It seems odd to me that you try to aggrandise existence by wanting to be eternal. Why does that make it more valuable? We are the product of 13.7 billion years of cosmic evolution. If I have an ambition, it would be to spread the idea that evidence-based decisions are the way to proceed rather than just making things up."

Stephen Hawking was just as forthright when he was asked about the existence of an afterlife by replying:

"The afterlife is a fairy story for people that are afraid of the dark."

Well, that's told you Sir Patrick! Sir Patrick's words implied that he, in common with many others, believed that our lives on Earth are a rehearsal for something better to come; some kind of test. Now, to use Sir Patrick's term, surely this 'would be pointless'. What would be the point of a test when an omniscient God would, by definition, know everything there is to know about us, past, present or future? We might as well go directly to, as Sir Patrick put it, 'the next stage'. What would be the point of spending, say, 70 years on Earth striving to complete some superfluous test and an eternity somewhere else? What chance would premature babies who die in an incubator shortly after being born have of passing the test? What chance do all those African infants who die of malnutrition in their thousands have of achieving a grade A? It seems that Sir Patrick told us what he believed using some abstruse reference to the universe as justification. Perhaps it's difficult for a scientist to admit a blind faith rather than attempt to gather some evidence in support of a deeply held point of view. Or, perhaps his desire to play his beloved cricket again overshadowed his reason. There are times, however, when it's simply better to say:

"I have no proof but this is what I believe."

In any case, in the likely event that there is no next stage, Sir Patrick has been so influential that his life could hardly be seen as pointless.

Charles Darwin took a more realistic view, worth repeating here, when he said:

"As for a future life, every man must judge for himself between conflicting vague probabilities."

Clearly, by his statement, he implied that the chance of an afterlife was, in his view, rather low. Many others are more emphatic and are not persuaded by the concept of an afterlife, seeing it as risible. As long ago as the 6th century BC, Gautama Buddha expressed a sceptical attitude to anything supposedly supernatural when he wrote:

"Since neither soul nor aught belonging to soul can really and truly exist, the view which holds that this I who am 'world', who am 'soul', shall hereafter live permanent, persisting, unchanging, yea abide eternally; is not this utterly and entirely a foolish doctrine?"

In the 3rd century BC, Epicurus became known for his disbelief in an afterlife and his conviction that, using the right approach, people could achieve eudemonia, the highest human good. He believed that humans were capable of great virtue without the incentive of a next stage. He used persuasion to allay the general fear of death. This fear, he felt, was based on anxiety induced by the anticipation of an unpleasant afterlife. Epicurus professed that this anxiety should be dispelled by the realisation that death means annihilation and that the mind is simply a group of atoms dissipated on death. He argued that since death is annihilation, it does not affect the living and, therefore, is not bad for the living, disregarding the transitory grief a person suffers when a loved one dies. For something to be bad for somebody, he stated, that person had to exist. The dead do not exist, the corollary of which is that death cannot be bad for the dead. He concluded, therefore, that death is not bad for either the living or the dead. Furthermore, he posited, that if death causes no pain when you are dead, it would be foolish to permit the fear of death to cause you pain when you are alive.

Had it been possible, a meeting between Jesus and Epicurus would have been illuminating and ground breaking. With Epicurus adopting the role of benevolent inquisitor, one can envisage his penetrating questioning as he skillfully sought the truth. The dialogue might have been as follows:

Epicurus: "My Lord Jesus, I concede that your moral teachings are the finest ever presented to mankind but, with your permission, I'd like to delve deeper into the substance that lies beneath. I understand that none of the ancient prophets such as Abraham, Moses and Elisha had any awareness of the place you refer to as the Kingdom of Heaven. Is this so?"

Jesus: "It is so."

Epicurus: "Can you explain why the prophets were unaware of such an important place?"

Jesus: "God must have had a reason to keep it from them. We cannot know God's mind."

Epicurus: "But, as I understand it, at no time did God mention it to you either. Am I right?"

Jesus: "Yes, you are right."

Epicurus: "Then how did you learn of this place?"

Jesus: "John the Baptist spoke of it when he preached. I adopted the term and incorporated it into my preaching."

Epicurus: "Do you think that God told John the Baptist about his kingdom instead of you?"

Jesus: "That I could not say."

Epicurus: "So, all this talk of the Kingdom of Heaven stems from John the Baptist who may simply have made it up to add power to his sermons."

Jesus: "Perhaps, but it seems reasonable to assume that God has a kingdom."

Epicurus: "That I grant you, but I understand when you spoke of the Kingdom of Heaven you referred to it as a place of eternal life.

Jesus: "The Kingdom of Heaven is all around us but, yes, I particularly referred to it as a realm of eternal life."

Epicurus: "It seems that there is no evidence of the Kingdom of Heaven or eternal life. Would I be right in thinking that you encompassed it in your teaching as an incentive for people to live better, more considerate lives?"

Jesus: "Yes, you are right but I sincerely believe that eternal life is a reality for those that choose God's ways."

Epicurus: "You never explained what happens in the afterlife and the reason is clear; it was never actually explained to you. However, what do you imagine the afterlife to be like?"

Jesus: "I expect that one will be able to spend every day praising God for millions of years, indeed, eternally."

Epicurus: "Do think there might be a reprieve for bad behaviour?"

Jesus: "There is unlikely to be any bad behaviour in Heaven."

Epicurus: "I apologise for my bad joke but, more seriously, do you think that for those less suited to the life you describe there might be an option for eternal sleep?"

Jesus: "I suppose there could be. After all, there would be little point in journeying through eternity without peace of mind."

Epicurus: "Thank you, Jesus, for your time. Perhaps you could ask God for clarification and let everyone know what he says."

The most likely outcome from the meeting is that Epicurus would have reaffirmed his conviction that the concept of eternal life existed solely in the mind and, as such, would never be realised. After all, everything one can imagine from a microbe to a mountain or our globe to a galaxy has a finite life cycle. At some time, everything comes to an end. Eternal life contravenes the pattern of behaviour of every known phenomenon and is thrown into question by all available evidence. Why should it stand alone in disharmony with trillions of entities that eventually die? It seems the answer is that it is referenced as hearsay in some ancient (perceived holy) text from where it became embedded in the psyche of aspirants only too anxious to spread the word to future generations. In reality, when the emotion is stripped away, does it make any sense?

Chapter 9

Evolution

Charles Darwin

Charles Robert Darwin (1809 – 1882) has been described as one of the most influential figures in human history. He established that all species of life have evolved with the passage of time from a common ancestry and posited the scientific theory that this evolution occurred via a process called natural selection. He was born the fifth of six children in Shrewsbury, England, on the same day that Abraham Lincoln was born in Kentucky. Shrewsbury was a busy market town overlooking the River Severn, near to the border between England and Wales. His father, Dr. Robert Darwin, was the leading physician of Shrewsbury, an imposing man standing 6 feet 2 inches tall and weighing over 330 pounds. Charles' mother, Susannah, was a member of the famous Wedgwood family, makers of fine pottery. Life for the young Charles was cultured and easy going with a large, comfortable home, fine gardens and servants. At nine years of age, he began his studies at Shrewsbury School, one of England's finest learning establishments. There was no science on the curriculum but, instead, he learnt Latin, Classics and

Ancient History, all of which he found uninspiring. Consequently, during his time at the school, he was a poor student. His two main passions were shooting and romping with his dogs in the countryside. In the world of the English upper-middle classes, it was quite possible for the younger sons of a family to spend their lives in leisure pursuits providing they had, or could anticipate, an inheritance. However, his father, who could not tolerate idleness, admonished Charles one day saying:

"You care for nothing but shooting, dogs and rat-catching and you will be a disgrace to yourself and your family."

In October 1825, aged 16 years, Charles was removed from Shrewsbury School to learn a subject his father considered worthwhile. Accordingly, he was sent to study medicine at Edinburgh University. However, Charles had little intention of practising medicine as, not long after arriving in Edinburgh, he learned he would inherit enough money from his father to be able to live in comfort without having to work. This news, he admitted, encouraged a complacent attitude and was sufficient to deflect any dedicated effort to learn medicine. After two years of futile studies, Charles' father removed him from medical school and sent him to Cambridge University with a view to his becoming a minister of the Church of England. Charles took residence in Christ's College in January 1828, aged 19 years. With a penchant for enjoyment and, 'as ignorant as a pig' as he later put it, he found many friends among the easygoing fraternity who rode horses, went shooting and studied as little as possible. Almost the only thing the young Charles cultivated was a somewhat curious passion for collecting beetles. He later wrote:

"It was the mere passion for collecting for I did not dissect them and rarely compared their external characters with published descriptions."

There was, however, one man at Cambridge, John Henslow (1796 – 1861), the clergyman, botanist and geologist, who saw more in Charles than did anyone else. Henslow, in his early 30's, was Chairman of the Botany Department and he befriended the young beetle collector. He urged Darwin to take a more serious interest in science, but without success. To Charles, natural history was little more than a hobby.

In the winter of 1830, Darwin began reading a travel book written by Baron Alexander von Humboldt, the most famous scientific explorer of the day. It described his journey to the Canary Islands, South America, Mexico and the United States. Suddenly inspired, Darwin began to contemplate visiting the Canary Islands to see the tropical scenery for himself. He started studying Spanish and hoped that Henslow would accompany him. In January 1831, he graduated, coming tenth out of 178 candidates, although he had to remain at Cambridge until June to complete the final requirements for his Bachelor of Arts degree. He passed the time on long walks with Henslow and he began, gradually, to develop an interest in geology. He made a brief field trip into Wales but, as the autumn shooting season approached, he decided to return home to participate. When he arrived at Shrewsbury, a letter from Henslow awaited him. It informed him that a Captain Robert Fitzroy, the 26-year old commander of the Royal Navy's HMS Beagle, was to carry out a detailed survey of the southern coast of South America for the British Admiralty. He was looking for a young naturalist to accompany him without pay. Darwin was selected, joined the Beagle on the 15th November 1831 and, on the 27th December, the ship hoisted anchor and set out to sea. On the trip Darwin collected, sketched and studied all the available fauna and flora and began to develop the rudiments of his revolutionary hypothesis concerning the origin and progression of the different species he studied. The Beagle entered Falmouth on the 2nd October 1836 after having been away for almost five years. On his return, Darwin was being regarded as a highly promising naturalist due, primarily, to the fact that Henslow had circulated his letters from the Beagle. He spent his time reviewing and collating all the data he had gathered and reading all the available scientific literature. By late September 1838, almost two years after the Beagle's return, he had pieced together his theory of evolution by natural selection. However, 21 years were to go by before it was announced to the world.

The known events in his life over this period are quite limited. He was delivering lectures and writing about his discoveries during the voyage of the Beagle and, in 1839, he was elected a Fellow of the Royal Society. In January 1839, he married Emma Wedgwood and they were to have seven children; five sons and two daughters. Almost immediately after he married, he became poorly with a debilitating illness. However, with his father's inheritance and a generous dowry from Emma, they lived a happy and comfortable life. In September 1842, they moved to the country when they purchased Down House. Although only 16 miles from London Bridge, the setting was rural, quiet and secluded; a place where Darwin could work and rest. He remained at Down House for the rest of his life, a period of almost 40 years. Although he had intended to commute into London every two or three weeks to converse with his scientific colleagues, he found the two to three hour journey exhausting and, after a few years, he capitulated. Except for his wife and children and his correspondence, he was a virtual recluse and had become a semi-invalid.   Life at Down passed uneventfully as he filled his days writing, playing with his children, reading, resting and carrying out simple experiments. He spent the years of 1842 to 1846 working, principally, on books describing his geological observations although, in 1842, he drafted a 35-page pencil abstract of his theory on the origin of species. In 1844, he enlarged this work into a 230-page outline but then went no further as he became deflected by a lengthy project about barnacles.

Darwin's Major Work

In late 1856, Darwin finally started to author his theory of natural selection for publication into an anticipated 1000-page book. Then, on the 18th June 1858, he received a letter from Alfred Russell Wallace (1823 – 1913), a 35-year old English naturalist who was exploring the West Indies. Wallace had enclosed an essay he had recently written and, as Darwin read it, he was astonished. The essay contained point by point an identical theory of evolution by natural selection. In a letter to a friend he wrote:

"I never saw a more striking coincidence. If Wallace had my manuscript sketch written out in 1842, he could not have made a better short abstract."

It was truly a remarkable coincidence, one of history's most extraordinary cases of two scientists working independently, yet coming to precisely the same conclusion. Darwin and his friends acted swiftly. At a meeting of the Linnean Society for naturalists, on the 1st July, they presented both Wallace's essay and Darwin's outline of 1842 / 1844 so both men shared the credit, though Darwin was clearly seen as the senior figure. Subsequently, Wallace refused to take any of the limelight away from Darwin. He had great respect for his eminence as a naturalist and was proud to have been included in such an equitable way. Wallace had asked only that Darwin forward his essay to Charles Lyell (1797 – 1875), the foremost geologist of the time, if it was of sufficient merit. Darwin acceded to the request and he and Wallace remained friends thereafter.

As a result of recent events, Darwin was obliged to abandon his original plan for the 1000-page book and write a more modest version. By March 1859, the manuscript was completed and, after some modification, *On the Origin of Species by Means of Natural Selection, or the Preservation of Favoured Races in the Struggle for Life* went on sale in November 1859, priced 15 shillings. The entire first edition, comprising 1250 copies, was sold out on the first day. Darwin's book wasn't the first to deal with evolution as in 1844, some 15 years before *The Origin of Species* appeared, a book called *Vestiges of the Natural History of Creation* was anonymously published which revived an old hypothesis that 'lower animals' evolved into 'higher animals'. It created uproar in England and the geologist, Adam Sedgwick, likened the author to the serpent in the Garden of Eden who, he stated:

"Would poison the minds of our glorious matrons and maids by teaching them that they are the children of apes and the breeders of monsters."

After several months of curiosity and intrigue, the identity of the author, a certain Robert Chambers, was revealed. The book, in reality, was a jumble of vague and wafer-thin ideas but, despite being scorned by critics, it achieved no fewer than 10 editions. Darwin's book was different, having been based on many years of painstaking research. The basic principles of his theory can be briefly outlined yet, *The Origin of*

Species is 500 pages long and, as Darwin himself said on rereading his manuscript:

"Oh my gracious, it is tough reading."

Darwin felt that he had to do more than merely outline his theory. He had to convince others it was true so much of the book is devoted to handling anticipated objections. *The Origin of Species* is an unremitting exposition in support of the theory of evolution by natural selection with numerous examples. It was designed to persuade people to accept a theory that would challenge their innermost thoughts; one that they had not been conditioned, in their everyday lives, to acknowledge.

In short, according to Darwin's theory, the myriad of species that inhabit the Earth are all descended from a few, much simpler ancient species that gradually evolved, or mutated, over the course of millions of years. Not only had they mutated but they had done so by natural means. According to Darwin, the lion, the horse, the eagle and even the lowly ant, were not the special, individual handiwork of a divine Creator, as had long been accepted. Instead, they had developed by means of a completely natural process. Natural selection, he postulated, is the result of two fundamental principles. Firstly, that small hereditary variations occur at random in the descendants of all living things and, secondly, that there is a struggle for existence amongst these creatures; they strive to find more food, more space and a more efficacious means of survival. Moreover, he contends, the most important force in the life of any creature stems from the other creatures among which it dwells. He maintained:

"The struggle almost invariably will be the most severe between the individuals of the same species, for they frequent the same districts, require the same food, and are exposed to the same dangers."

Darwin posited that any favoured variants will generally become more unlike the original parent species so that, after hundreds of thousands of generations, the successful surviving varieties will be quite different from the original parent species (by then, most likely, extinct). To use an analogy, they will have sprung from the parent species like the countless branches from a gigantic tree trunk. The surviving species might look alike because they share physical characteristics inherited from their common ancestor. Naturalists had for many years realised that certain types of species, a genus, were strikingly similar. The genus *panthera,* for example, includes the lion, tiger, leopard, and jaguar. It never crossed the minds of naturalists who believed in the creation theory to question why God would have, pointlessly, made several species so similar. Darwin's theory provided a simple, yet elegant, answer; members of the same genus resemble each other because they are derived from a common ancestor.

He explained that natural selection does not rely on the chance appearance of significant and particularly useful variations, that even the most trivial advantage would be preserved by natural selection. Neither is natural selection limited to a few observable advantages like sharp teeth and claws or thick fur since each creature lives in a complex web of relationships with others. Even a minute change in any part of any creature might prove advantageous in the fight for life. In addition to the existence of small, hereditary variations, his theory encompasses the high birth rate of the Earth's inhabitants. The world is a place where natural selection has become a replacement for the Creator and where life is being continually destroyed. He hints that even man is naught but an animal that evolved, alongside everything else, in the constant struggle for existence. In 1859, these revelations shook society's foundations to the core and it is easy to understand why Darwin, in anticipation of such an anguished reaction, was reticent about publishing his work for so long. Shortly before the book's appearance, he had been nominated for a knighthood and Prince Albert had agreed. With the publication of *The Origin of Species*, however, Queen Victoria's advisers opposed the nomination and it was defeated.

In reality, few scientists have shared Darwin's gift of being able to analyse the everyday world around them with such inquiry and perceptive vision. Still fewer have demonstrated his open-minded capacity to cast aside preconceptions in order to test a revolutionary idea. Darwin's theory of evolution by natural selection astounded not only the scientists of the mid-nineteenth century but a world that was resigned to explaining nature's riddles as God's work. Debate was always stifled by people saying:

"Well, how can we expect to understand God's ways?"

In the months following the book's publication, men of science and the church joined the clamour against its assertions. An article in the *Quarterly Review* of July 1860 called Darwin a flighty man who had crafted an 'utterly rotten fabric of guess and speculation'. The Harvard naturalist, Louis Agassiz, dismissed the theory by stating:

"It was a scientific mistake, untrue in its facts, unscientific in its method, and mischievous in its tendency."

Religious men accused Darwin of destroying the foundations of religion and degrading the human race though he had barely referred to the origin of man in the book. Darwinism was equated with blasphemy and atheism in an attitude that still abides today, particularly in the United States. In the final analysis, for Darwin, the truth revealed by science was more important than any religious furore that he had instigated. He was a deeply moral man but, although once destined to be a cleric, he was not profoundly religious. The current view of science is so firmly entrenched in evolution that it is difficult, nowadays, to appreciate how colossal a blow the revelation of Darwin's theory struck at the reputations of most scientists as well as their religious convictions. It required the genius of a number of England's leading zoologists, botanists and geologists to recognise how much sense the theory of evolution made before beginning to apply it to their own work.

When *The Origin of Species* first appeared, there were only two committed Darwinians in the world and one of them, Alfred Russell Wallace, was far away in the Dutch East Indies. So it was that in late 1859 and early 1860, Darwin stood alone to bear the attacks of eminent scientists and respectable clergymen. The hostility was to find a ready forum in national magazines. He was assailed by prejudice, deep religious conviction, misunderstanding and professional jealousy. All Darwin possessed was a book that was hard to read and a theory that, apparently, sidelined a divine Creator. He remarked:

"I fear I shall be greatly abused."

Darwin was not well equipped for fierce public combat. Not only did he have constant bouts of illness but he was too diffident even to argue with his friends, let alone stand his ground against eloquent and quick-witted antagonists. He was a man who did his thinking slowly, with precision, and often found it difficult to articulate his ideas, particularly at short notice. He remarked at the time:

"It is something unintelligible to me how anyone can argue in public as orators do."

He admitted the first retort that came to his mind was usually the worst one possible. Prior to its publication, in October and November 1859, Darwin sent a number of advance copies of his book to friends and fellow scientists. There were three men above all others whom he hoped would accept his theory. If these three men would support him, he said:

"I should feel that the subject is safe, and all the world may rail, but ultimately the theory of Natural Selection - though, no doubt, imperfect in its present condition and embracing many errors - would prevail."

These three men were Joseph Hooker, the country's leading botanist, Sir Charles Lyell, the leading geologist and Thomas Henry Huxley who, despite being only 34 years of age, was the country's leading zoologist. Hooker and Lyell had read and criticised each stage of the book over the past year but neither was prepared to lend him complete support. He felt somewhat more hopeful with Huxley. After years of discussion with Darwin, Hooker was a convert to evolution but not by natural selection. As for Charles Lyell, there was no one, Darwin thought, whose opinion had more authority than that of his 62-year old friend and advisor. To Lyell, Darwin wrote:

"Remember your verdict will probably have more influence than my book in deciding whether such views as I hold will be admitted or rejected at present."

The old geologist was in a dilemma. He wished to give backing to his friend but he was unsure and could never quite make up his mind. Early on, Darwin claimed:

"Lyell is nearly a convert."

Unfortunately, however, Lyell's commitment never exceeded the 'nearly' stage. Huxley was different and after reading Darwin's theory he exclaimed:

"How extremely stupid not to have thought of that!"

He wrote to Darwin:

"I am prepared to go to the stake if requisite. And as to the curs which will bark and yelp, you must recollect that some of your friends, at any rate, are endowed with an amount of combativeness which (though you have often and justly rebuked it) may stand you in good stead. I am sharpening up my claws and beak in readiness."

Thomas Henry Huxley (1825 – 1895), a foremost biologist and zoologist, came to be known as 'Darwin's Bulldog'. He was an agnostic who understood the gospels and deeply mistrusted them. He could not comprehend how Christian theology was founded on the untrustworthiness of the Hebrew scriptures. He doubted that Abraham enjoyed a covenant with God, that sacrifices and circumcision could have been ordained and that the commandments could have been written by God's hand on stone tablets. He believed that Abraham was a mythical hero much like Theseus, that Noah's flood was a fiction, that Adam and Eve's fall from grace was a legend and that the story of the creation was the dream of a seer. All these definite and detailed narratives, he felt, had no historical authenticity whatsoever and, as for the biographers of the New Testament, he had no doubt that they had accepted fiction in place of truth. All this, to the learned Huxley, meant that they had constructed the foundation of the Christian doctrine upon a legendary quicksand.

In the mid-19th century, he made clear his views by stating:
"I have never had the least sympathy with the a priori reasons against orthodoxy and I have by nature and disposition the greatest possible antipathy to all the atheistic and infidel school. Nevertheless I know that I am, in spite of myself, exactly what the Christian would call, and, so far as I can see, is justified in calling, atheist and infidel. I cannot see one shadow or tittle of evidence that the great unknown underlying the phenomenon of the universe stands to us in the relation of a Father who loves us and cares for us as Christianity asserts. So with regard to the other great Christian dogmas, immortality of soul and future state of rewards and punishments, what possible objection can I—who am compelled perforce to believe in the immortality of what we call Matter and Force, and in a very unmistakable present state of rewards and punishments for our deeds—have to these doctrines? Give me a scintilla of evidence, and I am ready to jump at them."

In a later statement to clarify further clarify his views, he said:
"When I reached intellectual maturity and began to ask myself whether I was an atheist, a theist, or a pantheist; a materialist or an idealist; Christian or a freethinker; I found that the more I learned and reflected, the less ready was the answer; until, at last, I came to the conclusion that I had neither art nor part with any of these denominations, except the last.

The one thing in which most of these good people were agreed was the one thing in which I differed from them. They were quite sure they had attained a certain 'gnosis', – had, more or less successfully, solved the problem of existence; while I was quite sure I had not, and had a pretty strong conviction that the problem was insoluble. So I took thought, and invented what I conceived to be the appropriate title of 'agnostic'. It came into my head as suggestively antithetic to the 'gnostic' of Church history, who professed to know so much about the very things of which I was ignorant. To my great satisfaction the term took."

It is likely that Huxley's agnosticism was, in part, a consequence of ecclesiastical intolerance and visceral repression of any scientific discoveries which conflicted with the literal word of the Book of Genesis and other Christian and Jewish texts.

Meanwhile, the battle lines of opposing forces were being drawn. In December 1859, almost immediately after his book was published, Darwin received a severe letter from an erstwhile Cambridge friend and teacher, Adam Sedgwick, Professor of Geology and Canon of Norwich Cathedral. Sedgwick wrote:

"I have read your book with more pain than pleasure. Parts of it I admired greatly, parts I laughed at 'til my sides were almost sore; other parts I read with absolute sorrow, because I think them utterly false and grievously mischievous. The theory would sink the human race into a lower grade of degradation than any into which it has fallen since its written record tells us of its history."

Sedgwick claimed that Darwin was not even an honest scientist, that he was a vicious atheist in masquerade. Similar assertions were made by the Archbishop of Dublin and other, lesser clergymen who wrote that evolution was 'degrading' and 'materialistic' and proclaimed that it meant:

"There is no God and the ape is our Adam."

Darwin had expected criticism from all pious churchmen but he received an encouraging and friendly letter from the Reverend Charles Kingsley, the novelist, who said he had no trouble reconciling evolution and God. He described in his letter how disturbing he found the highly negative scientific opinion. One scientist told him that he would read *The Origin of Species* but would never believe it, a curious prejudgment, Kingsley thought, for a scientist to make. Shortly after the book's publication, Darwin undertook one of his rare trips to London. He called at the British Museum where many of his old scientific colleagues worked but had the feeling he was entering hostile territory. It became clear later that the head of the palaeontology department, Sir Richard Owen, was determined to discredit Darwin's theory in any way possible. When Darwin called at the museum, however, Owen greeted him pleasantly. Many scientists realised that Darwin's theory severed the alliance between science and religious faith and, by opposing the theory, they were defending their position as believers. Louis Agassiz, the icon of Boston intellectual society, stated that science was theology's sister. Darwin fully anticipated that Agassiz would disagree with him and, in January 1860, Agassiz announced to the Boston Natural History Society that Darwin's new idea was:

"An ingenious but fanciful theory. The arguments presented by Darwin's book have not made the least impression on my mind."

The Agassiz mind, of course, wasn't sufficiently open to permit any impression to be left. To him, evolution was not a theory but a threat. It was a danger to religion, to science and, above all, to Louis Agassiz who harboured the unshakeable belief that each species is, 'a thought of God'. He could not reconcile himself to a process that did not invoke design. He held a series of debates at the Natural History Society with Asa Gray, Professor of Botany at Harvard and a staunch Darwin supporter. Many Agassiz admirers were disappointed to see their champion squirm, misrepresent facts and contradict himself when under pressure from Gray's arguments.

By the spring of 1860, Darwin's confidence was becoming shaken. The attacks were being intensified while his few supporters had not yet publicly supported him.   Even his friend, Thomas Huxley, had not openly declared his views.   In an anonymous review in the London Times, he had stated only that Darwin's theory should be treated with respect.   Joseph Hooker was saying the same to colleagues in private whilst Sir Charles Lyell continually referred to Darwin's work as a hypothesis.   Adam Sedgwick condemned the theory in the influential weekly, *The Spectator*, and Sir Richard Owen finally disclosed his views with a 45-page treatise in the prestigious *Edinburgh Review.*   Under a cloak of anonymity, Owen's article was duplicitous and dishonest and it was but an opening gambit.

The most prestigious scientific meeting of the year, the annual conference of the British Association for the Advancement of Science, was due to take place at the end of June.   The week-long meeting was attended not only by scientists but also by large numbers of an admiring public.   Owen felt that this was an excellent opportunity for science to demonstrate its propriety and crush Darwinism for ever.   He wouldn't even have to overtly involve himself as the venue was Oxford University and the Bishop of Oxford was eager to criticise Darwin from a public platform. A witty and gifted orator, Bishop Samuel Wilberforce, also known as Soapy Sam, had great confidence in his ability and claimed that all he needed was some rudimentary instruction in biology. Owen was only too pleased to further ingratiate himself as the pair had already collaborated on a 17,000-word, anonymous appraisal of Darwin's book that was due to appear in the *Quarterly Review* in July. They viewed the British Association meeting as ideal publicity for their article but they were not to know that the ensuing debate was to become one of the most unforgettable dramas in the history of science.

The presiding officer was Darwin's old friend and mentor from Cambridge, John Henslow. Darwin was missing as he was too ill and depressed to attend. The debate was to occur on the third day of the meeting, Saturday the 30th June 1860, when Thomas Huxley was expected to speak in support of Darwinism. On the Friday, however, he began to lose confidence saying:

"I do not see the good of giving up peace and quietness to be episcopally pounded."

He felt it would be most difficult to verbally strike back at a clergyman in a public debate. He was, however, eventually persuaded by Robert Chambers, the author of the much criticised *Vestiges*, to stay and contest the case. With more than 700 people in attendance, too many for the lecture hall, the meeting had to be reconvened in the library of the University Museum. A group of clergymen, ready to cheer their champion, were seated in the centre of the room. Huxley and Hooker sat on the platform alongside Bishop Wilberforce and, when the time came for the bishop to speak, he strode to the podium resplendent in his stately gown and announced:

"The permanence of specific forms is a fact confirmed by all observations."

He then enquired:

"Has anyone ever seen a single case of a species evolving? Can we really believe that all favourable varieties of turnip are tending to become men?"

Demonstrating considerable deftness, he moved from one point to the next, ridiculing Darwin's work and heaping scorn on Huxley. Such was the general tone of the bishop's rendition, self-assured and witty, that the audience was enthralled. Towards the end of his oratory, he announced that the evolutionists must be men with a preference for having apes as their ancestors. Turning to Huxley, he asked whether it was through his grandfather or his grandmother that he claimed his descent from a monkey. This insulting remark was a blunder, though the bishop didn't know it at the time, and Huxley instantly recognised it as such. When the time came for Huxley's riposte he delivered a polite, controlled rebuttal to each of the bishop's arguments. He claimed there was nothing new in the bishop's speech except for the question about 'my personal predilections in the matter of ancestry'. In reply, Huxley said:

"If the question is put to me, 'Would I rather have a miserable ape for a grandfather, or a man highly endowed by nature and possessed of great means and influence, and yet who employs these faculties and that influence for the mere purpose of introducing ridicule into a grave scientific discussion' - I unhesitatingly affirm my preference for the ape."

At this, the place was in uproar with Darwin's supporters cheering, the clergy uttering their outrage and undergraduates yelling.   As the pandemonium abated, John Henslow invited Hooker to the podium to deliver the closing arguments. The audience that had come, primarily, to jeer at Darwin then heard the nation's finest botanist dismantle Bishop Wilberforce's argument step by step and expose his objections as worthless.   He claimed that it was evident the bishop had not read Darwin's book and that he was equally unaware of the rudiments of botanical science. Hooker added:

"I knew of this theory 15 years ago. I was then entirely opposed to it … but since then I have devoted myself unremittingly to natural history; in its pursuit I have traveled around the world. Facts in this science which before were inexplicable to me became, one by one, explained by this theory and conviction has been thus gradually forced upon an unwilling convert."

Bishop Wilberforce and Owen had been routed. Darwin had merely sought the truth through the application of science and had never mentioned religion in any of his work. It was the implication of his theories that had caused so much offence but what is it that possesses a churchman, like Samuel Wilberforce, to believe that he can defeat a scientist in debate when totally unqualified in the subject matter? The answer would seem to be dogma. The literal truth of the Bible was indirectly challenged by a scientist and the churchman's natural impulse was to refute the findings instead of considering the facts. Did it never occur to him that the scientist had centuries of scientific discovery to provide him with a foundation for his work whilst all the cleric had was the revered text of a few, primitive, impressionable people, completely ignorant of the world around them? It wasn't really a contest, was it?

The bishop was an expert in theology and, without doubt, an intelligent man which qualified him to pontificate on religious matters but, not necessarily, scientific ones. He should have realised that he was ill-equipped to debate with Huxley but a combination of intellectual arrogance and the compulsion to defend his beliefs was impossible to resist. The church has always attempted to maintain the status quo by resisting change and repressing new ideas. The perpetual ignorance of its congregation has long been its greatest asset, facilitating a ministry that ruled largely by invoking the twin emotions of hope and fear.

Nicolaus Copernicus (1473 -1543), one of the great polymaths of the Renaissance, was a Polish astronomer and the first person to formulate a heliocentric cosmology. His book, *On the Revolutions of Celestial Spheres,* published just before his death, is often regarded as the starting point of modern astronomy. Until then, the received wisdom, tentatively supported by passages in the Bible, was that the Sun moved in orbit around the Earth. In contrast, as early as 1532, Copernicus had completed his manuscript which stated that the Earth orbited around the centre of the then known universe, namely, the Sun. Despite being urged by his friends to publish his findings he resisted, not wishing to risk the scorn 'to which he would expose himself on account of the novelty and incomprehensibility of his theses'. Copernicus was right to be fearful as, with the passage of time, the opprobrium his work attracted was intensified. Melanchthon rejected Copernicanism specifying:

"The evidence of the senses, the thousand-year consensus of men of science, and the authority of the Bible."

On the basis of Bible passages, he declared:

"Encouraged by this divine evidence, let us cherish the truth and let us not permit ourselves to be alienated from it by the tricks of those who deem it an intellectual honour to introduce confusion into the arts."

Another Protestant theologian, John Owen, stated:

"The late hypothesis, fixing the sun as in the centre of the world was built on fallible phenomena, and advanced by many arbitrary presumptions against evident testimonies of Scripture."

In Roman Catholic circles, German Jesuit Nicolaus Serarius was one of the first to describe the Copernicus theory as heretical. Cardinal Robert Bellarmine condemned the theory writing:

"Not only the Holy Fathers, but also the modern commentaries on Genesis, the Psalms, Ecclesiastes, and Joshua, you will find all agreeing in the literal interpretation that the sun is in heaven and turns around the earth with great speed, and that the earth is very far from heaven and sits motionless at the centre of the world … Nor can one answer that this is not a matter of faith, since if it is not a matter of faith as regards the topic, it is a matter of faith as regards the speaker and so it would be heretical to say that Abraham did not have two children and Jacob twelve, as well as to say that Christ was not born of a virgin, because both are said by the Holy Spirit through the mouth of prophets and apostles."

No wonder Copernicus was worried. One of the strongest opponents of Copernican theory was Francesco Ingoli, a Catholic priest, who wrote a January 1616 essay condemning it as, 'philosophically untenable and theologically heretical'. Had Copernicus been alive, it is most likely he would have been condemned as a heretic and burned at the stake. As later scientific discoveries showed beyond doubt, he was completely right and his critics spectacularly wrong but, as so many have found in the past, being right is no trustworthy defence when the established church is offended.

The parallels between the Copernicus and Darwin cases are unmistakable and without a further three centuries of scientific discovery and a more enlightened populace to support him, Darwin would have been even more vilified and branded a heretic. However, once the Oxford University debate was over, genuine scientists were compelled to treat *The Origin of Species* with respect. There was still opposition against 'the monkey theory', as evolution was often called, and attacks continued to appear even in the most reputable magazines like *Punch*. To many non-scientists, the theory remained a threat to their faith and the dignity of mankind but, within about two years, almost all scientists had accepted evolution without being as certain about natural selection. Even Sir Richard Owen was persuaded to shift his stance on evolution and, in 1863, Charles Kingsley wrote:

"Darwin is conquering everywhere and rushing in like a flood, by the mere force of truth and fact."

Charles Darwin, this gentle, unassuming and most honourable of men was, by this time, a recluse but he had triumphed after all. Since Darwin's day, advances in the study of heredity, mutations and genetics have uncovered some errors in his theory, hardly surprising given the state of knowledge at the time. However, the great body if his work stands firm for, as the distinguished biologist, Sir Julian Huxley, the grandson of Thomas Henry Huxley, said:

"Not only is natural selection inevitable, not only is it an effective agency of evolution, but it is the only effective agency of evolution."

In December 1881, Darwin suffered a mild heart seizure and in April the following year he suffered a more severe attack and went into a coma. He regained consciousness briefly but in the afternoon of the 19th April 1882, aged 73 years, Darwin died. One week later, he was buried in Westminster Abbey in London where so many of England's men of towering achievement lie interred. His coffin was placed near that of Sir Isaac Newton, one of the greatest scientists ever. Does anything more need to be said?

Darwin's Religious Beliefs

Darwin's father and grandfather were freethinkers whilst his baptism and boarding school were Church of England. Freethinkers hold that individuals should not blindly accept ideas proposed as truth without recourse to knowledge and reason. Thus, they strive to build their opinions on the basis of facts, scientific enquiry and logical principles, independent of any intellectually limiting effects such as prejudice, popular culture, tradition, sectarianism, legend and dogma. With regard to religion, freethinkers hold that there is insufficient evidence to support the existence of supernatural phenomena. A line from *Clifford's Credo* by the 19th century British mathematician and philosopher, William Kingdon Clifford, perhaps best describes the freethinker's premise:

"It is wrong always, everywhere, and for anyone, to believe anything upon insufficient evidence."

When going to Cambridge to become an Anglican clergyman, Darwin did not doubt the literal truth of the Bible. On board HMS Beagle, he was quite orthodox and would often quote the Bible as an authority on morality. He, initially, saw the adaptation of species as evidence of design and searched for 'centres of creation' to explain animal dispersion. By his return, of greater maturity, he was critical of the Bible as history and wondered why all religions should not be equally valid. In the next few years, while contemplating geology and the transmutation of species, he gave considerable thought to religion. He openly discussed it with his wife, Emma, whose beliefs also derived from intensive study and questioning. To Darwin, natural selection fully explained the adaptation of species and obviated the need for design. He could not see the work of an omnipotent deity in all the pain and suffering such as that experienced in the animal kingdom.

Darwin remained close friends with the Vicar of Downe, John Innes, and continued to be involved in the parish work of the church. In a letter written to Darwin in December 1878, Innes explains how he described his friend to bishops at a Church Congress in Dundee:

"I have the pleasure of the intimate friendship of one of the very first Naturalists in Europe. He is a most accurate observer, and never states anything as a fact which he has not most thoroughly investigated. He is a man of the most perfect moral character, and his scrupulous regard for the strictest truth is above that of almost all men I know. I am quite persuaded that if on any morning he met with a fact which would clearly contradict one of his cherished theories he would not let the sun set before he made it known. I never saw a word in his writings which was an attack on Religion. He follows his own course as a Naturalist and leaves Moses to take care of himself."

From around 1849, he would go for a walk on Sundays while his family attended church. His daughter, Annie, died in 1851 and by then his faith in Christianity had dwindled. He considered it 'absurd to doubt that a man might be an ardent theist and an evolutionist' and, though reticent about his religious views, in 1879 he wrote:

"I have never been an atheist in the sense of denying the existence of a God. I think that generally ... an agnostic would be the most correct description of my state of mind."

He didn't deny the existence of God but, clearly, had his doubts. Though he thought of religion as a kind of tribal survival strategy, Darwin still kept part of his mind, however small, open to the possibility that God was the ultimate power. However, because of all the pain and suffering he witnessed as a naturalist, he must have been disappointed that if God does exist, he is the God of the Old Testament and not the loving, merciful God as described by Jesus. Claims that Darwin had reverted back to Christianity on his sickbed were strenuously repudiated by his children and also by historians.

Chapter 10

Evolution or Intelligent Design?

The Animal Kingdom

The ichneumon wasp searches for a caterpillar which it intends to utilise for the rearing of its young. On locating a suitable host, it injects a virus and a wasp egg into the body of the caterpillar to commence incubation. The virus suppresses the caterpillar's immune system ensuring that the wasp egg is not destroyed and leads to the hatching and complete development of the immature wasp inside the caterpillar. On hatching, the larval wasp gains in strength by eating away at the caterpillar from the inside. The host is killed when the wasp is ready to pupate. Darwin questioned how anything so horrifying could possibly occur by design. What kind of designer could formulate such an aberration let alone implement it? Even Edgar Allan Poe (1809 – 1849), the American author of tales of mystery, couldn't have imagined a story so macabre.

Not every freak of nature is quite so exotic. Certain species of cuckoo are known as brood parasites in that they do not rear their own young. Their eggs are unusually thick with two distinct layers, the outer chalky layer providing a resistance to cracking when the eggs are dropped into the nests of other birds. Female parasitic cuckoos specialise in the laying of eggs that closely resemble the eggs of a chosen host, a habit that has been produced by natural selection. Without this capability, the cuckoo's egg would be thrown out of the nest by birds that are able to distinguish a foreign egg from their own. Once the cuckoo has hatched, it tends to grow more quickly than the young of the host species and, at the first opportunity, it drags them to the edge of the nest to evict them. The usurper flourishes and its companions die. It is understandable that we have arrived at this point as a result of the evolutionary process but how can anyone believe that this murder has been designed?

Herds of zebra graze on the African savannah. They are rather benign creatures in that they don't prey on other species, their survival depending on the vegetation around them. The savannah is also the habitat for lions and they, being carnivores, survive purely by predation, zebra forming part of their staple diet. A lioness with hungry cubs to feed will stealthily approach a herd and frequently select one of the weakest members. Even an animal with her speed and strength can be injured when trying to bring down a mature, male zebra so, in this case, she focuses on a 10-week old baby zebra eating alongside its mother, then charges with alarming speed. The herd scatters and there is nothing that the mother zebra can do to protect the baby who instinctively recognises the danger. It anxiously runs after its mother but within 30 metres the lioness has caught up with its prey. At this point, the terrified animal has only a couple of seconds of life left. It is clawed to the ground, its throat is torn apart and its frantic mother can only look back helplessly. This beautiful creature had lived for a mere 10 weeks. How can such slaughter be the work of a grand designer? When most human beings with their limited intelligence could propose a more compassionate, less traumatic system of life, how can it be that an omnipotent, ostensibly merciful designer, a Supreme Architect, could not?

Each year, grey whales migrate northwards to their feeding grounds with a calf alongside. Most will reach their destinations without incident but about a third will not be so fortunate, particularly if they are detected by a pod of orcas (killer whales). A mother grey and her calf are proceeding harmlessly along their route when they suddenly become aware of three orcas preparing to attack. The greys attempt to swim out of trouble but, being limited by the speed of the calf, they are quickly overhauled. The mother will not leave her calf even if she has to forfeit her own life so, in great anguish, she does all she can to protect her offspring. The terrified youngster, the target of the assault, swims as closely as possible to its mother as it has no way of protecting itself. The parent is a large animal, six times the weight of an orca and, though powerful, is relatively cumbersome. Her darting adversaries seem to be everywhere – one moment in front, the next instant at her rear. She charges at them with her huge head and drives them off momentarily with her formidable tail but, at intervals, the orcas find a way through her defences. Their aim is to drown the helpless calf which they butt and slash with every advantage. If they can turn the calf upside down so that its blowhole is submerged for a while, the hapless creature would be unable to breathe.

After four hours of violent struggle, the mother is beginning to tire whilst the orcas are relentless. How debilitating it must be for both mother and calf to be in a state of heightened terror for this length of time. Despite her heroic efforts, there was only ever going to be one outcome. The calf is eventually drowned, torn to pieces and a forlorn, exhausted mother can do nothing but continue on her journey. No one knows how long it will take for her trauma to subside. And yet, there are people who believe that this is all part of a loving Creator's design.

Sir David Attenborough, a most respected broadcaster, enjoyed a career presenting natural history programmes which endured for more than 50 years. When asked whether his observation of the natural world had given him faith in a divine Creator, he responded by making reference to the Loa loa parasitic worm, also known as the eye worm. He said:

"My response is that when Creationists talk about God creating every individual species as a separate act, they always instance hummingbirds, or orchids, sunflowers and beautiful things. But I tend to think instead of a parasitic worm that is boring through the eye of a boy sitting on the bank of a river in West Africa, a worm that's going to make him blind. And I ask them, 'Are you telling me that the God you believe in, who you also say is an all-merciful God, who cares for each one of us individually, are you saying that God created this worm that can live in no other way than in an innocent child's eyeball?' Because that doesn't seem to me to coincide with a God who's full of mercy."

In a BBC Four interview, Sir David was asked if he'd ever had any religious faith. He replied simply, "No." He also said:

"It never really occurred to me to believe in God."

In another interview he stated:

"It's true that we don't know everything but that doesn't mean that I've got to believe in some old guy with a white beard floating around on a cloud" – as depicted in Renaissance Art.

In early 2009, the BBC broadcasted an Attenborough one-hour special, *Charles Darwin and the Tree of Life*. In reference to the programme, Sir David stated that:

"People write to me that evolution is only a theory. Well, it is not a theory. Evolution is as solid a historical fact as you could conceive. Evidence comes from every quarter. What is a theory is whether natural selection is the mechanism and the only mechanism. That is a theory. But the historical reality that dinosaurs led to birds and mammals produced whales, that's not theory."

He strongly opposed creationism and its offshoot intelligent design. A survey found that a quarter of science teachers in state schools believed that creationism should be taught alongside evolution in science lessons. He called this 'really terrible'. Most people would agree with Sir David. By all means teach the history of religion and religious instruction but let us not mislead students into the belief that God's creation of the Earth in six days has any factual basis.

The Involvement of Man

Perhaps the consequences of evolution will have a more compassionate face when we see how man behaves as he takes his place at the pinnacle of the animal kingdom. Perhaps we might even see evidence of some grand design – less cruelty, less exploitation, more kindness.

Elephants are wonderful creatures and, living in family groups, they nurture their young for years before daring to allow them their independence. The largest land mammals are herbivores so they don't threaten to tear other creatures to pieces in order to feed their young. If intelligent design were a fact, it would, surely, have made all creatures more like elephants. Theirs would be a benign world enabling them to pursue as much happiness as possible as if aware that they have a limited lifespan. Instead, the evidence suggests that evolution has swept aside design and placed creatures like elephants in the minority.

One can, surely, witness no better example of happiness than baby elephants at play. They exhibit such unbridled exuberance and joy, safe in the knowledge that their mothers are nearby. No earthly creatures would dare to spoil their fun save for one and that, of course, is man. As the babies run, charge at each other and entwine their trunks, it is as if they are smiling all the while when a shot from a high velocity rifle rings out. A large female drops to the ground as the herd scatters in terror leaving a solitary baby behind. It was expecting to follow its mother but she is lying prostrate on the ground. The baby is in great distress as it tries desperately to revive its mother by tapping her with its trunk, nudging her and nuzzling against her – but nothing works. Presently, a truck arrives and the occupants hastily drive the terrified baby elephant off. The poachers have come to claim the ivory tusks which will be used to make ornaments and various utilitarian objects. A magnificent animal has died for the sake of such items or, rather, for profit.

The baby elephant is later encountered by some rangers who transport it to an elephant sanctuary. There, it is cared for day and night but it has suffered such trauma by the loss of its beloved mother that, despite the best efforts of the nurses, it cannot eat. The poor, beautiful creature, once so joyful, dies of a broken heart. And some people think all this is part of a grand design, a so-called intelligent design. What sense does that make?

Every year, between November and May, tens of thousands of harp seals are slaughtered on Canadian ice floes. The creatures are no more than babies around a fortnight old. Kill quotas set by the Canadian Department of Fisheries and Oceans have been in excess of 250,000 for a number of years. Whilst the Inuit people kill adult seals for survival, the baby seals are killed, primarily, for their fur which is sold to the world's fashion houses. The resultant fur coats are worn by people who are ignorant of the way the fur is acquired or, simply, uncaring or both.

Seal hunters are armed with a rifle or a hakapik, a fearsome weapon in the form of a heavy wooden club with a combined metal hammer head and a sharp hook. The hammer head is used to crush a baby seal's skull whilst the hook is used to snag and move the carcass. There are few more barbaric practices than a Canadian seal hunt. The defenceless creatures look pleadingly at the hunters but to no avail. After being clubbed, they are skinned and the ice floes run red with blood. It is alleged that, occasionally, the pups are skinned alive and it's probably fair to assume that anyone who could smash the skull of a beautiful creature would have little compunction in taking the next step and skinning it with its heart still beating. After all, time is money. Yes, it is easy to see how some humans could have evolved this capability but it's impossible to comprehend that they could have been specifically designed this way.

Thousands of Asiatic black bears, also known as moon bears, are kept in captivity in China and Vietnam for the harvesting of bile, a digestive juice produced by the liver and stored in the gall bladder. When extracted, the bile is a valuable commodity for sale as an ingredient in traditional Chinese medicine. The living conditions of the bears and the extraction process can only be described as heinous. The bile is usually extracted twice a day through a tube implanted into the abdomen. To facilitate the bile milking process, the bears are forced into extraction cages (also called crush cages) which are so small that they can barely move. Such is the pain these magnificent creatures have to endure that they moan, bang their heads against the sides of the cage and chew their paws. Living in such circumstances for up to 12 years or so causes severe mental stress and muscular atrophy. It was once reported in the Chinese media that a mother bear had strangled her own cub and then killed herself to spare them both from such a life. When the bears are no longer able to produce bile, they are killed and their suffering is at an end. Such exploitation is utterly heartbreaking and yet there are some people who claim, almost certainly without thinking, that this is all part of life's rich pattern, a grand design.

There seems to be no respite for the unfortunate Asiatic black bear. In Pakistan, bears are used in the cruel blood sport of bear baiting organised by powerful local landlords who own trained fighting dogs. Bear baiting is banned by the Pakistan Wildlife Act and contravenes Islamic teachings but these take second place when there is a profit to be made; the contests are as lucrative as they are brutal. During the contest, the bear is tethered by a rope which is two to five metres long to prevent any chance of escape. To even up the contest, the bear's canine teeth have been removed and its claws filed down. Experienced bears know what is to come and tremble in fearful anticipation as two powerful fighting dogs are unleashed. They throw themselves at the unfortunate creature targeting hindquarters, muzzle and ears. The handicapped bear has no advantage apart from its great strength and, if it can remain upright, each contest lasts for three minutes after which time its flesh, particularly around its muzzle, will have been badly torn. The novice bear facing its first contest has no idea what to expect when, as if from nowhere, it is confronted by two terrifying adversaries which tear into it. It squeals in pain as teeth puncture its skin and it is quickly hauled to the ground. Handlers drive the dogs off but this is only the start of the bear's agony as each bear has to endure several contests during the day. The bears suffer horrifying wounds which eventually heal only to be to be torn open again in subsequent sustained attacks. But why should religious apologists worry; it is, after all, just part of a grand design.

The list of atrocities perpetrated by mankind on other members of the animal kingdom is, virtually, endless. Tigers are an endangered species yet they are being killed to provide tiger bone for use in Chinese medicines. Another endangered species, the rhinoceros, is being slaughtered so that its horn can be used as a constituent in expensive prescriptions. There is no efficacy in the medicinal products; how could tiger bone and rhino horn possibly have greater beneficial impact than other forms of widely available calcium? It is simply that ignorant people in their tens of thousands believe in the myth that the power of these animals will, in some way, be conferred on themselves. Though completely fallacious, all that is necessary for beautiful creatures to be driven another step towards extinction is misguided belief.

There can be no sight more harrowing and heartbreaking than a rhino in a state of severe shock, its horn having been hacked off, bleeding to death and barely able to breathe. A creature of such colossal size can take a long time to die. The lucky one would be compassionately euthanased by a vigilant bush ranger; the one less fortunate would die a slow, agonising death. We see all this suffering for a morally worthless, ineffable deception. And what's God got to do with it? Well, very little it seems, although we're assured that God loves the poor, desolate, afflicted quarry. It makes you feel like crying out:

"For goodness sake, God, do something!"

Instead of inducing revelations in the minds of a handful of prophets, couldn't God provide some divine guidance to the murderous poachers, the fraudulent producers of the traditional medicines and all the ignorant, susceptible consumers? He could stop the evil trade in animal parts at a stroke. Of course, all those religious apologists out there wouldn't be able to accept such striking simplicity.   To them, God moves in mysterious ways which puny mortals could not be expected to understand and, in any case, mankind has been endowed with free will. Isn't it remarkable that when something wondrous occurs, it is imputed by these people to God's benevolence as they purport to know exactly what's in his mind? Yet, when something truly abhorrent happens, they argue that God's motives are too complex for us to comprehend. A little less free will and a little more compassion and kindness would have resulted in a far better balance in the recipe of life. Even in the United Kingdom, a country of reputed animal lovers, dogs, bewildered and terrified, have been left on motorways to perish under the wheels of onrushing traffic. Riding horses, beautiful and gentle, have been slain as they grazed by machete-wielding intruders.   It is all so agonisingly baffling yet, according to the indoctrinated, it's all just part of a grand design. And if you believe that, you'll believe anything!

Every day, billions of fearful creatures have to be exceedingly vigilant lest they are killed by predators that are simply trying to stay alive. Millions of the less fortunate meet terrifying ends so that others might live because, in reality, what we have is a world that is predicated on death. Those who believe in a Supreme Architect think of it as part of an intelligent design even though it doesn't seem at all intelligent. It may be a Merciless Design or a Thoughtless Design but how can it be called 'intelligent'? How could a merciful, omnipotent Creator design such a world? The only plausible answer seems to be that there is no design, there is only evolution which explains elegantly and completely what we see. Witnessing sectarianism and strife in 19th century Scotland, the great Andrew Carnegie kept away from organised religion and theism. Instead, he preferred to see things in naturalistic and scientific terms, stating:

"Not only had I got rid of the theology and the supernatural, but I had found the truth of evolution."

Of course, there are those among us whose belief and faith substitute as knowledge and nothing, not even direct evidence thrust at their feet, will change their minds. These people take the Book of Genesis literally and are fundamentalist creationists. Intelligent design is an offshoot of creationism and its advocates recognise that it is futile to deny the sheer weight of scientific evidence supporting evolution. Consequently, they try to usurp evolution by claiming that it is all part of the design when in fact the two cannot be reconciled; they are mutually exclusive. Evolution fully explains the timeline from the formation of Earth to the present day but evolutionary intelligent design doesn't make any sense; it is an oxymoron.   As for fundamentalist creationism, it should be consigned to the dustbin of fantasy along with the Flat Earthers whilst the intelligent designers, having been trumped by evolution, should look for another theory. Perhaps they will find one that answers the question that has exercised philosophers for centuries. Perhaps they will solve the conundrum which asks why an omniscient, omnipotent God needed billions of years to render planet Earth habitable when it would be expected to take only seconds. Nobody, however, is holding their breath in anticipation.

Whilst the most compelling argument against any form of supernatural design is the monumental elapse time before the appearance of mankind, what about the design of mankind itself? Meniscal and articular cartilage wears away in our joints, our fingers become arthritic, our bones become brittle, our arteries clog with detritus and we succumb to a plethora of diseases long before our lives have run their potential course. There's not much evidence of omniscient design here is there, given the countless modifications that mere mortals could suggest?

Early in the 21st century, average life expectancy in the United Kingdom was fast approaching 80 years (leaving aside differences of gender). In Medieval Britain, the figure was only 30 years with a high rate of infant mortality and women frequently dying in childbirth. Other significant factors were untreatable diseases, malnutrition and injuries sustained in accidents which caused infection or were beyond the scope of the medical help available. By the early 1900's, the average life expectancy had barely changed at 31 years. The genetics of humans and the rate of aging were no different in pre-industrial societies than today but early deaths continued until the 20th century when startling advances in medical science and general standards of living took place. It is evident, therefore, that the vast increase in life expectancy can in no way be imputed to design. Medical and surgical techniques, genetics and efficacious drug development are by far the greatest contributors. Anatomically enfeebled and with an immune system vulnerable to all manner of viruses and bacteria, humans cannot be the product of good design. Dionysus, the god of the grape harvest and wine making, could scarcely have made a worse attempt, and he was inebriated most of the time.

Though humans are by far the most intelligent members of the animal kingdom, they have brains which are under-developed and, consequently, are simply not intelligent enough. To counteract this contention, some might point to mankind's huge achievements; jet planes, skyscrapers, ocean-going liners, vast bridges, computers, satellites and magnificent churches, to name but a few. It should be borne in mind, however, that developments such as these were brought to fruition by relatively few, extremely talented individuals, a tiny fraction of the world's population, past and present. Most people have but limited applicative intelligence and, unfortunately, for the world at large, their rational thought too frequently succumbs to emotion, resulting in pointless anger and hatred. Imagine if the intellect of a Newton or a Spinoza were but the average. Unimpeded by the obscurantism of the church, scientific discoveries would have occurred hundreds of years earlier and the moon landings, for example, might have taken place in the 18th century. The Great War would not have taken place, neither would World War II. Religion would have died long ago and, most likely, there would have been no mad priests. There would have been no religious hatred, no slavery and people of a different race or skin colour would simply have been regarded as superficially, but not fundamentally, different. Whenever a 'different' person was encountered, the observer's brain would have resolved the image transmitted by the eyes into just another human being. Certainly, our limited intelligence countermands arguments for design whilst evidence from the beginning of human history to the present day indicates that continuous improvement has occurred. By extrapolation, we can adduce that our average intelligence is evolving to a higher plane, to a level that might have been conferred on us had we been the product of a supernatural design.

The issue of disease is worth expounding because *it* doesn't make any sense in terms of design either. Consider the Black Death, for example, one of the most devastating pandemics in human history, peaking in Europe between 1348 and 1350. While there were several competing theories as to the etiology of the Black Death, analysis of ancient DNA from plague victims has conclusively proven that the pathogen responsible was the *Yersinia pestis* bacterium. It is thought to have started in China and travelled along the Silk Road to reach the Crimea by 1346. From there, it spread throughout the Mediterranean and Europe, probably carried by Oriental rat fleas living on the black rats inhabiting merchant ships. The Black Death, a bubonic plague, is estimated to have killed up to 60 percent (around 100 million) of Europe's population. The plague returned at various times, killing more people until it left Europe in the 19th century. The Great Plague (1665–1666) was the last major epidemic of the bubonic plague to occur in the England, killing an estimated 100,000 people.

If the *Yersinia pestis* bacterium had been just a few percentage points more virulent, the whole of Europe (and possibly the world) could have been extirpated. Today, mosquitoes act as a vehicle for many disease-causing viruses and parasites as they transfer these organisms from one person to another without themselves exhibiting any symptoms. Mosquito-borne diseases include yellow fever, dengue fever, malaria and lymphatic filarisis, the main cause of elephantiasis. Mosquitoes are estimated to transmit disease to more than 700 million people annually in Africa, South America, Central America, Mexico, Russia and much of Asia resulting in millions of deaths. How can this be called design? Did God really create man on Earth to co-exist with countless micro-organisms endowed with the capacity to wipe him out? If, for some inexplicable reason, it suited God's purpose to fill the world with bacteria, wouldn't it have made sense to equip humans with a prophylactic immune system instead of the delicate one afforded us? You can approach these questions from every conceivable angle but, however much time you spend in thought and debate, you can conclude only that any real evidence of design (let alone a loving, merciful deity's design) is impossible to find.

There are countless designs that would have been preferable to the world we inhabit today. For a start, the whole of the animal kingdom could have been herbivores which, at a stroke, would have obviated the pain and terror suffered daily by millions of creatures because of predation. A plentiful supply of plant life would have been easy to summon by an omnipotent deity. Imagine a world without famine, without killer whales tearing seals apart, without crocodiles drowning and devouring wildebeest and without raptors killing blue tits and water voles. Imagine the words of Thomas Jefferson's United States Declaration of Independence, '…inalienable Rights, that among these are Life, Liberty and the pursuit of Happiness' being extended beyond humanity to all the creatures on Earth. Instead, we have world in which his ideal has never even been achieved by mankind, let alone the animals. Everything becomes clear when one takes the view that there is no design because no all-powerful, all-knowing supernatural being could possibly have designed the interminably flawed natural world we have today, taken billions of years in its making and be tinkering with it still. The most elegant explanation of such unmanaged, unmitigated randomness is, clearly, afforded by Darwinian evolution, the very antithesis of design.

Of course, had mammals suddenly appeared millions of years ago, fully formed as we see them today in all their variety and complexity, the case for a Supreme Architect would be incontrovertible. Instantaneous formation of something as stupefyingly intricate as a horse, for example, would be the very definition of 'supernatural'. However, because of countless scientific discoveries, we know that this is not what happened. Many millions of years ago, the horse would have started life as something as simple as a single-celled micro-organism and evolved, in time, through a vast number of mutations into the beautiful creature we currently behold. Along with other mammals, it purports a seemingly infinite complexity, no longer comprising a single cell, but billions. It is clearly a product of evolution, not of design.

Every day products such as automobiles, passenger aircraft and railway trains are always subject to copious design before they are manufactured. Even here, however, it is evolution that plays by far the most significant part. The current designs were developed on the foundations provided by thousands of earlier designs stretching back over centuries. Isaac Newton (1642 -1727), one of the most influential scientists in history, recognised the importance of evolution when he said:

"If I have seen farther it is by standing on the shoulders of giants."

Newton was a man of vast intelligence but, constrained by the technology of his day, there was no way he could have designed a modern automobile. Science had much more work to do before that could be achieved. As he stated:

"To explain all nature is too difficult a task for any one man or even for any one age. 'Tis much better to do a little with certainty, and leave the rest for others that come after you, than to explain all things by conjecture without making sure of anything."

The one step at a time process of evolution explains everything about the natural world, from its mountains, seas and rivers to all its inhabitants. Thousands of years ago, the Americas were attached to the continents of Europe and Africa and thousands of years hence, our mountain ranges, for example, will look entirely different. The infinite complexity should not be misappropriated to supernatural design because it is implicit that, with the benefit of omniscience and omnipotence, constant redesign would be superfluous. Continual redesign (which is what we have) leads us to the conclusion that the Creator's initial design was flawed but that, of course, would be a contradiction. After billions of years of change, we've still ended up with Al-Qaeda, the Klu Klux Klan and Anders Behring Breivik, the Norwegian mass murderer. The English author, Thomas Hardy (1840 – 1928), put it a little differently in his poem, *Christmas: 1924*, when he wrote:

"After two thousand years of mass, we've got as far as poison gas."

What could God possibly have to do with all this change? Moreover, when some people attest that the world's sheer complexity is proof of design, they should reflect on the fact that good design equates to less complexity, not more. On this basis, one has little alternative but to conclude that there was no initial design. Only the evolutionary process fully accommodates and explains the inexorable change, variety and complexity witnessed on our planet and will continue to do so.

The Flying Spaghetti Monster

The Flying Spaghetti Monster is the deity of the parody religion, the Church of the Flying Spaghetti Monster or Pastafarianism. It first appeared in a satirical letter, written by Bobby Henderson in 2005, as a protest against a decision by the Kansas State Board of Education to allow the teaching of intelligent design as an alternative to evolution in state school science classes. In the letter, he parodied the intelligent design concept by professing belief in a supernatural creator that comprised spaghetti and meatballs. He, furthermore, requested that Flying Spaghetti Monsterism should be appropriated equal time in the classroom alongside intelligent design and evolution.

Pastafarian 'beliefs' are, in general, satires on creationism. The central tenet is that an invisible and undetectable Flying Spaghetti Monster created the universe. Pirates are revered as the original Pastafarians (a portmanteau of pasta and Rastafarian) and it is claimed that the steady decline in the number of pirates over the years has resulted in global warming. Because of its wide appeal, the Flying Spaghetti Monster is often used as a contemporary version of Russell's teapot, the vehicle for the philosophical argument which posits that theories that cannot be falsified must be proven true by those who propose them, or be rejected. Whilst praised by the media and endorsed by scientists, the Flying Spaghetti Monster has, unsurprisingly, offended members of the intelligent design community.

Bobby Henderson was a 24-year old Oregon State University physics graduate when he wrote his letter to the Kansas State Board. The letter was sent in time for the Kansas evolution hearings as an argument against the teaching of intelligent design in biology classes. He described himself as a 'concerned citizen' representing more than ten million others and argued that his theory and intelligent design were equally valid. In his letter he noted:

"I think we can all look forward to the time when these three theories are given equal time in our science classrooms across the country, and eventually the world; one third time for intelligent design, one third time for Flying Spaghetti Monsterism and one third time for logical conjecture based on overwhelming observable evidence."

According to Henderson, since the intelligent design movement uses ambiguous references to a designer, any conceivable entity could fulfill the same function including a Flying Spaghetti Monster. Henderson explained:

"I don't have a problem with religion. What I have a problem with is religion posing as science. If there is a god and he's intelligent, then I would guess he has a sense of humour."

When Bobby Henderson received no reply from the Kansas State Board, he displayed the letter on his website and it did not take long before Pastafarianism became an internet phenomenon. This prompted responses from the Board members which he also published. Three members, all of whom were opposed to changes to the curriculum, responded favourably whilst a fourth member replied:

"It is a serious offence to mock God."

Within a year of his website publications, Henderson received tens of thousands of emails about 95 percent of which supported his views. The remainder constituted hate mail, a proportion of which were tantamount to death threats. The website garnered tens of millions of hits and as public awareness grew exponentially, the mainstream media began to express interest in the phenomenon. Henderson's original letter was published in many large circulation newspapers including the New York Times, the Washington Post and the Chicago Sun-Times. In consequence, the Flying Spaghetti Monster became a symbol for the case against the teaching of intelligent design in school education. The newspaper articles attracted the attention of book publishers and, at one point, no fewer than six publishers courted the Flying Spaghetti Monster. In November 2005, Henderson received an $80,000 advance from Villard to write a book. The book, entitled *The Gospel of the Flying Spaghetti Monster,* was released on the 28th March, 2006 and has sold over 100,000 copies. It begins with the creation of the universe by an invisible and undetectable Flying Spaghetti Monster. On the first day, the Flying Spaghetti Monster separated the water from the heavens. On the second, because he could not tread water for long and had grown tired of flying, he created the land complemented by a beer volcano. Satisfied, the Flying Spaghetti Monster overindulged in beer and woke up with a hangover. Between drunken nights and clumsy afternoons, the Flying Spaghetti Monster, accidentally, produced seas and land for a second time because he forgot that he had created them the day before.

He also created Heaven and a midget which he named Man. Man and an equally short woman lived happily in the Olive Garden of Eden for some time until the Flying Spaghetti Monster caused a global flood in a cooking accident.

The creation, claimed by Pastafarians to be only 5,000 years ago, is considered laughable by most scientists. To this, Henderson satirically retorts that the Flying Spaghetti Monster presented evidence contrary to scientific opinion in order to test Pastafarians' faith. In addition to parodying certain biblical literalists, Henderson uses his unorthodox method to lampoon intelligent design proponents who, he asserts, first 'define their conclusion and then gather evidence to support it'. When scientific measurements such as radiocarbon dating are taken, the Flying Spaghetti Monster tampers with the results using his Noodly Appendage. The Pastafarian conception of Heaven includes a beer volcano and a stripper factory. The Pastafarian Hell is quite similar but, in this case, the beer is stale and the strippers have sexually transmitted diseases.

The book contains the Eight 'I'd Really Rather You Didn'ts', strict adherence to which enables Pastafarians to ascend to Heaven. According to *The Gospel*, Mosey, the Pirate Captain, received 10 stone tablets as instruction from the Flying Spaghetti Monster. Of the original 10 'I'd Really Rather You Didn'ts', two were dropped and broken on the way down from Mount Salsa. This event accounts, in part, for Pastafarians' feeble moral standards. The advice addresses a broad array of behaviour from sexual conduct to nutrition. One commandment is:

"I'd really rather you didn't build multi-million dollar synagogues, churches, temples, mosques, shrines to His Noodly Goodness when the money could be better spent ending poverty, curing diseases, living in peace, loving with passion and lowering the cost of cable."

According to Pastafarian beliefs, pirates are 'absolute divine beings' and became the original Pastafarians. Furthermore, Pastafarians believe that the pirates' image, tarnished as 'thieves and outcasts', is misinformation disseminated by Christian theologians in the Middle Ages and by Hare Krishnas. Instead, Pastafarians believe that they were 'peace-loving explorers and spreaders of good will' who distributed candy to small children adding that modern pirates do not resemble 'the fun-loving buccaneers from history'. Furthermore, they believe that ghost pirates are responsible for the mysterious disappearance of ships and planes in the Bermuda Triangle. They celebrate International Talk Like a Pirate Day on the 19th September each year.

The inclusion of pirates in Pastafarianism was part of Henderson's original letter to illustrate that correlation does not imply causation. He proposed that global warming, earthquakes, hurricanes and other natural disasters are a direct effect of the shrinking numbers of pirates since the 1800's. A chart accompanying the letter illustrated a fascinating correlation: as the number of pirates decreased, global temperatures increased. This parodies the much-proffered suggestion from some faith groups that the high numbers of disasters, famines and wars in the world are due to the dwindling role of religion. In 2008, Henderson claimed the growing pirate activities in the Gulf of Aden as confirmation, pointing out that Somalia has 'the highest number of pirates and the lowest carbon emissions of any country'.

The point of Henderson's letter was that there is no more scientific evidence for intelligent design than there is for the notion that an omnipotent, omniscient being made of pasta and meatballs created the universe. If intelligent design advocates could demand a platform in a science class, why not anyone else? The only acceptable solution is to put nothing into science classes but the best available science. The great Thomas Jefferson would have approved of Henderson's use of parody and satire because he once said:

"Ridicule is the only weapon which can be used against unintelligible propositions. Ideas must be distinct before reason can act upon them; and no man ever had a distinct idea of the trinity. It is the mere Abracadabra of the mountebanks calling themselves the priests of Jesus."

The probability that a Flying Spaghetti Monster actually exists is about the same as that for the parting of the Red Sea, the creation of Adam from dust or, according to Islam, a drop of congealed blood. All are infinitesimally small yet, whilst few believe in His Noodly Goodness, many millions believe the literal words of ancient scriptures. The real purpose of the Flying Spaghetti Monster is to provoke rational thought, to encourage people to question rather than accept everything at face value. Where did the congealed blood come from, by the way?

It seems that intelligent design has been dealt a severe blow by the Henderson satire and, if so, it means that more people are facing reality instead of indulging in the pure fantasy of the paranormal. There are, of course, places that will never learn of the Flying Spaghetti Monster, cocooned as they are from his idiosyncrasies, which is a pity. Some people just seem to live in a world of their own. In August 2011, a story emerged in the USA about four-year old Kanon Tipton who first held a microphone at his family's church when he was just 21 months old. From then on, he developed a reputation as a preacher and appeared on NBC's *The Today Show*. When his parents were asked if Kanon had a true calling for the ministry or whether he was merely mimicking what he had seen from others, his father, Pastor Damon Tipton said:

"I think it's a little of both … I do feel like the hand of God is on him in a special way."

At least Pastor Damon acknowledged the mimesis. The story of Kanon found its way from the USA, across the Atlantic, to ITV's *News at Ten*, the producers of which thought it significant enough to displace other news items. In the recording, Kanon resembled a 30-year old midget with an oversized microphone in his hand as he exclaimed, in his deepest voice:

"Praise the Lord." "The one true God" and several similar phrases.

The audience was in raptures believing they were witnessing a rare talent that had been kissed by the angels. Or, was it all just a little weird? Kanon was the third generation of preachers in his family and, given his fascination for the microphone, there didn't seem to be much chance of a normal childhood ahead. There may, however, have been 'method in the madness' because, by the time he actually reaches 30, he may well have stashed away millions of dollars in appearance money.

Chapter 11

The Dénouement

The Debate about Belief

Gloria Hunniford, the well known Irish radio and television personality, had the misfortune to lose her lovely daughter, Caron Keating, to breast cancer. Her faith seems to have helped her through her grief as she believed that Caron was in a good place. After Stephen Hawking had stated, in effect, that the universe did not need God, Gloria pointed out during a TV debate that, equally, Stephen Hawking could not disprove the existence of God. She was absolutely right, of course, but was she missing the point? Does it actually make sense to believe in something just because you can neither prove nor falsify its existence? The onus was not on Stephen Hawking to prove that God doesn't exist; rather it was on Gloria Hunniford to prove that he does exist or, at least, explain why she believed he exists.

Russell's teapot is an analogy first proffered by the philosopher, Bertrand Russell, to illustrate the notion that the philosophical burden of proof lies with a person making claims that cannot be scientifically falsified rather than shifting it to sceptical others, specifically in the case of religion. Russell wrote that if he claimed a teapot were orbiting the Sun somewhere in space between the Earth and Mars, it would be nonsensical for him to expect others to believe him on the grounds that they could not prove him wrong. Russell's teapot is still referred to in discussions concerning the existence of God. It has attracted criticism, particularly from those who missed the point of his argument, for comparing God's existence to that of a teapot. He did not, however, seek to trivialise God but to emphasise that the burden of proof relating to something's existence lies with the believer, whether that belief is in an orbiting teapot or in God.

In an article entitled, *Is There a God?*, Russell wrote, in 1952:
"Many orthodox people speak as though it were the business of sceptics to disprove received dogmas rather than of dogmatists to prove them. This is, of course, a mistake. If I were to suggest that between the Earth and Mars there is a china teapot revolving about the sun in an elliptical orbit, nobody would be able to disprove my assertion provided I were careful to add that the teapot is too small to be revealed even by our most powerful telescopes. But if I were to go on to say that, since my assertion cannot be disproved, it is intolerable presumption on the part of human reason to doubt it, I should rightly be thought to be talking nonsense. If, however, the existence of such a teapot were affirmed in ancient books, taught as the sacred truth every Sunday, and instilled into the minds of children at school, hesitation to believe in its existence would become a mark of eccentricity and entitle the doubter to the attentions of the psychiatrist in an enlightened age or of the Inquisitor in an earlier time."

In 1958, Russell elaborated on the analogy as a reason for his own atheism. He stated:

"I ought to call myself an agnostic; but, for all practical purposes, I am an atheist. I do not think the existence of the Christian God any more probable than the existence of the Gods of Olympus or Valhalla. To take another illustration, nobody can prove that there is not between the Earth and Mars a china teapot revolving in an elliptical orbit, but nobody thinks this sufficiently likely to be taken into account in practice. I think the Christian God just as unlikely."

During a Sunday morning BBC TV programme, in 2011, called *The Big Questions*, the host, Nicky Campbell, asked one of the participants if she believed in God. She replied:

"No, because I'm not stupid."

It wasn't the most diplomatic answer, given that several members of the audience were devout believers. Perhaps, she really meant to say that she'd given the question a great deal of thought over several years and had come to the conclusion that, owing to lack of evidence, she was unable to believe that God exists. Campbell asked the same question about the existence of God several months later, in January 2012, during a new series of the programme. Initially, the question was addressed, somewhat circumspectly, to the Reverend Dr. Andrew Pinsent, eminent physicist and theologian, who failed to answer convincingly why he was a believer. By referring to the scientists, Georges Lemaitre (1894 – 1966) and Gregor Mendel (1822 – 1884), he postulated that science and faith could co-exist without conflict. Lemaitre was a Belgian Catholic priest who was the first to propose the Big Bang theory for the origin of the universe.   Gregor Mendel, an Austrian Augustinian friar, gained posthumous fame as the founder of the science of genetics.   However, Dr. Pinsent failed to explain why *he* believed in the existence of God. Campbell tried again, in a different way, by asking:

"Dr. Andrew Pinsent, what can only be explained by God?"

Dr. Pinsent's answer, again indirect, tangentially alluded to materialism being prevalent in societies without God.   Had he never heard of Buddhism?   The question asked of Dr. Pinsent demanded an answer in the affirmative, not the negative; that is, 'with God', not 'without God'. He may have intended to be deftly evasive; otherwise, one could only assume that some form of scientific-theological schizophrenia had stultifyingly affected his reasoning.   He must have been asked a similar question a thousand times, so one would have expected a well-rehearsed answer to be somewhat more cogent.   The author, broadcaster and journalist, David Aaronovitch, gently admonished the good doctor by stating:

"Aren't you just saying that you prefer a society in which people believe in God?   You're not actually suggesting that there is any evidence for God.   The evidence is that man created God and continues to create God."

From that point, the sophistry of the believers continued unabated. Campbell asked someone described as a Muslim thinker:

"What's the greatest piece of evidence you can bring to the table for the existence of God?"

The thinker replied that it was the origin of the universe, the Big Bang, because every cause had to have a causer (in this case God). When Campbell cleverly asked:

"Then what caused God?" the best reply that the thinker could muster was:

"Well, that's a ridiculous question."

Completely outflanked, the thinker clearly hadn't previously applied much thought to this most fundamental question and contributed little further to the debate. A Muslim from the Manchester Mosque contended that the Quran made reference to the Big Bang which was a controlled explosion (controlled by God) resulting in a predictable outcome rather than, presumably, the unpredictable outcome of the Hiroshima atom bomb (which was, in fact, fairly predictable). Former Anglican bishop, the Right Reverend Stephen Lowe, stated that he becomes elevated by a piece of beautiful music and considered that as proof of the existence of God. Is that a proof; did he really believe that atheists are musically illiterate, incapable of appreciating Mozart and Beethoven? One supposes the reverend wouldn't include Lennon's *Imagine* as one of his beautiful and uplifting pieces given its anti-religious sentiments which, had they been realised, would have put him out of a job.

A preacher, a former triad gangster, explained that when he was in prison, God spoke to him and changed his life. An atheist comedian remarked:

"What a shame that God didn't speak to you *before* you committed all your crimes."

The preacher claimed that he, at least, believed in something whereas atheists believe in nothing and, directing a question at David Aaronovitch, he asked:

"What do you believe in, David?"

Aaronovitch replied that he didn't believe in God but he had been asked 'what he believed in', not 'what he didn't believe in'. Again, he should also have answered in the affirmative and, by failing to do so, he had missed an opportunity to put the former gangster and preacher 'on the back foot'. He should have said:

"I believe in lots of things. I believe in human rights, in liberty, morality, tolerance, respect for the individual and in being kind to people. I just don't happen to believe in God, nor do I believe that God is a precondition to the things I've just mentioned."

By the end of the programme, the unbelievers had, by applying logic and reason, routed the sophistry of the dogmatists. The arguments for God amounted to the effects of materialism, the origin of the universe, musically elevated feelings and a voice from an invisible source. Despite such abstraction, the believers remained as convinced as ever that God exists which is hardly surprising given that no belief is as strong as that which requires no evidence. As Voltaire said:

"The truths of religion are never so well understood as by those who have lost the power of reasoning."

The Analysis into God's Existence

During his latter years, Thomas Jefferson wrote:

"Fix Reason firmly in her seat, and call to her tribunal every fact, every opinion. Question with boldness even the existence of a God; because, if there be one, he must more approve the homage of reason than of blindfolded fear. Do not be frightened from this inquiry by any fear of its consequences. If it end in a belief that there is no God, you will find incitements to virtue in the comfort and pleasantness you feel in its exercise and in the love of others which it will procure for you."

Clearly, Jefferson was doubtful about God's existence though he realised also that his thought processes would not lead him to a definitive answer. How can you verify the unverifiable or refute the irrefutable? William of Ockham (1288 – 1348), an English Franciscan friar and scholastic philosopher, would have agreed. He is regarded, along with Thomas Aquinas, as being one of the greatest thinkers of medieval times. Unlike Aquinas, however, he did not advocate killing people who did not share his religious views. With regard to faith and reason, he wrote:

"The ways of God are not open to reason, for God has freely chosen to create a world and establish a way of salvation within it apart from any necessary laws that human logic or rationality can uncover."

Ockham's views on apostolic poverty brought him into conflict with the Catholic Church. His controversial doctrine was a challenge to the wealth of the church and its consequent corruption. Despite the fact that Jesus and his apostles had little wealth, apostolic poverty was condemned as heresy in 1323 and, fearing confinement and possible execution, Ockham fled from Avignon to the court of the Holy Roman Emperor, Louis IV of Bavaria. Whilst under the protection and patronage of the court, Ockham wrote a number of treatises proposing that Louis should have supreme control over the church and state in his empire. This was too much for Pope John XXII. Having already been indirectly criticised for his lavish lifestyle, pomp and finery, he excommunicated Ockham who spent the rest of his life writing about political issues encompassing the relative authority and rights of the spiritual and temporal powers.

Voltaire stated:
"If God did not exist, it would be necessary to invent Him."

Given his abundant wit and gift for satire, he probably meant that God doesn't exist and has been invented. In other words, it was man that created God, rather than vice versa. Throughout history, there have been attempts to prove the existence of God, all of which have proven futile owing to the lack of any empirical evidence. Arguments for and against have been proposed by philosophers, theologians, scientists and many others involving, at different times, epistemology, metaphysics, its sub-discipline ontology, and logic.

Some scientists believe that evidence for God should be readily detectable by scientific means and if a properly controlled experiment derived an observation that could not be explained naturally, science would have to take seriously the possibility of a supernatural world. Such experiments have been attempted. For example, scientists have empirically tested the efficacy of intercessory prayer aimed at healing the sick in double-blind (bias eliminated), placebo controlled trials. The results showed that prayer had no effect whatsoever and, though the trials cast considerable doubt on God's existence, they did not and could not prove conclusively that he does not exist. It may be that God wasn't answering prayers at the time of the trials, or refused to 'play ball' or that he never answers prayers, anyway. Similar trials have been performed involving near-death experiences but all observations had perfectly natural explanations.

Scientists argue that there is nothing in the world attributable to God that cannot be better explained by Darwinian evolution and that the intelligent design lobby (a resignation to 'if you can't beat 'em, join 'em') has been exposed as nothing more than chicanery. Theists claim that the parameters of the universe are fine-tuned for human life but scientists attest the reverse is true; we are fine-tuned for the universe. The conclusion is that the universe and life look exactly as they would be expected to look if there were no God. Over millennia, many people have reported mystical experiences during which they have communicated with one god or another. By now, we should have observed some confirmation of these phenomena, some evidence such as a verifiable fact that could not possibly have entered a person's mind unless by numinous revelation. This has never been achieved. The reformed triad gangster turned preacher, when claiming that God spoke to him in his prison cell, said:

"It was as if my cellmate was a ventriloquist or something."

A member of the audience instantly quipped:

"Which he might have been, of course," highlighting the unproven veracity of the basis of the preacher's conviction.

For all the powerful scientific arguments, however, conclusive proof, one way or the other, remains elusive. Perhaps, instead of attempting to establish the existence or non-existence of God with absolute certainty, we would be better served by trying to establish a probability for God. Whilst there is no absolute empirical evidence, an assessment, albeit subjectively derived, can be made on the basis of the available circumstantial evidence. A 'black box' approach, used by various disciplines from engineering to matters mysterious, can be used for the purposes of evaluation. The hypothesis would be that if God exists, he exists inside the box; if he does not exist, the box is empty. We can't see inside the box so we can only make a judgement as to whether anything exists within it on the basis of what happens outside the box. Arguments for and against God's existence can be evaluated by taking into account these external factors and the substance of each case. Individual arguments should be rated using the following scale as a guide:

0.   It is certain that God exists.
1.   It is almost certain that God exists.
2.   It is very likely that God exists.
3.   It is quite likely that God exists
4.   It is probable that God exists
5.   There is only a 50 percent likelihood of God's existence
6.   It is probable that God does not exist
7.   It is quite likely that God does not exist
8.   It is very likely that God does not exist
9.   It is almost certain that God does not exist
10. It is certain that God does not exist

Arguments for the Existence of God:

The Cosmological Argument has been used by many theologians and philosophers over the centuries including Plato, Aristotle and Thomas Aquinas. It postulates that since the universe exists, there must have been a first cause (an uncaused cause or an unmoved mover) and this must be God.

The first three of the Aquinas Five Proofs (*Quinque viae*) relate to the cosmological argument. The first 'proof' (the unmoved mover) attempts to explain motion in the universe and states:

- Some things are in motion.
- Everything that is moving is moved by something else.
- An infinite regress of movers is impossible.
- Therefore, there is an unmoved mover from whom all motion proceeds.
- This mover is called God.

The second 'proof' (the first cause) tries to explain the cause or creation of the universe and states:

- Some things are caused.
- Everything that is caused is caused by a causer.
- An infinite regress of causation is impossible.
- Therefore, there must be an uncaused cause of all that is caused.
- This causer is called God.

The third 'proof' (contingency) posits much the same as the first two and states:

- Many things in the universe may either exist or not exist. These are called contingent beings.
- Every contingent being fails to exist at some time. It is impossible, therefore, for everything in the universe to be contingent, for then

there would be a time when nothing existed, and so nothing would exist now, which is clearly false.

- Therefore, there must be a necessary being whose existence is not contingent on any other being.
- This being is called God.

Virtually all scientific discoveries have taken place during the last 300 years so that any knowledge that Aquinas possessed was extremely primitive. He would have understood nothing, for example, of abiogenesis, the study of how biological life arises from inorganic matter through natural processes. Most amino acids, often called the 'building blocks of life', form via natural chemical reactions and, in all living things, are organised into proteins. Life on our planet would, almost certainly, have started by such means, from the humblest of beginnings and wouldn't have needed any intervention from God. The first living things are thought to have been single-celled prokaryotes and reliable fossil evidence has been found in rocks 3.4 billion years old. Nor would Aquinas have known anything of the origin of the universe, the Big Bang, so he simply attributed it to God. Indeed, whilst current scientists believe they can explain the characteristics of the universe immediately after its inception entailing inconceivable pressure, temperature and energy density, they are unable to postulate a cause of the event. It is quite possible that science may never establish an answer but does that mean that the knowledge gap needs, inevitably, to be filled by God? According to Stephen Hawking, God wasn't needed by the Big Bang; nor was he needed by the chemical reactions from which life on Earth arose. So, has God been sidelined? Well, not according to Aquinas, of course, who either failed to recognise or chose to ignore the knockout blow to his cosmological arguments. To curtail the infinite regress, he introduced God without ever addressing the blatantly obvious question: "So, who or what created God?"

By failing to fully acknowledge the question of the regress, the Aquinas 'proofs' are, in effect, diluted to:
"God exists because I believe he exists."

An assessment of the flimsy cosmological argument, therefore, derives a score of between 9 and 10, though nearer to 10.

Score = 9.95

The Argument from Degree is the fourth of the Aquinas 'proofs' and states that there must exist a being that possesses all properties to the maximum possible degree. The elements of the argument are:

- Varying perfections of varying degrees may be found throughout the universe.
- These degrees assume the existence of an ultimate perfection.
- Therefore, perfection must have a pinnacle.
- This pinnacle is called God.

In other words, Aquinas believes that God exists and he cannot conceive of anything more perfect. What kind of argument is this other than a completely worthless one? Clearly, it is not evident that simply because we can conceive of an object with some property to an inestimable degree, that such an object exists. It might as well be claimed that the most perfect thing we can imagine is the Flying Spaghetti Monster, particularly by lovers of spaghetti and meat balls and, therefore, it must exist. Since when do thoughts and conceptions imply reality? The argument from degree is so flawed that its assessment derives a score near to 10.

Score = 9.95

The Teleological Argument posits that the order and complexity of the universe are best explained by reference to a creator God; that the universe exhibits aspects of design. The Thomas Aquinas 'proof' is as follows:

- All natural bodies in the world have objectives.

- These bodies are not in themselves intelligent.

- Acting towards an end is characteristic of intelligence.

- Therefore, there exists an intelligent being that guides all natural bodies towards their objectives.

- This being is called God.

In typical Aquinas fashion, he starts with the premise that God exists and then, with no knowledge of cosmology, geology and palaeontology, for example, and little knowledge of the natural world, he makes spurious assumptions to support his argument. David Hume (1711 – 1776), the great Scottish philosopher, historian and economist, presented a criticism of the teleological argument in his *Dialogues Concerning Natural Religion*. The character Philo, a religious sceptic, voices Hume's criticisms. He contends that the design argument is built upon a flawed analogy as, unlike with man-made objects, we have not witnessed the design of a universe so we cannot tell whether the universe was the result of design. Moreover, the sheer size of the universe makes the

analogy unsafe.   Although our experience of the universe is of order,
there may be chaos elsewhere. Philo argues:

"A very small part of this great system, during a very short time, is very
imperfectly discovered to us; and do we thence pronounce decisively
concerning the origin of the whole?"

Philo further proposes that any order in nature may be due to nature
alone. If nature contains a principle of order within it, the need for a
designer is removed. Philo further posits that if the universe is indeed
designed, it is unreasonable to conclude that the designer must be an
omnipotent, omniscient, benevolent God. Hume also contended that the
argument does not necessarily lead to the existence of one God by
stating:

"Why may not several deities combine in contriving and framing the
world?"

When Philo proposed that the order in nature might be due to nature
alone, his insight was compliant with Darwinian evolution. Without the
benefit of science and portent, the Aquinas bias is understandable
though, in line with most other ecclesiastical pedants, it is likely he
would have vigorously opposed any evidence that ran counter to his
religious views.

The teleological argument proposes that the universe and natural
world exhibit design features and that, therefore, a designer must exist.
However, the claims can be shown to be fallacious in a number of ways:

- Scrutiny of the appearance of a vast entity to determine whether it
  has been designed is subjective, open to conjecture, equivocal and
  inconclusive.

- Just because there is a perception of design in the eyes of the beholder is not proof of design.

- When observing the night sky, one cannot fail to be impressed by its sheer randomness. Had it been subject to design, one would have anticipated at least a modicum of symmetry; but there is none.

- We have been able to observe but a tiny fraction of the universe and, even if a semblance of design were perceived, it does not mean that the undisclosed parts exhibit similar indications.

- Our observations of distant parts of the universe can convey to us only the characteristics as they were millions of years ago. Any hint of design (however arguable) could long since have been ceded to randomness and chaos.

- If our natural world has been designed, the design is error strewn as it is riddled with countless imperfections including catastrophic events, predation, disease and killer micro-organisms.

- An omnipotent, benevolent God would not design anything with inherent imperfection.

It can, in fact, be argued that there is no evidence of design in the cosmos or our natural world, whatsoever; that there is no evidence of an intelligent designer and that all natural phenomena are more concisely and persuasively explained by Darwinian evolution. An assessment of the teleological argument derives a score of between 9 and 10.

Score = 9.90

The Ontological Argument starts simply with a concept of God and is formulated to show that if it is logically possible for God to exist, then he must exist. There are a number of variations of the ontological argument though the exact criteria for their categorisation are not widely agreed. Typically, however, the arguments start with a definition of God and conclude with his necessary existence using *a priori* reasoning i.e. with no reference to empirical observations of the world. It is widely accepted that the first ontological argument was proposed by Anselm of Canterbury (1033 – 1109), a Benedictine monk, philosopher and Archbishop of Canterbury for 16 years until his death. He posited the following:

- No greater being than God can be conceived.
- The idea of God exists in the mind.
- A being that exists both in the mind and in reality is greater than a being that exists solely in the mind.
- If God only exists in the mind, then we can conceive of a greater being, one which exists in reality.
- We cannot imagine something that is greater than God.
- Therefore, God exists.

Avicenna (980 – 1037), the most famous and influential polymath of the Islamic Golden Age, developed his own ontological variation. Rene Descartes composed a number of ontological arguments which differed from the Anselm formulation. He wrote in the *Fifth Meditation*:

"But, if the mere fact that I can produce from my thought the idea of something that entails everything that I clearly and distinctly perceive to belong to that thing really does belong to it, is not this a possible basis for another argument to prove the existence of God? Certainly, the idea of God, or a supremely perfect being, is one that I find within me just as surely as the idea of any shape or number. And my understanding that it belongs to his nature that he always exists is no less clear and distinct than is the case when I prove of any shape or number that some property belongs to its nature."

The great German mathematician and philosopher, Gottfried Wilhelm Leibniz (1646 – 1716), did not entirely agree with the Descartes argument. However, he reasoned that since it is possible for all perfections to exist in a single entity, the argument was valid. Mulla Sadra (1572 – 1640), the Persian Shia Islamic philosopher and theologian, disagreed with Avicenna's ontology claiming that it was not *a priori*. Sadra posited his own version, summarised as follows:

- There is existence.
- Existence is a perfection above which no perfection may be conceived.
- God is perfect and perfection in existence.
- Existence is a singular and simple reality.
- That singular reality is graded in intensity in a scale of perfection.
- That scale must have a limit point, a point of greatest intensity and of greatest existence.
- Hence God exists.

Every ontological argument is problematic as even the formulators disagree with each other. Thomas Aquinas, for example, while proposing his five proofs in his *Summa Theologica*, objected to Anselm's argument. He suggested that people do not know the nature of God and, therefore, cannot conceive of God in the manner Anselm proposed. The ontological argument would make sense only to someone who understands the essence of God completely. Aquinas reasoned that, as only God can completely know himself, only he can use the argument.

His rejection of Anselm's ontological argument caused many Catholic theologians to do likewise.

David Hume argued that nothing can be proven to exist using only *a priori* reasoning. In his *Dialogues Concerning Natural Religion*, the character Cleanthes proposes this criticism:

"...there is an evident absurdity in pretending to demonstrate a matter of fact, or to prove it by any arguments *a priori*. Nothing is demonstrable, unless the contrary implies a contradiction. Nothing, that is distinctly conceivable, implies a contradiction. Whatever we conceive as existent, we can also conceive as non-existent. There is no being, therefore, whose non-existence implies a contradiction. Consequently there is no being, whose existence is demonstrable."

Hume also purported that, as we have no abstract idea of existence, we cannot claim that the idea of God implies his existence. He suggests that any conception of God we may have, we can conceive either of existing or of not existing. Existence is not a quality (or perfection), so the concept of a totally perfect being need not actually exist. Thus, he claims that it is not a contradiction to deny God's existence. The great German philosopher, Immanuel Kant (1724 – 1804), objected to ontological arguments, particularly those expounded by Descartes and Leibnitz, and by applying philosophical reasoning showed them to be bogus. Kant questioned the intelligibility of the concept of a necessary being. He considered examples of necessary propositions such as a triangle having three angles and dismissed the transfer of this logic to the existence of God. He argued that such propositions are necessarily true only if such a being exists i.e. if a triangle exists, it must have three angles. The necessary proposition, he claimed, does not make the existence of a triangle necessary. Thus, he argued that, if the proposition 'X exists' is posited, it would follow that, if X exists, it exists necessarily which does not mean that X exists in reality.

Kant went on to explain that 'being' is obviously not a real predicate and cannot be part of the concept of something. He proposed that existence is not a predicate or a quality because existence does not add to the essence of a being, indicating merely its real occurrence. He stated that by taking the subject of God with its entire predicate and then asserting that God exists:

"I add no new predicate to the conception of God."

He argued that the ontological argument works only if existence is a predicate and, if this is not so, then it is conceivable for a completely perfect being to not exist, thus defeating the ontological argument. In addition, Kant claimed that the concept of God is not of one particular sense; rather, it is an object of pure thought. He asserted that God exists outside the realm of our experience and nature. Because we cannot know God through experience, Kant argued that it is impossible to know how we would verify God's existence. This is in contrast to material concepts, which can be verified by means of the senses.

So much has been written about the ontological argument by both its advocates and detractors that it seems to have become over-complicated. The proponents start with the belief that God exists and attempt to apply statements of proof rather than beginning without a bias, neither in favour of existence or non-existence. The essence of the argument is that if God can be imagined or conceived in the mind, he must exist in reality. The naivety at play here is staggering isn't it? A scintilla of common sense sweeping aside a poverty of rationality tells us quite clearly that something imagined isn't necessarily real. We can all conjure up images of fairies living amongst garden flowers, leprechauns, unicorns and flying horses without assuming their credence in the real world. Furthermore, in the imagination, God is always anthropomorphic isn't he? No one ever has a conception of God looking like a dinosaur, like *King Kong* or an alien, as depicted in science fiction, with a huge head and bulging eyes. The advocates of the ontological argument can, of course, be as unrealistic as they like (and they are) but their opponents have not been fooled. The characteristics of the argument are worth presenting as a matter of historical record but their very effeteness rules them out from reasonable debate. The problem with the ontological argument, in short, is that it confuses perception with reality and, as such, its assessment derives a score of between 9 and 10.

Score = 9.95

The Argument from Beauty is an argument for the existence of God in the sense that God must have created the objects we consider beautiful. The awesome splendour of Earth's landscape including mountains, valleys and lakes can only, theists argue, be appropriated to God. If this is so, what about the ugliness of the aftermaths of countless natural disasters such as earthquakes, volcanic eruption, tsunamis and hurricanes? Shouldn't these be imputed to God as well and, if so, isn't the argument from beauty completely neutralised? Also, if God created the beauty in the world, why didn't he get it right first time? Why does he continually find it necessary to re-decorate (a most unlikely divine or supernatural trait) the panorama it is our privilege to observe. The American continents were once joined to Europe and Africa and one simply cannot speculate as to why they had to be separated. Several ice ages, each with their own glacial phases, have occurred over millions of years changing the features of the planet beyond recognition. We currently enjoy a warmer (interglacial) period known as the Holocene which began more than 11,000 years ago but it is likely that, within a few thousand years, much of the Earth's surface will once again be shrouded in ice. Although the last glacial period ended several thousands of years ago, its effects can still be seen today. For example, the moving ice carved out the landscape in Canada, Greenland, northern Eurasia and Antarctica. The erratic boulders, till, drumlins, eskers, fjords, kettle lakes, moraines and cirques are typical features left behind by the glaciers. Moreover, within another 10,000 years or so, further vast changes will have taken place. Few would argue that the English Lake District in Cumbria is one of the most beautiful places on Earth and most observers who have been privileged to enjoy its surroundings would plead for it to remain unchanged forever. Sadly, it will not stay the same. In the distant future, its landscape will be unrecognisable after being besieged by all manner of hostile forces. It could easily become an arid wasteland. If so, a whole series of random events would have played their part; it is virtually impossible to contemplate a divine hand deliberately guiding such decline. It would, after all, be pointless, wouldn't it? Could it really be that God is perpetually changing his mind or is the evidence for change, yet again, best explained by the gradual, small steps of evolution? It would be a contradiction for an omniscient God to have need of continual modification so we are left with evolution to provide the only plausible answer. From the assessment of the tepid argument from beauty, therefore, a score of between 8 and 10 is derived.

Score = 9

The Argument from Religious Experience claims there are persuasive reasons that at least some religious experiences validate spiritual realities in ways that surpass material manifestations, thereby, implying the existence of God. The primary reasons are:

- Substantial numbers of ordinary people report having had such experiences.

- These experiences often have very significant effects on people's lives, frequently inducing in them acts of extreme self-sacrifice well beyond what could be expected from evolutionary arguments.

- These experiences often seem very real to the people involved, and are quite often reported as being shared by groups. Although mass delusions are not inconceivable, one needs compelling reasons for invoking these as an explanation.

The counter arguments, disputing the above are as follows:

- The number of people claiming religious experiences as a percentage of historical humanity is minute. Why are these experiences not more commonplace? Therefore, whilst one would not doubt the sincerity of such people, veracity and reality remain very much in question. No scientific proof exists thus far.

- It seems strange that revelation is, almost exclusively, experienced by monotheists when those who would benefit most, one would have thought, are polytheists. God could convert these unbelievers in an instant with a word or a sign yet appears reluctant to do so which, logically, raises the suspicion that monotheists created God rather than the converse.

- There is little doubt that some reports of religious experience have naturalistic or psychological explanations and are thus mistaken. If some reports are misconceptions, perhaps all such reports are equally fallacious.

- Religious texts such as the Bible that speak of revelations are of disputable, if not refutable, historical accuracy.
- It is conceivable that some claimed religious experiences are lies, possibly fabricated for attention or acceptance.
- People have had revelations which are inconsistent across the spectrum of religions. Only some of these, if any, can be correct.
- It has been argued that religious experiences are little more than hallucinations aimed at fulfilling basic psychological desires of immortality, destiny and purpose. For example, Sigmund Freud (1856 – 1939), the famous Austrian neurologist and founder of psychoanalysis, considered God to be simply a psychological illusion, created by the mind rather than existing in reality. He considered the illusion to be based upon the infantile emotional desire for a powerful, supernatural father of the family. He maintained that religion, once necessary to restrain man's violent nature in the early stages of civilisation could, nowadays, be set aside in favour of reason and science. Freud noted the similarities between religious belief and neurotic obsession.

With the counter arguments heavily outweighing religious experience as a proof for the existence of God, a score of 9 is derived.

Score = 9

The Transcendental Argument attempts to prove God's existence by the contention that God must be the source of logic, morals and science. It posits that God is the precondition of all human knowledge and experience by demonstrating the impossibility of the contrary. In other words, that logic, reason, or morality cannot exist without God. The argument proceeds as follows:

- If there is no God, knowledge is not possible.
- Knowledge is possible (as is logic and morality).
- Therefore, God exists.

The chief criticism of this argument is directed at the premise that without God, knowledge cannot exist. Whilst acceptance of this premise can lead to the conclusion that God must exist, there is no demonstrated necessity to accept the premise. One might just as well say that without God, nothing can exist (which would take us back to Aquinas). The invalidity of the assertion is demonstrated by a reformulation, the 'transcendental argument for the non-existence of God', using the equally unsubstantiated premise that 'the existence of knowledge presupposes the non-existence of God'. Couldn't knowledge simply exist because it has been acquired, bit by bit, by countless generations of humans and their predecessors as part of the evolutionary process? The assessment of the transcendental argument, given its weakness, derives a score somewhere between 9 and 10.

Score = 9.5

There are several other arguments posited for the existence of God but they are all so feeble that they are hardly worthy of expansion and assessment. Among these are, for example, the *anthropic argument* and the *argument from reason*. The former credits God with setting the laws of nature and the parameters of the universe such that they are consistent with the support of life on Earth. It does not attempt to address why it took billions of years for life to emerge nor why it should be any source of wonder given the existence of billions of galaxies. The *argument from reason* was developed primarily by Clive Staples Lewis (1898 – 1963), a lay theologian and famous author of *The Chronicles of Narnia* and a body of other fictional work. However, Elizabeth Anscombe (1919 – 2001), a British analytic philosopher, so demolished the validity of Lewis's argument that he, utterly humiliated, never again ventured into theological writing.

Arguments against the Existence of God:

The Dysteleological Argument or *Argument from Poor Design* posits against the existence of God because of the colossal number of imperfections, both moral and physical that exist in the world. Examples of poor design are illness, disease, predation, natural disasters, cruelty, murder (particularly on religious grounds), homosexuality (and its vilification), sub-optimal creatures and specifically, the ichneumon wasp and the Loa loa parasitic worm. The argument is based on the following chain of reasoning:

- An omnipotent, omniscient, benevolent God would create a world that exhibited optimal design.
- The world is full of features that are sub-optimal.
- Therefore, either God does not exist or is not omnipotent, omniscient, and benevolent.
- It is inconceivable that God would not have the faculties of omnipotence, omniscience, and benevolence.
- Therefore, God does not exist.

The Roman poet and philosopher, Lucretius, captured the argument quite succinctly when he wrote:

Had God designed the world, it would not be
A world so frail and faulty as we see.

Woody Allen, perceiving God to be an under-achiever, would no doubt agree. One suspects that he would, along with many others, vote God out of office if the machinery allowed and if they could have confidence in the alternative. The argument from poor design is one that was used by Charles Darwin. It is consistent with the predictions of the scientific theory of evolution by means of natural selection. This advocates that features that were evolved for certain uses are then reused or co-opted for different uses and, sometimes, completely abandoned. A sub-optimal state is due to the inability of the hereditary system to eliminate specific vestiges of the evolutionary process. Because the existence of God is incompatible with a sub-standard design and the evolutionary process fully explains the world we experience, the assessment of the argument derives a very high score.

Score = 9.95

The Argument from Time posits that an omnipotent God would not require billions of years to create life on Earth. Any objective should be secured with immediacy; it clearly isn't, so the evolutionary process provides the only logical explanation. The basis for the argument is as follows:

•   If God exists, he must be omnipotent.

- If God is omnipotent, he must be capable of any accomplishment in a very short space of time.
- Over 9 billion years elapsed after the origin of the universe before Earth's formation and mankind did not appear for another 4 billion years or so.
- These times are of very long duration.
- Therefore, an omnipotent God does not exist.

Score = 9.9

The Argument from Sin takes into account the inconsistencies in mankind's existence and postulates that a benevolent God, if he existed, would be more equitable towards his subjects. Religions place great emphasis on our leading good and kindly lives, free from sin and also, on redemption, absolution, salvation and eternal damnation in the afterlife. Is it not bewildering, therefore, that decent people frequently die at a young age after suffering dreadfully whilst the most evil often live full lives, relatively unscathed? Either God is not merciful, or he is non-existent and the rich tapestry of life is simply governed by the laws of chance.

Score = 8.5

The Argument from Non-intervention contends that since God never appears to intervene even when his reputed love and mercy is most acutely required, it is highly unlikely that he exists. As well as appearing as a vision to Abraham, it would have been most bounteous had God appeared at the sacrificial altars of the Aztec priests before they plunged their razor-sharp obsidian knives into the breasts of their captives to rip out their hearts in propitiation of their gods. This would have had the simultaneous benefit of converting the Aztecs to monotheism and saving hundreds of thousands of innocent people from the most horrifying of deaths. Surely, an omniscient God would have contemplated both the necessity and the expedience. The extirpation of the Aztec's victims and the existence of God seem, to the logical mind, irreconcilable.

The First Crusade culminated in the storming of Jerusalem and its capture from Fatimid Egypt on the 15th July, 1099. On entering the city, the Crusaders behaved as a raging torrent of barbaric and indiscriminate slaughter. During a killing frenzy, thousands of Muslim and Jewish men, women and children were butchered with a ferocity unsurpassed even in medieval times. With a distorted conception of their religion, the Crusaders saw the 'killing for Christ' as an act of supreme devotion. The eve of the 14th July was a time when revelation would have been most beneficial. God could have chosen to reveal himself to Godfrey de Bouillon to say:

"When your armies break through the walls of Jerusalem, be merciful to all those living within."

Thousands of innocent lives would have been saved and the Crusaders would have been judged by history to be magnanimous liberators rather than savage murderers. But, Godfrey de Bouillon was not privileged to experience such a revelation, one which would have had far-reaching significance. Instead, if we are to believe the claim, centuries later God spoke to a criminal who was so impressed by his experience that he became a preacher. Whilst one can but applaud the preacher's persuasion from a life of crime, doesn't it seem rather trivial when compared to the sacking of Jerusalem?

Baibars (1223 – 1277), Mamluk Sultan of Egypt, was one of the commanders of the forces that inflicted a devastating defeat on the Seventh Crusade of King Louis IX of France. He also led the vanguard of the Mamluk army at the Battle of Ain Jalut in 1260 which marked the first substantial defeat of the Mongol forces previously inspired by Genghis Khan.   The Mamluks are among the most ferocious, accomplished warriors in history and in 1268, they turned their attention towards the remaining Christian dominions of the Middle East. Antioch had been in Christian hands for almost two centuries, ever since the successful First Crusade and, on the 18th May 1268, the city capitulated to the Mamluks. Doubtless influenced by the savagery of the Crusaders towards the Muslim population of Jerusalem in 1099, Baibars ordered the city gates to be shut so that there was no escape for the inhabitants and a terrifying massacre ensued.   It is believed that as many as 40,000 Christians were put to death and another 100,000 enslaved. Prior to the siege, God could have spoken to Baibars urging compassion, but he didn't, and all those people perished needlessly. Instead, God addresses himself to the odd petty thief who is so chastened by the experience that he becomes a born-again Christian. Unfathomable, isn't it?

Tony Blair, a former UK Prime Minister and a man of religion, was in 2003 contemplating whether to support the United States by invading Iraq. This would have been an opportune time for God to intervene by inducing a Blair revelation and advising him not to go to war. Blair could then have contacted George W. Bush and relayed his experience saying:

"George, God has just spoken to me and has commanded me to find another way."

Tens of thousands of lives might have been spared but, instead, what does God do? He appears before a young woman who takes it as a sign that she should take holy orders and dedicate her life to him by becoming a nun. If God really wanted to maximise the impact of revelatory experiences he should have appeared before Adolf Hitler, Joseph Stalin or Pol Pot, the Cambodian Maoist revolutionary leader of the Khmer Rouge. Just imagine the effect if Hitler, on God's instruction, had addressed the Wehrmacht's generals by saying:

"I've had a rethink and have decided to put Operation Barbarossa on hold along with our other expansionist plans."

The invasion of the Soviet Union might never have taken place and the lives of tens of millions could have been saved. It is truly baffling that despotic leaders never seem to have revelations that cause them to 'stay their hands'; rather, when and if they have them, they are invariably used to justify death and destruction in the name of God.

Score = 9.5

The Argument from Non-belief or *Argument from Divine Hiddenness* is a philosophical argument against the existence of God. The premise of the argument is that if God existed (and wanted humanity to know it), he would have brought about a situation in which every reasonable person believed in him. However, there are reasonable unbelievers and, therefore, this weighs heavily against God's existence. If God does exist, is it not baffling that only around half of the world's population believes in his existence and, after thousands of years, there is still no uniformity of religion. Instead of communing with a few prophets, why hasn't God addressed himself unequivocally to everybody to avoid confusion?

Despite the millions of lives that have been lost and continue to be lost in his name, he still remains invisible and provides no clear message. The clerics, interpreters of the errant scriptures, and their incongruous claims are all we have; claims which are so suspect and fanciful that they cannot be trusted.

Score = 9.95

The Argument from Parsimony posits the non-existence of God using Ockham's Razor, sometimes expressed as the law of parsimony, economy or succinctness. The principle, in general, suggests that from amongst competing hypotheses, selecting the one that makes the fewest assumptions usually provides the correct one and that the simplest explanation will be the most plausible until evidence is presented to the contrary. The argument contends that since natural theories adequately explain the development of religion and belief in gods, the actual existence of such supernatural agents is superfluous and may be dismissed. Therefore, as too many assumptions are required and as it is so unlikely, there is no reason to believe in God's existence.

Score = 9

The Argument from Evil finds the existence of a deity that is benevolent, omnipotent and omniscient logically incompatible with all the evil that is evident in the world. The logical problem of evil, an elaboration of the Epicurean paradox, states:

• God exists.

• God is omnipotent, omniscient, and perfectly good.

• A perfectly good being would want to prevent all evils.

• An omniscient being knows every way in which evil can occur.

- An omnipotent being, who knows every way in which an evil can occur, has the power to prevent that evil from coming into existence.

- A being who knows every way in which an evil can occur, who is able to prevent that evil from coming into existence, and who wants to do so would prevent the existence of that evil.

- If there exists an omnipotent, omniscient, and perfectly good being, then no evil exists.

- Evil exists (a logical contradiction).

On the basis of this argument, God can't exist. An American preacher, when asked by a member of his congregation why God allows so much evil in the world, replied with a few assumptive, stock answers:

"We cannot hope to understand God."

"God gave mankind the benefit of free will."

"God is testing us."

"Only when we confront evil can we improve as human beings."

"God needs to know which people to punish when they die."

There are probably dozens of other answers he could have given, all equally speculative. It would never have occurred to him to apply Ockham's Razor and derive one simple answer; there is so much evil because there is no God to prevent it.

Score = 9.5

The Ultimate Boeing 747 Gambit is a counter-argument to the argument from design which claims that a complex or ordered structure must have been designed. However, a God that is responsible for the creation of a universe would be at least as complicated as the universe that he creates. Therefore, he too must require a designer and its designer would require a designer also, ad infinitum. The argument for the existence of God is then a logical fallacy. The Ultimate Boeing 747 gambit points out that God does not provide an origin of complexity; it simply assumes that complexity always existed. It also points out that design fails to account for complexity which evolution and natural selection fully and plausibly explain. Indeed, it is an objective of good design to reduce complexity, not to increase it, so claiming complexity as evidence of design is rather self-refuting.

Score = 9

In total, 15 arguments have been considered and assessed, seven for and eight against the existence of God. The analysis undertaken reveals that the arguments supporting the existence of God have very little substance in that, generally, the advocates postulate that God exists because they believe he exists. Perhaps unsurprisingly, there are no real proofs or even near proofs; only blind faith. The average of the scores is 9.5 which when multiplied by a consistency factor (see the Addendum) derives a value of 9.785 meaning that, rounding up, there is a 98 percent certainty that God does not exist. In other words, the probability of God's existence is about the same as the chance of putting one's hand into an opaque bag of billiard balls, one white and 49 black, and drawing out the white one. If God does not exist as the score suggests, conundrums which have plagued civilisation for centuries are resolved at a stroke. God doesn't answer prayers because he doesn't exist. God didn't intervene when millions of people died unnecessarily in his name because he doesn't exist. There is no unification of religion because God doesn't exist. God has never addressed himself to the masses because he doesn't exist, and so on. The corollaries are many:

- Whilst their sincerity is not in question, it is almost certain that the prophets were deluded and did not actually commune with God. Any communion may have taken place in minds conducive to misconception, hallucination, dreams or various alternative phenomena.

- It is most unlikely that Jesus died on the cross to save anybody.

- It is most unlikely that a virgin birth or resurrection actually took place.

- Heaven, Hell, the afterlife, salvation and eternal damnation are very unlikely to exist and, therefore, when we die, with the passage of time, we simply become elements in the atmosphere.

- The chances are that there are no angels and that all forms of sainthood are a mere contrivance.

- It is likely that holy books such as the Bible, Quran and the Tanakh are based almost entirely on misconception and have been augmented by successive accretions and embellishments to become works of fiction.

- It is almost certain that all manner of ecclesiastical liturgy, ritual and thousands of hymns and prayers have been derived on a false premise.

- It is highly likely that millions of clerics – priests, bishops, popes, cardinals, rabbis, imams, ayatollahs, mullahs, and lay preachers, owe their vocations to myth and superstition.

- Auricular confession, the practice of confessing one's sins to a priest to pave the way to Heaven is, almost certainly, nonsense.

- It is virtually certain that millions of people have died needlessly due to holy wars, inquisitions, witch-hunts, religious intolerance, unfounded doctrines and conflicting beliefs.

- It is highly likely that when millions of people perform acts of worship every day, they are praying to something that exists only in their imagination; nothing real, a mirage.

Bertrand Russell would not have been surprised by the results of the analysis having, for most of his life, seen the existence of God as chimerical.   He noted that the religious have a tendency to hold passionate beliefs and for them he had this to say:

"The opinions that are held with passion are always those for which no good ground exists; indeed the passion is the measure of the holder's lack of rational conviction.   Opinions in politics and religion are almost always held passionately."

Both passion and faith are poor substitutes for truth though, frequently, both hinder its emergence.

Morality and Kindness

Some people say that you have to believe in something.   Bertrand Russell declared that he thought the existence of the Christian God no more probable than the existence of the gods of Olympus and Valhalla. So, what should you believe in?   Well, you can always believe in the Flying Spaghetti Monster or, perhaps, Russell's teapot.   Or, what about believing in Russell's teapot with the word, 'kindness', written all over it?   If this sounds a little too absurd, what about keeping the Flying

Spaghetti Monster and Russell's teapot in the background to be brought forth only when a significant point needs to be made in an amusing way? This leaves us with 'kindness' and if, alongside it, we include John Lennon's 'brotherhood of man', we arrive at something really worth believing in. Is there anything more apposite, more likely to unify a global brotherhood, than kindness? The brilliant Thomas Paine would have agreed wholeheartedly because he said:

"To do good is my religion."

Kindness transcends the protectionist self-interest of organised religion which Paine addressed when he wrote:

"All national institutions of churches, whether Jewish, Christian, or Turkish, appear to me no other than human inventions set up to terrify and enslave mankind, and monopolise power and profit. I do not believe in the creed professed by the Jewish church, by the Roman church, by the Greek church, by the Turkish church, by the Protestant church, nor by any church that I know of. My own mind is my own church."

Life on planet Earth is very short, seemingly passing by in a flash. Wouldn't it be worth a try; perceiving all people as just people, without labels, and treating them all with the religion of kindness? Bertrand Russell put it rather well when he said:

"A good world needs knowledge, kindliness, and courage; it does not need a regretful hankering after the past or a fettering of the free intelligence by the words uttered long ago by ignorant men."

Religion, without doubt, has been one of the greatest curses of mankind, millions of people having lost their lives because of primitive ideologies in conflict, even when the object of their adulation was frequently the same God. So often, the driving force behind all the slaughter has been a priesthood reliant upon fear and ignorance and, with self-interest transforming it from a witch doctorate into interpreters of holy text and ecclesiastical law, it acquired unassailability. Along with John Adams and James Madison, the fourth President of the United States, Thomas Jefferson held a life-long abhorrence of the priesthood and its hierophants. His administration was probably the most secular his country has seen and during his eight years as incumbent, not a single religious proclamation was issued. Referring to this, he said:

"I know it will give great offence to the clergy, but the advocate of religious freedom is to expect neither peace nor forgiveness from them."

Long before his presidency, when he was the United States Minister to France, he wrote from Paris:

"If anybody thinks that kings, nobles and priests, are good conservators of the public happiness, send him here. It is the best school in the universe to cure him of that folly. He will see here with his own eyes that these descriptions of men are an abandoned confederacy against the happiness of the mass of the people."

Jefferson detested the entire clergy, regarding them as a worthless class living like parasites on the labours of others. He evinced:

"The Christian priesthood, finding the doctrines of Christ levelled to every understanding, and too plain to need explanation, saw in the mysticisms of Plato materials with which they might build up an artificial system, which might, from its indistinctness, admit everlasting controversy, give employment for their order and introduce it to profit, power and pre-eminence."

With a forthright candour, he wrote:
"In every country and in every age the priest has been hostile to liberty; he is always in alliance with the despot, abetting his abuses in return for protection to his own."

Though they had frequently been politically opposed, towards the end of their lives Jefferson and Adams corresponded with regularity. Adams wrote:
"This would be the best of all possible worlds if there were no religion in it."

Jefferson replied:
"If by religion we are to understand sectarian dogmas, in which no two of them agree, then your exclamation on that hypothesis is just."

It is utterly extraordinary that the two great men died on the 50th anniversary of the Declaration of Independence (the 4th July, 1826), Adams outliving Jefferson by just a few hours.

Jefferson would have so enjoyed discussions with Bertrand Russell, had they been possible, in an engagement of two great intellects. Clearly, they were of like mind as Russell has stated:
"I am as firmly convinced that religions do harm as I am that they are untrue."

He saw them as the principal enemy of moral progress in the world. When the sentiments of Adams and Jefferson come to pass, as they most surely will, clerics will have to find alternative means of employment which are likely to be more taxing and, hopefully, based on truth rather than superstition. One can't help but feel a pang of remorse when one considers the kindly and virtuous, clergyman of the local church but he is just as likely to do good work in another vocation. Religion's legacy will be outstanding works of art, wonderful churches and a rich history of misguided belief and its ramifications. The architecture and stonemasonry skills which constructed magnificent cathedrals, mosques and synagogues are of a bygone age when they were inspired by an absolute and unconditional faith and a thirst for salvation and eternal life. Their like will never be seen again because, even if the skills could be relearned, the cost would be prohibitive and, more essentially, the commitment to faith has waned and will continue to be diluted.

Within a century or so, it is likely that blind religious belief will have run its course though, somewhat surprisingly, this was not a view entirely shared by Christopher Hitchens (1949 – 2011), the brilliant British American journalist, author and debater who wrote, amongst other polemics, *God Is Not Great: How Religion Poisons Everything*. On the 26th November 2010, he debated with Tony Blair the subject, 'Is religion a force for good in the world?' The debate took place in Toronto, Canada and, by the end, Blair must have felt intellectually mugged. With breathtaking eloquence, Hitchens metaphorically finessed one rapier thrust after another to win the debate, leaving Blair shaken.

At one point, this doyen of debaters stated that he did not believe religion would ever be eradicated, his view being gratefully seized upon by Blair. Perhaps Hitchens was unduly influenced by the slow rate of decline to irreligion in the United States, his country of residence, without giving due consideration to a completely different picture in Europe.   Perhaps also, he had not taken into account the transparent disparity in belief between the younger and older generations and its inevitable impact on religion's demise.

Christopher Hitchens, the champion of reason and logic against the metaphysical, died from oesophageal cancer on the 15th December, 2011. On the death of his former debating adversary, Blair commented:

"Christopher Hitchens was a complete one-off, an amazing mixture of writer, journalist, polemicist, and unique character.   He was fearless in the pursuit of truth and any cause in which he believed.   And there was no belief he held that he did not advocate with passion, commitment, and brilliance.   He was an extraordinary, compelling and colourful human being whom it was a privilege to know."

Richard Dawkins was effusive in his praise for his like-minded opponent of religion and its clerisy when he said:

"I think he was one of the greatest orators of all time.   He was a polymath, a wit, immensely knowledgeable, and a valiant fighter against all tyrants including imaginary supernatural ones."

The current rate of change in religious commitment is moderate but inexorable and is likely to increase exponentially with the passage of time as others follow the Scandinavian lead.   Because of an outmoded adherence to the Sabbath, for example, the first Sunday Football League matches did not take place in England until the 20th January, 1974; now they are commonplace.   The Sunday Trading Act of 1994 permitted Sunday shopping in England and Wales for the first time.   Prior to this, buying and selling on a Sunday had, in general, been illegal and the Act repealed the ancient observance of the Sabbath as a 'day of rest'.

In February 2012, a judge ruled that local authorities cannot hold prayers as part of formal council meetings following a legal objection from an atheist town councillor. The case was brought against Bideford Town Council by former Liberal Democrat, Clive Bone, who was backed by the National Secular Society. Bone had complained about the custom which saw the prayers formally minuted and, subsequently, resigned from the council due to its refusal to adjust its policy. The High Court backed Bone's argument that the practice was not lawful but rejected two other claims that his human rights were infringed and that he was being discriminated against. Mr Justice Ouseley's judgement stated:

"A local authority has no powers under section 111 of the Local Government Act 1972 to hold prayers as part of a formal local authority meeting, or to summon councillors to such a meeting at which prayers are on the agenda. The saying of prayers in a local authority chamber before a formal meeting of such a body is lawful, provided councillors are not formally summoned to attend."

Other religious bastions will fall as science gains the upper hand and better education becomes more widely and freely available, enlightening communities everywhere. Thus far, religion has come to recognise, indeed is reeling from, the scientific threat. Its spiritual heads are trying to find ways of co-operating with the scientific community prompted, no doubt, by an agenda of self-preservation. In the 2012 BBC Television programme entitled, *Rosh Hashanah: Science vs. Religion*, Lord Jonathan Sacks, Chief Rabbi of the British Orthodox Synagogues, met three non-believing scientists; neuroscientist Baroness Susan Greenfield, theoretical physicist Professor Jim Al-Khalili and Professor Richard Dawkins. Lord Sacks hoped to establish that religion and science could, in his own words, make a great partnership. He was encouraged by the baroness's laissez faire attitude but made no progress with Al-Khalili save that they were both in awe of the wonder of the universe. The professor had no belief in a creator God whilst, without any supporting evidence, Sacks was convinced that his religion's contrary view was the right one.

The final meeting took place at the Royal Society, Carlton House Terrace, London. Lord Sacks anticipated that this would be his sternest test; he was meeting Richard Dawkins whom he described as a militant atheist. Professor Dawkins, concerned about the literal truth of holy books, asked:

"Do you actually think it happened? Do you actually think that Abraham did truss Isaac on an altar then let him off?"

Lord Sacks responded by saying:

"I definitely believe that something happened that made Jews value their children more than in any other civilisation I know. I really think that God wanted Abraham and Jews from that day to this to know - don't sacrifice your children."

He did not explain why this self-evident sentiment was necessary. However, undeterred, Professor Dawkins tried again by asking:

"Do you think that Abraham really did truss Isaac on an altar? I want to know if you think it's literally true."

Once again circumspect, Lord Sacks replied:

"Well, first of all, I think that story is a protest against the belief throughout the ancient world that parents owned their children."

For some reason, the professor failed to point out that his question had not been answered and to ask, once again:
"Do you think it's literally true?"

Was Lord Sacks being deliberately evasive? If so, was it because he feared the follow-up questioning that would inevitably have ensued had he answered robustly in the affirmative. Be that as it may, did he not see that God could have instructed Abraham and his people never to sacrifice their children without insisting that Isaac be tethered to an altar? Imagine the permanent psychological damage that this terrified child might have experienced as a consequence of seeing a sacrificial blade hovering inches from his throat. Even so, one suspects that Lord Sacks would have found such violence completely reconcilable with a benevolent God.

As the interview began to draw to a close, the chief rabbi claimed there was common ground between himself and Dawkins in that both were committed to question. On this foundation, he asked:
"Could we not work together to value human rights, human dignity, where we engage in the collaborative pursuit of truth?"

Faced with such a reasonable proposition, Dawkins replied:
"Yes, people of goodwill could and should work together."

This conciliatory response led Lord Sacks to declare that a real breakthrough had been made when, in fact, according to his original terms of reference, he had not advanced his proposition at all. This was not science and religion in partnership; it was a case of two individuals from entirely different backgrounds agreeing that they had the interests of humanity at heart. With considerable eloquence, and not a little sleight of hand, he had extrapolated from the individuals to their disciplines though science and religion remained diametrically opposed, one relying on evidence, the other relying on faith without evidence. There was no reason whatsoever why Dawkins and Sacks should not work together as friends but the truth of their fundamental differences could not be disguised. Lord Sacks, perhaps deceived by his desire to demonstrate some success, had derived false conclusions. Though his sophistry might have had some viewers fooled, there was no fooling many, least of all Richard Dawkins.

Judaism is likely to be the last religion to expire. Founded as it is on the misguided slaying of 3,000 Israelites by brother Israelites and having suffered centuries of intense persecution which it resignedly ascribed to the will of God, it clearly has staying power. The continuance of religion has always relied on ignorance. Centuries ago, for example, the Catholic Church was reluctant about its adherents reading the Bible as it believed this would lead to Protestantism. Inevitably, with the passage of time, more and more Bible translations followed. Progress can be impeded but it cannot be halted. Rather than seeing religion as a bulwark in their lives, people will increasingly see it as a hindrance, maintaining division when there should be unity. The signs are already here as churches continue to be closed and turned into coffee bars. In common with everything else, religions have their own life cycles as they expand from birth, flourish for a time, wane and eventually decline into oblivion. The scholarly Italian cardinal, Carlo Maria Martini (1927 – 2012), once described the Catholic Church as being 200 years out of date. In an interview published in the Italian daily newspaper, *Corriere della Sera*, he warned:

"Our culture has aged, our churches are big and empty and the church bureaucracy rises up, our rituals and our cassocks are pompous. The Church must admit its mistakes and begin a radical change, starting with the pope and the bishops. The paedophilia scandals oblige us to take a journey of transformation."

The cardinal's views were frequently controversial but, in the minds of many, were both necessary and progressive. These included commentaries on the role of women in the church, the use of condoms and divorce. He believed that the use of condoms could be acceptable in some cases, particularly in relation to the spread of AIDS and that the church should be receptive to new kinds of families or risk losing its followers. He told the newspaper:

"A woman is abandoned by her husband and finds a new companion to look after her and her children. A second love succeeds. If this family is discriminated against, not just the mother will be cut off but also her children."

Martini was a liberal voice in the church and might have become pope had it not been for the onset of Parkinson's disease. He was clearly a man who thought deeply about the issues and was unafraid to express his views. However, even if the church hierarchy had taken his advice, it would have served only to delay the inevitable.

The number of people appearing in TV debates who admit that religion plays no part in their lives and that they see no reason to believe in God is increasing year on year. There are many high profile cases. Jonathan Edwards became one of Britain's most decorated athletes as a triple jumper. The son of a vicar, he spent most of his adult life as a devout Christian. Initially, he even refused to compete on Sundays, his faith costing him a place in the 1991 World Athletic Championships. He once stated:

"My relationship with Jesus and God is fundamental to everything I do. I have made a commitment in that relationship to serve God in every area of my life."

He was a regular presenter of the BBC Christian television show, *Songs of Praise,* until 2007 when he renounced his faith and his belief in God. In an interview with *The Times*, he stated:

"When you think about it rationally, it does seem incredibly improbable that there is a God."

In the same interview, he added:

"I feel internally happier than at any time in my life."

No single reason for his loss of belief in God has been made public but it seems most likely that instead of blindly following the faith of his upbringing, he began to apply rationality and logic to his thought processes; perhaps for the first time. It may be he realised that the spurious scriptures provide the flimsiest of foundations for a belief in God and that, if a Supreme Being existed, there would be much more order and equality in the world.

Today, we live in a communications age, the like of which has never been seen before. News is reported globally within minutes of an event, 24 hours a day, and the internet has encouraged erudition on an unprecedented scale via powerful search engines. The facilities are such that millions of people can be influenced by a single opinion, a single debate. More than any other factor, it is the individual's increased knowledge and awareness sponsored by the communications age that will hasten religion's demise. Thus far, however, despite challenges to ecclesiastical authorities in the past, churches throughout the world still wield excessive power. The Age of Enlightenment took place in 18th century Europe and America as a cultural movement whose aim was to reform society using reason. It rejected the influence of faith, revelation, superstition and tradition, believing in the advancement of knowledge by means of science. Intellectual interchange was seen as the way forward whilst opposing intolerance and the many abuses perpetrated by both church and state.

Originating in the late 17th century, the Enlightenment was ignited by brilliant thinkers such as Baruch Spinoza, John Locke, Isaac Newton, Voltaire and the French philosopher, Pierre Bayle. In France, the movement was based in the salons where groups of like-minded intellectuals increased their knowledge through discussion. The most tangible culmination of the meetings was the *Encyclopédie* (1751 – 1772), edited by the French philosopher and writer, Denis Diderot, which included contributions from hundreds of the greatest academics of the time. The new ideals spread throughout Europe and across the Atlantic to North America where they influenced Benjamin Franklin, Thomas Jefferson and many distinguished others. They played a significant role in the American War of Independence (1775 – 1783), the American

Declaration of Independence and the United States Bill of Rights. Around 25,000 copies of the 35 volumes of *Encyclopédie* were sold but after flourishing for well over 100 years, the Enlightenment was displaced by Romanticism and its emphasis on emotion. The Enlightenment, despite its noble intent, had not permeated the hearts and minds of the masses of ordinary people. The papers written by the advocates of the movement were largely for the consumption of their peers and lacked the common touch. Consequently, the 'man in the street' was never introduced to views that differed from those of an anachronistic church whose direction, through fear and ignorance, he continued to obey. Nowadays, however, almost everyone is exposed to a thousand times more information than could possibly have been imparted during the Age of Enlightenment. It is the impact of the age of communications on knowledge, opinion and evidence-based decision making that will be the final arbiter in ensuring religion's terminal decline and disbelief in a judgmental sky God.

Decades ago, most people were afraid, at least reluctant, to reveal their atheism; not any more. Famous atheists from the world of film and theatre include Woody Allen, James Cameron, George Clooney, Paul Bettany, Emma Thompson and Daniel Radcliffe; from literature – Sir Kingsley Amis, Douglas Adams, Tariq Ali, Ken Follett, Stephen Fry and Graham Greene; from science – Brian Cox, Richard Dawkins, Peter Atkins, Francis Crick and Stephen Hawking; from comedy – Billy Connolly, Alan Davies, Eddie Izzard, Ben Elton and Dave Allen, who famously said:

"I'm an atheist, thank God."

These people didn't need religion to direct them to lead fulfilling lives based on moral values; morality being largely inherent and instinctive, derived from human intelligence and awareness. Does religious belief reinforce morality? It almost certainly can have that beneficial effect but then, you couldn't expect it to do less, could you? Is morality dependent upon religious belief? Certainly not, is the answer; there are millions of decent, kindly people who are profoundly irreligious. It was Bertrand Russell who wrote:

"I do not think that the real reason why people accept religion has anything to do with argumentation. They accept religion on emotional grounds. One is often told that it is a very wrong thing to attack religion, because religion makes men virtuous. So I am told; I have not noticed it."

In August 2011, some of England's greatest cities were consumed by the most destructive riots seen in a generation as protests against economic stringency escalated. Such was the violence that thousands of police officers lost control of the city centres and could only stand by as property damage and looting was rife. In the aftermath, the faithful were quick to bemoan that it was due largely to the decline in religious belief that had beset society. This is almost certainly a fallacious explanation because history has repeatedly shown that religious belief is quickly jettisoned at times of mass hysteria by adrenalin fuelled mobs. Moreover, many of the rioters could later have been seen in the confessional seeking absolution whilst others were kneeling on their prayer mats facing Mecca. Apart from any physical damage, the real casualties were morality and kindness.

Also in 2011, a number of Muslim men were convicted in Birmingham, England, of organising dog fights. They were aware that dog fighting is illegal and morally reprehensible, yet they carried out their grotesque, clandestine practice regardless of the consequences. The dogs involved in the fights tend to be Staffordshire Bull Terriers which as puppies are naturally docile. As they mature, however, if trained to be aggressive, they become powerful and lethal. It is quite common for contests between a pair of these animals to last for over two hours and for the dogs to be so badly lacerated that they frequently die from their wounds. What is it that incites the dog handlers to involve themselves in such wanton cruelty? Is there a distorted thrill in seeing their charges in action or is it simply the prize money? Whatever the reason, it's almost certain that when they're released from custody, they'll visit the local mosque as frequently as before and indulge in their evil practice all over again. The teachings of their religion will be conveniently sidelined.

Some so-called Christians are just as morally bankrupt. Small groups of men roam the countryside to perpetrate the unspeakable crime of badger baiting. They locate the setts and dig the badgers out, hitting them with their spades before releasing specially bred dogs (lurcher and pit bull cross-breeds) to confront them. The badgers fight valiantly but are inevitably vanquished as they are torn to pieces by their swift and powerful adversaries. In this case, there is no prize money to act as an incentive; only deranged minds and an inflated desire for cruelty. Some might confess their activities to their priest who might admonish them but any effect would be short lived; their blood lust fuels their hobby and they find it impossible to resist.

Notwithstanding the obvious exceptions, morality and kindness come quite naturally to most of human kind but some of it is learned from introspection and experience. Ronald Reagan was the 40th president of the United States. George H.W. Bush, his successor in office, paid a moving tribute to his friend during his memorial service saying it was from him he learned kindness and decency. The capacity for kindness was, no doubt, within Bush all along but it was, it seems, his interaction with Reagan that encouraged it to grow.

Many years ago, a 12-year old boy was playing in the countryside with a small group of friends when they espied some water voles by a river bank. One of the boys began throwing stones at the voles and, without thinking, the others joined in the fun. The voles quickly dispersed, running into the water for cover, pursued by the group who, gripped by hysteria, continued their harassment unabated. The 12-year old picked up a small rock and dropped it from a point directly above one of the submerged creatures. Water resistance gave the water vole just enough time to evade the rock and it was then, as if a light had been switched on in his mind, he realised that he could have killed an innocent little animal. He called for his friends to desist and, fortunately, as far as the boys knew, no water voles had been hurt. From that day forth, the 12-year old never knowingly hurt any living creatures, doing all that he could to protect them. He had learned the lesson of morality and kindness and, with hindsight, he could confidently claim that religion played no part.

The benign teachings of current religions have value in their own right without anyone having to accept the religions as a whole. Why does anyone have to accept all the accessories such as the ceremony, the rituals and incantations, the angels and the effigies of hundreds of saints? It is knowledge derived from the benefit of education that will, increasingly, change our religious thinking; a thinking which hasn't shifted fundamentally since the Middle Ages. Christian values, without all the paraphernalia, providing a moral compass laced with kindness would be an elixir for happiness. Why not be happy in this life without agonising about or hoping there is another one? Paradoxically, religion is for those that don't think about religion; those that do think about it invariably arrive at a position of disbelief. The expectation of the church has always been one of blind acceptance. Those that expressed a contrary view, in days gone by, were often burned alive whilst priests looked on and prayed for their souls.

Once religion has been consigned to mythology, nobody will be able to say that they committed some atrocity because they were directed by God or that God was on their side. Had a Thomas Jefferson been President of the United States in 2001, there would have been no invasion of Iraq. First of all, he would not have claimed to have had his actions sanctioned by God, unlike George W. Bush and Tony Blair. Isn't it curious that the likes of Bush and Blair readily claim that they have God's approval to initiate death and destruction but are never told by God to preserve life by taking *no* action? Secondly, such was Jefferson's capacious intellect, he would have found another way of resolving the dichotomy posed by Saddam Hussein. There is no way that he would have caused the deaths of thousands of innocent people by going to war on a false and, quite possibly, contrived premise. Thirdly, as an accomplished historian, he would have understood that, in the aftermath of war, another conflict would arise between the Sunni and Shia Muslims. He would have known that after centuries of enmity between the two factions, more loss of life would be inevitable as they pursued vengeance and reprisal. Jefferson would have known in advance that

American bombs and missiles would devastate the buildings in Baghdad and that as the TV images of the carnage were relayed into the comfortable homes of western society, the real tragedy would not be counted in the cost of the bricks and mortar. He would have seen through the buildings to a terrified populace huddled within. No matter how assured he might have been by his generals that only military and control establishments would be targeted, he would have known that collateral damage could not be avoided; that civilian casualties would be high. He would have fully understood the enormity of the potential death toll and the number of residents maimed for life. He once stated:

"I value peace, and I would unwillingly see any event take place which would render war a necessary resource. I do not believe war the most certain means of enforcing principles. Those peaceable coercions which are in the power of every nation, if undertaken in concert and in time of peace, are more likely to produce the desired effect."

A couple of centuries later, Winston Churchill, Prime Minister of the United Kingdom, echoed these sentiments even more succinctly when he stated:

"Jaw-jaw is always better than war-war."

Bush and Blair could not have seen beyond the collapsing buildings. To them, the people damaged inside must have been, simply, statistics. They needed the prescience to see behind the statistics to the reality of men, women and children with broken bodies and missing limbs. Perhaps, if each of them had suffered a long period of nightmares graphically presenting children having their arms and legs blown from their torsos, they might have come to a different conclusion. Who knows, they might even have interpreted it as a message from God and been persuaded to find an alternative solution to the problem that was Iraq. Instead, they followed the proverbial muck cart and thought it was democracy.

Some time ago, police in Warwickshire, England, opened a garden shed and discovered inside a whimpering, cowering dog. The dog, having been locked in the shed and abandoned, was dirty, malnourished and in poor health. In an act of kindness, the police took the dog, a female greyhound, to the Nuneaton Warwickshire Wildlife Sanctuary, well known as a haven for animals abandoned, orphaned or otherwise in need. The staff tried to restore the dog to full health and to, simultaneously, win her trust. Several weeks passed but eventually both goals were achieved. They named the dog Jasmine and began to consider finding her an adoptive home.

Jasmine, however, had another agenda as she began to welcome all new arrivals at the sanctuary. She didn't discriminate between a puppy, a fox cub, a rabbit or any other animal in distress. She would simply peer into the box or cage and, whenever she could, she would deliver a welcoming lick. Relating one of the early incidents, the sanctuary manager said:

"We had two puppies that had been abandoned by a nearby railway line. One was a Lakeland Terrier cross and the other was a Jack Russell Doberman cross. They were tiny when they arrived at the centre. Jasmine approached them and grabbed one by the scruff of the neck and put him on the settee. Then she fetched the other one and sat down alongside, cuddling them. But she is like that with all of our animals, even the rabbits. She takes all the stress out of them and it helps them to not only feel close to her but to settle into their new surroundings. She has done the same with the fox and badger cubs; she licks the rabbits and guinea pigs and even lets the birds perch on the bridge of her nose."

Jasmine, the timid, abused, deserted waif, had become the animal sanctuary's resident surrogate mother.   The list of orphaned and abandoned youngsters she has cared for comprises five fox cubs, four badger cubs, 15 chicks, eight guinea pigs, two stray puppies, 15 rabbits and Bramble, a roe deer fawn. Tiny Bramble was 11 weeks old when she was found semi-conscious in a field. Upon her arrival at the sanctuary, Jasmine cuddled up to her to keep her warm before adopting the role of foster mother. She showered the roe deer with affection and kept her clean, making sure that her fur was never matted. They became inseparable.

Jasmine knew nothing about religion and nobody had told her about God. No matter; she showed love and kindness to a variety of creatures that, under different circumstances, she might have been expected to harm. The fact that she was equipped with a level of intelligence way below that of humans was irrelevant. She didn't have to rationalise kindness; it came naturally to her from within. Couldn't we learn from Jasmine's example and try being kind to one another, irrespective of race, skin pigmentation or creed? It all starts with tolerance and the triumph of reason over emotion. The next step is kindness and, if that became universal, the John Lennon aspiration of a brotherhood of man as expressed in *Imagine* would be tantalisingly close. Lennon's great song, though he may not have been fully aware of its prescient significance, showed us the way; now it's up to us to banish superstition and unfounded belief in the supernatural and make it happen. Without our being endowed with the wisdom of a Jefferson, it may take some time but it will be realised. When that time comes, in the unlikely event that he could witness it, John Lennon would be well pleased.

A Summation

When the author began his analysis into God's existence, he believed there might be some evidence, however tentative, to suggest there is a God. As it turned out, no evidence was forthcoming; not a shard or a shred. Consequently, the arguments for God's existence scored no better than the arguments against.

Some of the greatest minds in history such as Epicurus, Spinoza, Einstein and Russell have questioned the existence of a Supreme Being and concluded that, in reality, there isn't one. They are not alone; around half of the world's populace agrees with them. If over three billion people are wrong, God must be very tolerant, not at all like the jealous God of Moses.

It appears that God twiddled his thumbs for billions of years and then, following the advent of mankind, was extraneous to human consciousness for hundreds of millennia. Around 4,000 years ago, we are led to believe, he must have thought humans were ready for revelation but, curiously, he decided not to announce his presence to all of the world's people. Instead, he confided in a single peripatetic tribesman. Is it any wonder that the scriptures are considered an untrustworthy source?

The only reason to believe in God emanates from the scriptures but it is widely acknowledged that they have been fabricated, abridged, adulterated, contrived and falsified. Biblical scholars, such as Professor Francesca Stavrakopoulou, confirm that the holy texts are works of dubious authenticity with virtually no basis in historical fact. Even with our limited cerebral faculties, we know that nobody can calm storms, walk on water, travel hundreds of miles in an instant and bring the dead back to life. In short, the scriptures constitute a fiction on a spectacular scale, a foundation for God as irresolute as quicksand. It is hardly surprising that Freud asserted that God is a psychological illusion and religious belief is similar to a neurotic obsession. In affirmation, we note that God remains hidden, tolerates evil and required billions of years to create a world that is crammed with imperfections. He frequently seems to reward the most sinful and his policy of non-intervention is truly baffling. As a mother and child were led to the gas chamber or the heart was being ripped from a sacrificial victim, we are to be reassured that God's love surrounded them. What kind of love, what kind of consolation is that?

The complexity of our world does not provide evidence of God as is claimed; on the contrary, far from increasing complexity, good design minimises it. The discrepant features of nature, its countless imperfections and intricacy can in no way be synonymous with a divine deity's design. Some ancient philosophers failed to contemplate that the perfect being should have been able to create something equally, or almost, as perfect as himself. Their hypotheses and theories are discredited because they ignored this truism. The vagaries of the world we inhabit, however, are completely explained by the randomness of Darwinian evolution. The application of Ockham's Razor derives the same conclusion; too many assumptions are required to support the proposition that God exists whilst evolution, as a scientific fact, has no dependence on the transcendental. Moreover, morality, regarded by some to be the preserve of God and religion, is also explained by

Darwin's work; it has been assimilated into the human mind by means of trial and error over a million years of mankind's development.

It is, of course, possible that God exists but is not omnipotent, omniscient, benevolent and merciful but, if that were the case, why would you call him 'God'? Even though beliefs in the supernatural cannot be falsified empirically, the time will come when science gains dominion over emotion and God will be consigned to mythology alongside Zeus, whilst the prophets will become regarded as unwitting imposters. By then, the ecclesiastical clerisy will have joined a long line of deluded holy men and the debate about God's existence would simply be a philosophical one: "Can God exist if nobody believes in him?" Until then, God's actuality remains an exceedingly small probability.

Addendum

Martin Luther's 95 Theses

The 95 Theses, or the Disputation on the Power and Efficacy of Indulgences by Dr. Martin Luther, were written in response to the selling of indulgences by Johann Tetzel, a Dominican Friar and papal commissioner for indulgences. Luther wrote:

"Out of love and concern for the truth, and with the object of eliciting it, the following heads will be the subject of a public discussion at Wittenberg under the presidency of the reverend father, Martin Luther, Augustinian, Master of Arts and Sacred Theology, and duly appointed Lecturer on these subjects in that place. He requests that whoever cannot be present personally to debate the matter orally will do so in absence in writing."

The 95 Theses are as follows:

1. When our Lord and Master, Jesus Christ, said 'Repent', He called for the entire life of believers to be one of repentance.

2.   The word cannot be properly understood as referring to the sacrament of penance, i.e. confession and satisfaction, as administered by the clergy.

3.   Yet its meaning is not restricted to repentance in one's heart; for such repentance is null unless it produces outward signs in various mortifications of the flesh.

4.   As long as hatred of self abides (i.e. true inward repentance) the penalty of sin abides, viz., until we enter the kingdom of heaven.

5.   The pope has neither the will nor the power to remit any penalties beyond those imposed either at his own discretion or by canon law.

6.   The pope himself cannot remit guilt, but only declare and confirm that it has been remitted by God; or, at most, he can remit it in cases reserved to his discretion. Except for these cases, the guilt remains untouched.

7.   God never remits guilt to anyone without, at the same time, making him humbly submissive to the priest, His representative.

8.   The penitential canons apply only to men who are still alive, and, according to the canons themselves, none applies to the dead.

9.   Accordingly, the Holy Spirit, acting in the person of the pope, manifests grace to us, by the fact that the papal regulations always cease to apply at death, or in any hard case.

10.   It is a wrongful act, due to ignorance, when priests retain the canonical penalties on the dead in purgatory.

11.   When canonical penalties were changed and made to apply to purgatory, surely it would seem that tares were sown while the bishops were asleep.

12.   In former days, the canonical penalties were imposed, not after, but before absolution was pronounced; and were intended to be tests of true contrition.

13.   Death puts an end to all the claims of the Church; even the dying are already dead to the canon laws, and are no longer bound by them.

14.   Defective piety or love in a dying person is necessarily accompanied by great fear, which is greatest where the piety or love is least.

15.   This fear or horror is sufficient in itself, whatever else might be said, to constitute the pain of purgatory, since it approaches very closely to the horror of despair.

16. There seems to be the same difference between hell, purgatory, and heaven as between despair, uncertainty, and assurance.

17. Of a truth, the pains of souls in purgatory ought to be abated, and charity ought to be proportionately increased.

18. Moreover, it does not seem proved, on any grounds of reason or Scripture, that these souls are outside the state of merit, or unable to grow in grace.

19. Nor does it seem proved to be always the case that they are certain and assured of salvation, even if we are very certain ourselves.

20. Therefore the pope, in speaking of the plenary remission of all penalties, does not mean 'all' in the strict sense, but only those imposed by himself.

21. Hence those who preach indulgences are in error when they say that a man is absolved and saved from every penalty by the pope's indulgences.

22. Indeed, he cannot remit to souls in purgatory any penalty which canon law declares should be suffered in the present life.

23. If plenary remission could be granted to anyone at all, it would be only in the cases of the most perfect, i.e. to very few.

24.   It must therefore be the case that the major part of the people are
       deceived by that indiscriminate and high-sounding promise of
       relief from penalty.

25.   The same power as the pope exercises in general over purgatory is
       exercised in particular by every single bishop in his bishopric and
       priest in his parish.

26.   The pope does excellently when he grants remission to the souls in
       purgatory on account of intercessions made on their behalf, and not
       by the power of the keys (which he cannot exercise for them).

27.   There is no divine authority for preaching that the soul flies out of
       the purgatory immediately the money clinks in the bottom of the
       chest.

28.   It is certainly possible that when the money clinks in the bottom of
       the chest avarice and greed increase; but when the church offers
       intercession, all depends in the will of God.

29.   Who knows whether all souls in purgatory wish to be redeemed in
       view of what is said of St. Severinus and St. Pascal? (Note:
       Paschal I, pope 817-24. The legend is that he and Severinus were
       willing to endure the pains of purgatory for the benefit of the
       faithful).

30.   No one is sure of the reality of his own contrition, much less of
       receiving plenary forgiveness.

31.   One who bona fide buys indulgence is as rare as a bona fide
       penitent man, i.e. very rare indeed.

32.   All those who believe themselves certain of their own salvation by
       means of letters of indulgence, will be eternally damned, together
       with their teachers.

33.   We should be most carefully on our guard against those who say
       that the papal indulgences are an inestimable divine gift, and that a
       man is reconciled to God by them.

34.   For the grace conveyed by these indulgences relates simply to the
       penalties of the sacramental 'satisfactions' decreed merely by man.

35.   It is not in accordance with Christian doctrines to preach and teach
       that those who buy off souls, or purchase confessional licenses,
       have no need to repent of their own sins.

36.   Any Christian whatsoever, who is truly repentant, enjoys plenary
       remission from penalty and guilt, and this is given him without
       letters of indulgence.

37.   Any true Christian whatsoever, living or dead, participates in all
       the benefits of Christ and the Church; and this participation is
       granted to him by God without letters of indulgence.

38.   Yet the pope's remission and dispensation are in no way to be despised, for, as already said, they proclaim the divine remission.

39.   It is very difficult, even for the most learned theologians, to extol to the people the great bounty contained in the indulgences, while, at the same time, praising contrition as a virtue.

40.   A truly contrite sinner seeks out, and loves to pay, the penalties of his sins; whereas the very multitude of indulgences dulls men's consciences, and tends to make them hate the penalties.

41.   Papal indulgences should only be preached with caution, lest people gain a wrong understanding, and think that they are preferable to other good works: those of love.

42.   Christians should be taught that the pope does not at all intend that the purchase of indulgences should be understood as at all comparable with the works of mercy.

43.   Christians should be taught that one who gives to the poor, or lends to the needy, does a better action than if he purchases indulgences.

44.   Because, by works of love, love grows and a man becomes a better man; whereas, by indulgences, he does not become a better man, but only escapes certain penalties.

45.   Christians should be taught that he who sees a needy person, but passes him by although he gives money for indulgences, gains no benefit from the pope's pardon, but only incurs the wrath of God.

46.   Christians should be taught that, unless they have more than they need, they are bound to retain what is only necessary for the upkeep of their home, and should in no way squander it on indulgences.

47.   Christians should be taught that they purchase indulgences voluntarily, and are not under obligation to do so.

48.   Christians should be taught that, in granting indulgences, the pope has more need, and more desire, for devout prayer on his own behalf than for ready money.

49.   Christians should be taught that the pope's indulgences are useful only if one does not rely on them, but most harmful if one loses the fear of God through them.

50.   Christians should be taught that, if the pope knew the exactions of the indulgence-preachers, he would rather the church of St. Peter were reduced to ashes than be built with the skin, flesh, and bones of the sheep.

51.   Christians should be taught that the pope would be willing, as he ought if necessity should arise, to sell the church of St. Peter, and

give, too, his own money to many of those from whom the pardon-merchants conjure money.

52.   It is vain to rely on salvation by letters of indulgence, even if the commissary, or indeed the pope himself, were to pledge his own soul for their validity.

53.   Those are enemies of Christ and the pope who forbid the word of God to be preached at all in some churches, in order that indulgences may be preached in others.

54.   The word of God suffers injury if, in the same sermon, an equal or longer time is devoted to indulgences than to that word.

55.   The pope cannot help taking the view that if indulgences (very small matters) are celebrated by one bell, one pageant, or one ceremony, the gospel (a very great matter) should be preached to the accompaniment of a hundred bells, a hundred processions, a hundred ceremonies.

56.   The treasures of the church, out of which the pope dispenses indulgences, are not sufficiently spoken of or known among the people of Christ.

57.   That these treasures are not temporal are clear from the fact that many of the merchants do not grant them freely, but only collect them.

58.   Nor are they the merits of Christ and the saints, because, even apart from the pope, these merits are always working grace in the inner man, and working the cross, death, and hell in the outer man.

59.   St. Laurence said that the poor were the treasures of the church, but he used the term in accordance with the custom of his own time.

60.   We do not speak rashly in saying that the treasures of the church are the keys of the church, and are bestowed by the merits of Christ.

61.   For it is clear that the power of the pope suffices, by itself, for the remission of penalties and reserved cases.

62.   The true treasure of the church is the Holy gospel of the glory and the grace of God.

63.   It is right to regard this treasure as most odious, for it makes the first to be the last.

64.   On the other hand, the treasure of indulgences is most acceptable, for it makes the last to be the first.

65.   Therefore the treasures of the gospel are nets which, in former times, they used to fish for men of wealth.

66. The treasures of the indulgences are the nets which today they use to fish for the wealth of men.

67. The indulgences, which the merchants extol as the greatest of favours, are seen to be, in fact, a favourite means for money-getting.

68. Nevertheless, they are not to be compared with the grace of God and the compassion shown in the Cross.

69. Bishops and curates, in duty bound, must receive the commissaries of the papal indulgences with all reverence.

70. But they are under a much greater obligation to watch closely and attend carefully lest these men preach their own fancies instead of what the pope commissioned.

71. Let him be anathema and accursed who denies the apostolic character of the indulgences.

72. On the other hand, let him be blessed who is on his guard against the wantonness and license of the pardon-merchant's words.

73. In the same way, the pope rightly excommunicates those who make any plans to the detriment of the trade in indulgences.

74.   It is much more in keeping with his views to excommunicate those who use the pretext of indulgences to plot anything to the detriment of holy love and truth.

75.   It is foolish to think that papal indulgences have so much power that they can absolve a man even if he has done the impossible and violated the mother of God.

76.   We assert the contrary, and say that the pope's pardons are not able to remove the least venial of sins as far as their guilt is concerned.

77.   When it is said that not even St. Peter, if he were now pope, could grant a greater grace, it is blasphemy against St. Peter and the pope.

78.   We assert the contrary, and say that he, and any pope whatever, possesses greater graces, viz., the gospel, spiritual powers, gifts of healing, etc., as is declared in I Corinthians 12 [:28].

79.   It is blasphemy to say that the insignia of the cross with the papal arms are of equal value to the cross on which Christ died.

80.   The bishops, curates, and theologians, who permit assertions of that kind to be made to the people without let or hindrance, will have to answer for it.

81. This unbridled preaching of indulgences makes it difficult for learned men to guard the respect due to the pope against false accusations, or at least from the keen criticisms of the laity.

82. They ask, e.g.: Why does not the pope liberate everyone from purgatory for the sake of love (a most holy thing) and because of the supreme necessity of their souls? This would be morally the best of all reasons. Meanwhile he redeems innumerable souls for money, a most perishable thing, with which to build St. Peter's church, a very minor purpose.

83. Again: Why should funeral and anniversary masses for the dead continue to be said? And why does not the pope repay, or permit to be repaid, the benefactions instituted for these purposes, since it is wrong to pray for those souls who are now redeemed?

84. Again: Surely this is a new sort of compassion, on the part of God and the pope, when an impious man, an enemy of God, is allowed to pay money to redeem a devout soul, a friend of God; while yet that devout and beloved soul is not allowed to be redeemed without payment, for love's sake, and just because of its need of redemption.

85. Again: Why are the penitential canon laws, which in fact, if not in practice, have long been obsolete and dead in themselves,—why are they, today, still used in imposing fines in money, through the granting of indulgences, as if all the penitential canons were fully operative?

86. Again: since the pope's income today is larger than that of the wealthiest of wealthy men, why does he not build this one church of St. Peter with his own money, rather than with the money of indigent believers?

87. Again: What does the pope remit or dispense to people who, by their perfect repentance, have a right to plenary remission or dispensation?

88. Again: Surely a greater good could be done to the church if the pope were to bestow these remissions and dispensations, not once, as now, but a hundred times a day, for the benefit of any believer whatever.

89. What the pope seeks by indulgences is not money, but rather the salvation of souls; why then does he suspend the letters and indulgences formerly conceded, and still as efficacious as ever?

90. These questions are serious matters of conscience to the laity. To suppress them by force alone, and not to refute them by giving reasons, is to expose the church and the pope to the ridicule of their enemies, and to make Christian people unhappy.

91. If therefore, indulgences were preached in accordance with the spirit and mind of the pope, all these difficulties would be easily overcome, and indeed, cease to exist.

92.   Away, then, with those prophets who say to Christ's people, 'Peace, peace', and there is no peace.

93.   Hail, hail to all those prophets who say to Christ's people, 'The cross, the cross', where there is no cross.

94.   Christians should be exhorted to be zealous to follow Christ, their Head, through penalties, deaths, and hells.

95.   And let them thus be more confident of entering heaven through many tribulations rather than through a false assurance of peace.

Analysis Calculations

Argument Scores: 9.95, 9.95, 9.9, 9.95, 9, 9, 9.5, 9.95, 9.9, 8.5, 9.5, 9.95, 9.5, 9, 9.
Total = 142.55; Average = 142.55 / 15 = 9.5

The Consistency Factor reflects the number of 'For' arguments versus the number of 'Against' arguments i.e. the number of arguments with scores less than or greater than 5 multiplied by a constant of 0.002.

Consistency Factor = 1 + (No. of Arguments scoring above 5 − No. of Arguments scoring less than 5) x 0.002 = 1 + 15 x 0.002 = 1.03
Probability Score = Average x Consistency Factor
Therefore, Probability of Non-existence = 9.5 x 1.03 x 10 = 97.85 % which rounds up to 98 %.

References

Chapter 4. Movements supported by secularists. BBC Online Services, http://www.bbc.co.uk/religion/religions/atheism/types/secularism/shtml

Chapter 4. World Pantheist Movement Statement of Principles, http://www.pantheism.net/manifest.htm

Chapter 4. British Humanist Association, Are You a Humanist? http://www.humanism.org.uk/humanism

Addendum. The 95 Theses attributable to Phillip R. Johnson, http://www.spurgeon.org/~phil/history/95theses.htm

Index